Contents

1 Introduction   9

Part One: Attachment and Caregiving

2 What is Attachment?   15

An evolutionary perspective 16; The attachment behavioural system 17; Activation and termination of attachment behaviour 17; The development of attachment 18; Internal working models of attachment representations 21; Interplay between attachment and other behavioural systems 21; The exploratory behavioural system and the secure base 22; A safe or secure haven 22; Summary 23

3 The Classifications of Attachment   24

Organised attachments 25; Disorganised attachment 27; From disorganised to controlling attachment behaviour 29; An alternative classification 30; The distribution of attachment patterns 30; Stability or predictability of attachment patterns 32; Summary 36

4 What are the Factors Influencing Attachment Organisation (and Disorganisation)?   38

The contribution of caregiving to attachment organisation 38; What is caregiving? 38; Empirical evidence for the role of the caregiver in determining organisation (or disorganisation) of attachment security 41; **The role of the child's temperament and genetic factors in influencing attachment organisation 46**; Temperament factors 46; Attachment and autism 47; Specific genes 48; **The intergenerational transmission of attachment 49**; The link between parental state of mind with respect to attachment and infant security 50; The link between parental state of mind with respect to attachment and parental sensitive responsiveness (B) 51; The link between parental sensitive responsiveness and infant attachment security (C) 52; The transmission gap 52; Bridging the transmission gap 53; Summary 55

5 **Affectional Bonds and Attachment Figures** 56

What are affectional bonds? 56; How is an attachment figure
defined? 59; Are professional child-carers attachment figures? 60;
How are the representations of multiple attachment figures
structured? 63; Summary 69

6 **Is Attachment Theory Valid across Cultures?** 71

Ainsworth's Uganda study 71; The Gusii of Kenya 72; The Dogon
of Mali 72; The Israeli Kibbutzim 73; The Hausa of Nigeria 74;
The !Kung San of Botswana 75; The Efe or Pygmies of Zambia 75;
The academic debate 75; Comments 77; Summary 81

Part Two: Assessments
of Attachment and Caregiving

7 **Introduction** 85

Attachment 85; Caregiving 86; Structure for presentation of
assessments 87; Glossary of research and statistical terms 89

8 **Assessments of Attachment** 96

**Assessments of attachment based on observation of the child's
behaviour 96**; Separation–reunion procedure 96; Q-sort
methodology 105; **Assessments of attachment based on the
child's internal working model/representation 109**; Picture
response tasks 109; Narrative Story Stem techniques (NSSTs) 113;
Interview techniques 124

9 **Assessments of Caregiving** 139

Assessments based on observations of caregiving 139;
Maternal Sensitivity Scales 139; The CARE-Index 143; Atypical
Maternal Behavior Instrument for Assessment and Classification
(AMBIANCE) 145; Caregiver Behavior Classification System 147;
**Assessments/ measures of caregiving based on the caregiver's
internal working model/ representation of caregiving or
relationship with the child 150**; Parent Development Interview
(PDI) 150; Experiences of Caregiving Interview 152

Understanding Attachment and Attachment Disorders

Child and Adolescent Mental Health Series

Written for professionals and parents, these accessible, evidence-based resources are essential reading for anyone seeking to understand and promote children and young people's mental health. Drawing on the work of FOCUS, a multi-disciplinary project based at the Royal College of Psychiatrists' Research and Training Unit, each title in the series brings together practical and policy-level suggestions with up-to-the-minute analysis of research.

also in the series

Conduct Disorder and Offending Behaviour in Young People
Findings from Research
Kristin Liabø and Joanna Richardson
ISBN 978 1 84310 508 4
eISBN 978 1 84642 660 5

Cannabis and Young People
Reviewing the Evidence
Richard Jenkins
ISBN 978 1 84310 398 1
eISBN 978 1 84642 459 5

Deliberate Self-Harm in Adolescence
Claudine Fox and Keith Hawton
ISBN 978 1 84310 237 3
eISBN 978 1 84642 016 0

Mental Health Services for Minority Ethnic Children and Adolescents
Edited by Mhemooda Malek and Carol Joughin
Foreword by Kedar Nath Dwivedi
ISBN 978 1 84310 236 6
eISBN 978 1 84642 039 9

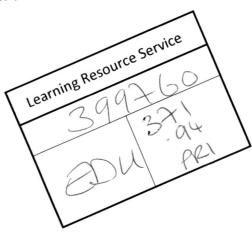

Child and Adolescent Mental Health Series

FOCUS

Understanding Attachment and Attachment Disorders

Theory, Evidence and Practice

Vivien Prior and Danya Glaser

The Royal College of
Psychiatrists' Research and Training Unit

Jessica Kingsley *Publishers*
London and Philadelphia

First published in 2006
by Jessica Kingsley Publishers
73 Collier Street
London N1 9BE, UK
and
400 Market Street, Suite 400
Philadelphia, PA 19106, USA

www.jkp.com

Library of Congress Cataloging in Publication Data
Prior, Vivien.
    Understanding attachment and attachment disorders : theory, evidence, and practice / Vivien Prior and
Danya Glaser.
        p. cm. -- (Child and adolescent mental health series)
    Includes bibliographical references and index.
    ISBN-13: 978-1-84310-245-8 (pbk.)
    ISBN-10: 1-84310-245-5 (pbk.)
    1. Attachment disorder in children. 2. Attachment behavior. 3. Attachment behavior in children. 4. Psy-
chology. I. Glaser, Danya. II. Title.
    [DNLM: 1. Object Attachment. 2. Reactive Attachment Disorder. 3. Parent-Child Relations. 4.
Parenting. 5. Child. WM 460.5.O2 P958u 2006]
    RJ507.A77U53 2006
    618.92'8588--dc22
                            2006022732

British Library Cataloguing in Publication Data
A CIP catalogue record for this book is available from the British Library

ISBN 978 1 84310 245 8
eISBN 978 1 84642 546 2

Part Three: Correlates of Attachment Organisation with Functioning

10 Which Domains of Functioning are Hypothesised to be Correlated with Attachment and What are the Possible Pathways of its Influence?   159

Which domains of functioning are hypothesised to be correlated with attachment? 160; What are the possible pathways of the influence of attachment? 161; Summary 165

11 Evidence for Correlations between Attachment Security/Insecurity and the Child's Functioning   166

Research issues 166; The evidence 168; Summary 179

Part Four: What is Attachment Disorder?

12 Two Versions of Attachment Disorder   183

International classifications 183; Another version 184; Summary 187

13 Research on Attachment Disorder   188

Issues regarding research methods 188; The evidence 189; Young children in residential nurseries in the UK and their later development 190; Children from Romanian orphanages adopted in Canada 195; Deprived children from Romania adopted in the UK 200; Children living in residential nurseries in Bucharest 206; US children in high-risk populations and maltreated children 212; Summary 216

14 The Nature of Attachment Disorder   218

No discriminated attachment figure 218; The nature of the difference between inhibited and disinhibited RAD 220; Alternative criteria for disorders of attachment 223; Disorganised and inhibited RAD 225; Reactive attachment disorder in children over the age of 5? 225; Summary 227

Part Five: Attachment Theory-based Interventions (and Some that are Not)

15 Introduction   231

16 Evidence-based Interventions: Enhancing Caregiver Sensitivity   233

Bakermans-Kranenburg, van IJzendoorn and Juffer (2003) 'Less is more: meta-analyses of sensitivity and attachment interventions in early childhood' 234; Cohen *et al.* (1999) 'Watch, wait and wonder: testing the effectiveness of a new approach to mother–infant psychotherapy' 239; van den Boom (1994) 'The influence of temperament and mothering on attachment and exploration: an experimental manipulation of sensitive responsiveness among lower-class mothers with irritable infants' 241; van den Boom (1995) 'Do first-year intervention effects endure? Follow-up during toddlerhood of a sample of Dutch irritable infants' 242; Benoit *et al.* (2001) 'Atypical maternal behavior toward feeding-disordered infants before and after intervention' 243; Toth *et al.* (2002) 'The relative efficacy of two interventions in altering maltreated preschool children's representational models: implications for attachment theory' 245; Marvin *et al.* (2002) 'The Circle of Security project: attachment-based intervention with caregiver–preschool dyads' 248; Summary 250

17 Evidence-based Interventions: Change of Caregiver   252

Rushton and Mayes (1997) 'Forming fresh attachments in childhood: a research update' 252; Dozier *et al.* (2001) 'Attachment for infants in foster care: the role of caregiver state of mind' 254; Steele *et al.* (2003a) 'Attachment representations and adoption: associations between maternal states of mind and emotion narratives in previously maltreated children' 256; Hodges *et al.* Changes in attachment representations over the first year (Hodges *et al.* 2003b) and second year (Hodges *et al.* 2005) of adoptive placement: narratives of maltreated children 258; Summary 260

18 Interventions with No Evidence Base   261

Direct intervention with the child 261; 'Attachment therapy' 262

19 Conclusions Regarding Interventions   267

References   269

Subject Index   281

Author Index   286

About FOCUS   288

1 Introduction

This book was initially conceived as an evidence-based document on attachment, along similar lines to other publications by FOCUS which have considered the evidence base for interventions in a number of different disorders. However, it became apparent early in the endeavour that a somewhat different format would be required. In discussing the clinical application of the concept of attachment, three aspects needed to be considered in detail: (1) attachment theory; (2) the assessment of attachment patterns; and (3) disturbances related to attachment. An evidence-based approach has been applied to considering these three aspects.

Attachment theory was introduced and described in detail by John Bowlby in his many papers and books. Bowlby regarded attachment as a biological instinct, evolved to ensure the survival of the vulnerable young. Bowlby's trilogy (1969/1982, 1973, 1980) considered the formation of attachment, separation and loss. Subsequent attention has become focused on the process of attachment of children to their caregivers, with much less emphasis on separation and loss. It is clear that separation and loss are painful and distressing and, if unresolved, may leave lasting emotional sequelae. Prior security of attachment is, however, protective of the effects of later stresses. Insecure attachment is best regarded as a vulnerability factor or a marker of risk to the child's functioning and wider social adaptation. How attachment behaviour becomes organised is largely determined by the caregiving environment. This places the onus of 'responsibility' for the formation of secure attachments on the young child's caregivers.

What is remarkable is the extent to which Bowlby's writing and predictions, which were based on extensive observations, have been proved correct. The theory has stood the test of empirical scrutiny and is referred to throughout the book, extending into the more uncertain territory of attachment disorders.

Attachment theory has generated a great deal of interest within the fields of psychology and child development and there is a wealth of scientific work and evidence relating to it. Much of it has been referred to in the *Handbook of Attachment* (Cassidy and Shaver 1999) and by Goldberg (2000; Goldberg, Muir and Kerr 1995). Our book is a further distillation of this vast knowledge base. The conclusions in the various Parts of this book are based on the available evidence base and its appraisal. In addition, Part Four presents a clarification of the meaning of attachment disorders, which is based both on attachment theory and the evidence base.

It has not been possible to mention, let alone appraise, every study in this field, some aspects of which are very richly researched. As well as using meta-analyses where these are available, the studies selected have included 'classic' ones as well as those illustrating different approaches or practice. The aim has been to bring a representative selection of the evidence which is based on attachment theory to guide practice.

Alongside the requirement to base the contents of this book on the appraisal of the available evidence, the needs of practitioners have also been considered. A number of questions that might be asked by practitioners were, therefore, posed by the authors at the outset. The questions were:

1. What is attachment?

2. Is attachment organisation continuous over time?

3. What determines attachment security?

4. What is the relationship between a parent's own attachment organisation, their parenting of the child and the child's own attachment organisation?

5. Does good overall parent–child interaction predict secure attachment?

6. When and how does an individual's attachment organisation move from being specific to particular caregivers to becoming consolidated into one organisation?

7. How does attachment develop with multiple caregivers?

8. Is attachment theory valid across different cultures?

9. How is attachment assessed?

10. What is the relationship between attachment organisation and the child's functioning and mental health?

11. Do life events or experiences, including therapy, alter an individual's attachment organisation?

12. What is the relationship between child abuse and neglect and attachment?

13. What are attachment disorders?

14. How can attachment security be enhanced and attachment disorders be treated?

As becomes evident, the answers to these seemingly straightforward questions are complex, emanate from different aspects of attachment theory and its application, and are therefore embedded throughout the book.

Part One (Chapters 2 to 6) presents an overview of attachment theory. Chapter 2 describes the nature and formation of attachment (question 1). The organisation of attachment security (question 2) is described in Chapter 3. The determinants of attachment organisation (questions 3, 4 and 12) are discussed in Chapter 4; the relatively sparse literature on domains of parenting and attachment (question 5) are also considered in this chapter. Chapter 5 considers the way in which attachment develops in relation to multiple caregivers (questions 6 and 7). Finally in Part One, the applicability of attachment theory across different cultures (question 8), which has been questioned and debated, is discussed in Chapter 6.

Part Two (Chapters 7 to 9) considers the measurement or assessment of attachment (question 9). As will be seen, there is less clarity about measuring attachment organisation in middle childhood. Moreover, some measures of attachment are based on behaviour; others use play and cognitions; yet others focus on cognition, coherence and expression of thought. There is now evidence to show that different ways of measuring attachment organisation do address the same underlying representations.

Practitioners have wondered what the relevance of attachment theory is to clinically-encountered difficulties (question 10). Part Three (Chapters 10 and 11) focuses on the correlates of attachment organisation with functioning. Chapter 10 considers which domains of functioning may be correlated with attachment and suggests possible pathways for its influence. Chapter 11 considers research issues and presents a summary of the evidence.

In contrast to the rich evidence base regarding the measurement of attachment and its development, a parallel and seemingly unrelated field has grown, concerning an entity termed attachment disorder. Other than the word 'attach-ment', much of it bears little resemblance to attachment theory. Attachment disorder (question 13) is discussed extensively in Part Four (Chapters 12, 13 and 14). Interest in this apparent entity has grown as professionals and (mostly 'alternative' – foster and adoptive) parents have become increasingly aware of the very serious difficulties which some of their children are showing. These children have suffered previous privation and abuse, mostly by their parents and some by institutions. However, aside from children who were adopted out of institutions, relatively little attention has been paid in the academic and profes-sional attachment field to the plight of these children. For instance, the *Handbook of Attachment* does not mention the term 'attachment disorder'. A clari-fication of the meaning of attachment disorders is developed in Chapter 14.

The lack of therapeutic resources, alongside a clear need to offer some help to these extremely troubled children, has led to the growth of an unevaluated and potentially abusive attachment therapy 'industry'. Part Five (Chapters 15 to 19) describes some evidence-based and successful interventions designed to change disorganised and insecure attachment organisations to secure ones (questions 11 and 14). Chapters 16 and 17 describe theoretically sound thera-peutic approaches which are appraised. Chapter 18 critiques the wholly unsub-stantiated theoretical basis for attachment therapy and its practice.

We have found this review of attachment theory and research a most exciting venture and we hope the reader will share this excitement.

Although readers may be inclined to turn to those parts of the book in which they have a particular interest, we would ask that readers who are not very familiar with attachment theory first turn to Chapter 2, which details the theo-retical and conceptual basis for all that follows.

We would like to acknowledge Helen Care for her significant contribution, and Justine Beriot for additional input, to Part Two. We would also like to thank Dr Jonathan Green, Dr Jill Hodges and Dr Howard Steele, the three peer review-ers, for their very helpful comments, and our families for their support and for-bearance, including, in particular, the unstinting and invaluable support of Denis Glaser.

Part One
Attachment and Caregiving

2 What is Attachment?

An attachment, in its literal meaning, is a tie or fastening. Attachment, especially between people, is often defined positively as affection, devotion (*Concise Oxford Dictionary*) or even love, although harmful attachments, for example to a damaging substance or person, clearly exist.

An attachment as it is defined in attachment theory has a specific meaning, both in terms of its nature and the person to whom it applies. According to attachment theory, an attachment is a bond or tie between an individual and an attachment figure. In adult relationships, people may be mutual and reciprocal attachment figures, but in the relationship between the child and parent, this is not the case. The reason for this clear distinction is inherent in the theory. In attachment theory, an attachment is a tie based on the need for safety, security and protection. This need is paramount in infancy and childhood, when the developing individual is immature and vulnerable. Thus, infants *instinctively* attach to their carer(s). In this sense, attachment serves the specific biological function of promoting protection, survival and, ultimately, genetic replication.[1] In the relationship between the child and the parent, the term 'attachment' applies to the infant or child and the term 'attachment figure' invariably refers to their primary carer. In the terms of attachment theory, it is incorrect to refer to a parent's attachment to their child or attachment *between* parents and children.

Attachment, therefore, is *not* synonymous with love or affection; it is not an overall descriptor of the relationship between the parent and child which includes other parent–child interactions such as feeding, stimulation, play or problem solving.

The attachment figure's equivalent tie to the child is termed the 'caregiving bond'.

An evolutionary perspective

Attachment theory is an evolutionary theory.[2] Species evolve by adapting to their environment, the most successful being those which adapt most effectively and efficiently. The mechanism by which this occurs is natural selection, which operates through successive reproduction over aeons of time. Bowlby uses the term 'environment of evolutionary adaptedness' (EEA) to refer to the environment from which biological systems are evolved. He suggests that the EEA for human instinctive behaviour, that is the environment in which our present behavioural equipment is likely to have been evolved, existed long before the increases in diversity of habitat that have occurred over the past few thousand years. This environment was one in which humans were predominantly hunter-gatherers and protection from predators and other dangers was best achieved by staying close to a protective adult. Bowlby stresses that placing humans' EEA in the primeval past implies no judgement on past or present existence. Rather, he is concerned with understanding: 'not a single feature of a species' morphology, physiology, or behaviour can be understood or even discussed intelligently except in relation to that species' environment of evolutionary adaptedness' (Bowlby 1969, p.64).

Attachment behaviour is proximity-seeking to the attachment figure in the face of threat. Bowlby termed this proximity the 'set-goal' of the attachment behavioural system. Fear is the appreciation of danger and calls for a response. There is a survival advantage in sensing danger before it occurs; that is, in knowing the conditions which are potentially unsafe. Among these 'natural clues to an increased risk of danger', Bowlby lists strangeness (unfamiliarity), sudden change of stimulation, rapid approach, height and being alone. These conditions tend to be appraised in terms of fear. Fear and attachment behaviour are often simultaneously activated. Conditions in which two or more natural clues to danger are present are likely to elicit an intense activation. The anticipated outcome of this activation is increased proximity to an attachment figure.

Bowlby uses the analogy of an army in the field. The safety of the army depends on both its defence against attack and its contact with and security of its base. The analogy is applied to a child sensing a clue to danger. The fear elicited by the clue to danger, Bowlby termed 'alarm'; the fear of being cut off or separated from one's base, he termed 'anxiety'. In attachment theory, the base is the attachment figure. Separation anxiety thus refers to separation from an attachment figure. Separation in this context, however, does not refer merely to the absence of the attachment figure. 'What is crucial is the availability of the figure. It is when a figure is perceived as having become inaccessible and unresponsive, that separation distress (grief) occurs, and the anticipation of the possible occurrence of such a situation arouses anxiety' (Ainsworth *et al.* 1978, p.21).

The attachment behavioural system

Attachment operates through the attachment behavioural system. This comprises many different behaviours which may, individually, also serve other behavioural systems. The feature that combines diverse behaviours into a behavioural system is that they serve a common outcome. Bowlby uses the term 'predictable outcome' for this, meaning that once the system is activated the outcome in question is likely to occur. The predictable outcome of the attachment behavioural system is to bring the individual into closer proximity, or to maintain proximity with his or her attachment figure, with the instinctive expectation that the attachment figure will remove the stressors, thus deactivating the need for the attachment behaviour.

Activation and termination of attachment behaviour

In his original formulation of attachment theory, Bowlby conceived of attachment as a start–stop system (1969, p.258). When the child is experiencing comfort (or an absence of discomfort) the system is relaxed. Attachment behaviour is activated by the child's sense of discomfort or threat and is (usually) terminated as the discomfort is relieved. However, as Main points out (1999, p.858), there is now a general acceptance that the attachment system is best conceived of as continually active. This modification, she informs, was proposed at an early stage by Ainsworth and Bretherton who realised that a 'turned off' system would leave the child vulnerable and at risk. Thus, in the absence of discomfort or alarm, the attachment behavioural system, rather than being inactive, operates by continuously monitoring the proximity and the physical and psychological accessibility of the attachment figure. Bowlby immediately accepted this early modification. The 'setting' or degree of proximity (set-goal) varies according to the level of activation. Thus, if the activation is intense (the child is intensely alarmed) the setting of the set-goal may require very close proximity to, or actual physical contact with, the attachment figure. If the activation is low, the setting of the set-goal may be such that merely gaining sight of the attachment figure will suffice to deactivate the attachment behaviour (Ainsworth *et al.* 1978, pp.10–11).

Activation of attachment behaviour

The level of activation depends on the level of the child's discomfort or their perception of the severity of the threat. At its simplest, the discomfort may be mere physical distance from the caregiver. Vocal signalling by the child may bring the carer back to a comfortable distance, or with locomotion, the child may restore a comfortable distance by moving towards the carer. Bowlby suggests that a similar stimulus for activation may be the time elapsed away from the carer.

Bowlby lists under the following three headings other conditions which activate attachment behaviour and influence its intensity:

1. *Condition of the child*
   fatigue
   hunger
   ill health
   pain
   cold

2. *Whereabouts and behaviour of the mother*
   mother absent
   mother departing
   mother discouraging proximity

3. *Other environmental conditions*
   occurrence of alarming events
   rebuffs by other adults or children

Termination of attachment behaviour

Termination of attachment behaviour varies according to the intensity of the activation. Following intense activation, possibly only physical contact with the carer will terminate the attachment behaviour, with much crying and clinging. Low level activation, however, in response to slight fear or discomfort, may be terminated by the child simply checking the whereabouts of the carer.

The development of attachment

There are four phases in the development of attachment. The boundaries between the phases are not clear-cut.

Phase 1

Orientation and signals without discrimination of figure (Bowlby)
Initial pre-attachment (Ainsworth)
This phase spans from birth to not less than 8 weeks of age. During this period the infant uses behaviours designed to attract and respond to the attention of caregivers. Behaviours such as grasping, smiling, babbling or crying are directed at anyone in the baby's vicinity. Studies have shown, however, that already during this phase infants are learning to discriminate between adults.

Phase 2

Orientation and signals directed towards one (or more) discriminated figure(s) (Bowlby)
Attachment-in-the-making (Ainsworth)
Typically, the second phase occurs from 8 weeks to approximately 6 months of age. With the development of improved vision and audition, the infant increasingly discriminates between familiar and unfamiliar adults and becomes particularly responsive towards his or her carer.

Phase 3

Maintenance of proximity to a discriminated figure by means of locomotion as well as signals (Bowlby)
Clear-cut attachment (Ainsworth)
This phase typically begins between 6 and 7 months but may be delayed until after one year of age. Bowlby suggests that this phase probably continues throughout the second and into the third year. This is a crucial phase of consolidation and has three components.

First, during this phase the child's behaviour to his mother becomes organised on a goal-corrected basis, 'and then his attachment to his mother-figure is evident for all to see' (Bowlby 1969, p.267). 'Thenceforward, it seems, he discovers what the conditions are that terminate his distress and that make him feel secure; and from that phase onward he begins to be able to plan his behaviour so that these conditions are achieved' (p.351). Second, the infant increasingly discriminates between adults. Third, with the development of locomotion, the infant begins to use his carer as a base and to explore.

Phase 4

Formation of goal-corrected partnership (Bowlby and Ainsworth)
Typically this phase does not begin until the second year and, for many children, not until near or after the third year. The central feature of this fourth

and final phase is the child's 'lessening of egocentricity' (Ainsworth *et al.* 1978, p.28). The child begins to see his mother-figure as an independent person with her own set-goals. This lays the foundation for a more complex mother–child relationship, which Bowlby terms a 'partnership'.

Attachment throughout the lifespan

Whilst Bowlby recognised that attachment behaviour continues throughout the lifespan, he did not consider that attachment behaviour in later childhood and adulthood was characterised by processes significantly different from those operating in Phase 4. After three years of age, attachment behaviour is less frequent and urgent, as the maturing child feels threatened less frequently, but it continues as 'a dominant strand' (Bowlby 1969, p.207) in the child's life. During adolescence the child's attachment to his parents typically begins to be superseded by ties to others, usually the child's peers. In adulthood, the attachment bond and behaviour is usually directed at partners or close friends. Finally, in old age, attachment behaviour often comes full circle and is directed from the old to the young, from the parents to the offspring.

A note about dependency

Bowlby and Ainsworth were repeatedly concerned to point out the differences between attachment and dependency (e.g. Bowlby 1969, 1988; Ainsworth 1969a; Ainsworth *et al.* 1978). That the two are not synonymous is evidenced by the following:

- During the first weeks of life an infant is dependent on his parent(s) but not yet attached.

- An older child in the care of others may not be dependent on his parent(s) but is likely to remain attached to them.

- Dependency in older children and adults is usually viewed as problematic, a condition or trait to be 'grown out of'. Mistaking attachment behaviour for dependency in older children or adults, such that the attachment behaviour may be 'dubbed regressive', Bowlby considered an 'appalling misjudgement' (1988, p.12).

- A secure attachment, i.e. having confidence in the availability of one's base, is associated with exploration and independence rather than dependence.

Internal working models of attachment representations

Bowlby postulated that the child constructs internal working models for each attachment figure on the basis of attachment–caregiving experiences with that person. Internal working models are predictions which the child develops about him- or herself, others, and the response of significant others to his or her attachment needs. Bowlby likened internal working models to cognitive maps, a map being a 'coded representation of selected aspects of whatever is mapped' (Bowlby 1969, p.80). A map, however, as Bowlby points out, is a static representation. Working models, on the other hand, enable the individual to 'conduct…small-scale experiments within the head' (p.81). Working models comprise two parts, an environmental model, based on accumulated experience, and an organismic model, based on self-knowledge of one's skills and potentialities.

To be useful, Bowlby states, both working models must be kept up to date. However, the extent to which internal working models can change remains a central question. Although models are influenced by new experience, the integration of the new experience is shaped by the existing model. 'Hence the effects of early experience are carried forward in these models, even as they undergo change' (Goldberg 2000, p.9). A second difficulty is that unconscious aspects of internal working models are likely to be particularly resistant to change. 'Clinical evidence suggests that the necessary revisions of model are not always easy to achieve. Usually they are completed but only slowly, often they are done imperfectly, and sometimes done not at all' (Bowlby 1969, p.82).

Bowlby implies rather than states that revision of models is best done by subjecting the model 'to whatever special benefits accrue from becoming conscious' (Bowlby 1969, p.83).

Interplay between attachment and other behavioural systems

A complex interplay operates between the attachment behavioural system and other biologically based behavioural systems. An example of behaviour which serves more than one behavioural system is sucking, which serves both the food seeking and attachment behavioural systems. Bowlby distinguishes nutritional and non-nutritional sucking. Infants spend far more time in non-nutritional sucking, of a nipple or nipple-like object, than in nutritional sucking. Moreover, infants especially engage in non-nutritional sucking when they are alarmed or upset. Thus, non-nutritional sucking is an activity in its own right and 'in man's environment of evolutionary adaptedness, non-nutritional sucking is an integral part of attachment behaviour and has proximity to mother as a predictable outcome' (Bowlby 1969, p.250).

The exploratory behavioural system and the secure base

Exploratory behaviour is the antithesis of attachment behaviour because it usually takes the child away from his or her attachment figure. For this reason, attachment is often assessed in relation to exploration, the object of interest being the child's behaviour when both systems are activated. Ainsworth's early work in Uganda (Ainsworth 1963, 1967) found that infant exploration was greater when the mother was present and diminished in her absence. This was anticipated, as attachment behaviour is strongly activated when the attachment figure is inaccessible and/or unresponsive. With the attachment figure present, the attachment system is relaxed and exploration can occur. Attachment and exploration are thus often in a state of balance or tension. Ainsworth's careful observations confirmed that infants use their attachment figure as a secure base from which to explore.

Bowlby viewed the provision of a secure base as a central feature of his concept of parenting. A secure base is described as a base

> from which a child or adolescent can make sorties into the outside world and to which he can return knowing for sure that he will be welcomed when he gets there, nourished physically and emotionally, comforted if distressed, reassured if frightened. In essence this role is one of being available, ready to respond when called upon to encourage and perhaps assist, but to intervene actively only when clearly necessary. (Bowlby 1988, p.11)

Thus, at the heart of attachment theory is the notion that exploration and autonomy are fostered by *responding* to the child's proximity-seeking attachment behaviour rather than resisting it; that is, the granting of proximity *promotes* autonomy rather than inhibits it. Daring to 'press forward and take risks' (Bowlby 1988, p.11) requires confidence in the security of one's base.

A safe or secure haven

Ainsworth *et al.* (1978) describe some infants in the strange situation (described in Chapter 8) who were so alarmed by the entrance of the stranger that strong attachment behaviour was activated. These infants behaved in a way described by the authors as 'retreat to the mother', moving into close proximity to or actual contact with her. On reaching the mother, the infant's intention seemed not to interact with her, but to turn back to or even smile at the stranger 'from the secure haven provided by the mother' (p.264). Although nearly all the children showed some wary behaviour, not all approached their mothers; for many the mere presence of the mother in the same room provided a safe or secure haven.

Ainsworth *et al.* acknowledge that the concept of a mother as a secure haven is similar to the concept of her as a secure base. Nevertheless, they believe that retaining the distinction is desirable. When the child uses the attachment figure as a secure base from which to explore, wariness or fear is not implied. However, when the infant seeks proximity to his mother as a secure haven, the implication is that he is to some extent alarmed. Once his alarm is moderated by proximity, he may explore again. In this way, 'the attachment figure shifts from being a secure haven to being a secure base from which to explore' (Ainsworth *et al.* 1978, p.265).

Summary

Attachment behaviour was defined by John Bowlby as a biological instinct in which proximity to an attachment figure is sought when the child senses or perceives threat or discomfort. Attachment behaviour anticipates a response by the attachment figure which will remove the threat or discomfort. Selective attachments develop in the first year of life, proceeding through several stages. Mental representations of the infant-child and their human environment are formed on the basis of early attachment experiences. They were termed by Bowlby 'internal working models' to denote the possibility of updating these representations. The role of the attachment figure is to provide a secure base from which the child can explore, and a safe haven to which to retreat when threatened.

Notes

1   For a discussion of this point, see Belsky, Chapter 7 in the *Handbook of Attachment* (1999).

2   For a description of the place of attachment theory in the hierarchy of evolutionary theories, see Simpson, Chapter 6 in the *Handbook of Attachment* (1999).

3 The Classifications of Attachment

Quantitative terms such as 'strong', 'intense' or 'weak' are not appropriate terminology in attachment theory and were very rarely used by Bowlby and Ainsworth. Instead, attachments are described and classified by their qualitative characteristics.

By the age of 18 months and probably earlier the young child has already developed discernible and specific attachment patterns to different attachment figures, based on the young child's cumulative attachment experiences with their attachment figures.

These attachment patterns are classified in two ways. One is according to whether the pattern represents an *organised* strategy for gaining the proximity of an attachment figure when the attachment behavioural system is activated, or the lack or collapse of such a strategy, termed *disorganised*. Children who have an attachment figure who is also the source of the fear which activated the attachment system are caught in an irresolvable conflict. This renders them at a loss, sometimes to the point of apparent paralysis, as to how to deactivate their attachment needs and restore a sense of comfort and security.

Attachment patterns are also classified according to whether the individual feels *secure* or *insecure/anxious* regarding the availability and responsiveness of the attachment figure.

As Bowlby points out, the term 'secure', in its original meaning, 'applies to the world as reflected in feeling and not to the world as it is' (1973, p.182). 'Safe' is perhaps a better term to describe the objective condition. Thus, a person may feel insecure although in reality they are safe and vice versa. Security and insecurity are feeling states.

Organised attachments

Individuals who have an organised strategy to achieve the set-goal of proximity to an attachment figure can be securely or insecurely attached to that attachment figure. A secure attachment indicates having confidence that the attachment figure will be available and respond, sensitively and benignly to the need for proximity and, if the attachment system is highly activated, the need for comfort. An insecure attachment can be described as anxious in this regard.

Insecure organised attachments are distinguished as either 'avoidant' or 'resistant' (also called 'ambivalent'). This tripartite classification (secure, insecure-avoidant and insecure-resistant) of different types of organised attachment resulted from the groundbreaking work of Mary Ainsworth and colleagues (Ainsworth and Wittig 1969; Ainsworth *et al.* 1978) and was based on extensive observation of infant attachment behaviour both in the laboratory-based strange situation procedure, carried out between 9 and 18 months of age (described in detail in Chapter 8), and at home.[1] Not wishing to assign descriptive labels, the three groups were called A, B and C (Ainsworth *et al.* 1978, p.58). The validity of this classification has stood the test of time and further scrutiny and the following descriptions of the three groups are taken broadly from Ainsworth *et al.* 1978. They apply to organisation of attachment behaviour in respect of a particular attachment figure.

Group B: secure attachment

The typical Group B infant is more positive in his or her behaviour toward his or her mother than Groups A and C infants. He is more harmonious and cooperative in his interaction with his mother and more willing to comply with her requests. He uses his mother as a secure base from which to explore. At home he is not likely to cry if his mother leaves the room. When his attachment behavioural system is intensely activated, as in the strange situation procedure, he seeks proximity to his mother and close bodily contact with her. He is quickly soothed, although may resist premature release, and within a few minutes returns to exploration and play.

Group A: insecure-avoidant attachment

In the strange situation, Group A infants tend to maintain a relatively high level of exploration across the separation and reunion episodes. They show little response to separation (clue to danger) and conspicuous avoidance of proximity-seeking, or interaction with, the mother in the reunion episodes. If the infant approaches her mother, she tends to show avoidant behaviour such as moving past her or averting her gaze. If picked up, she shows little or no tendency to cling or resist release.

Ainsworth *et al.* point out that we should not lose sight of the fact that Group A infants are anxious as well as avoidant. Their attachment need tends not to be terminated, for they rarely experience the soothing that most effectively terminates intense activation. Such continuing frustration may result in frequent expressions of anger. Moreover, at home (unlike in the strange situation) they were observed to cry more and show separation anxiety more often than Group B babies.

Group C: insecure-resistant/ambivalent attachment

Group C infants cry more than Group B infants both at home and in the strange situation. In the strange situation they respond to the mother's departures with immediate and intense distress. They show conspicuous contact- and interaction-resisting behaviour, but also moderate to strong proximity- and contact-seeking behaviour once contact is gained, thus giving the impression of ambivalence. They are less quickly soothed than Group B infants. When picked up they may mingle angry resistance with clinging and other contact-maintaining behaviour.

Groups A, B and C and subgroups on a continuum

Ainsworth *et al.* also identified eight subgroups, two in Group A, four in Group B and two in Group C. The main groups and the subgroups may be presented along a continuum reflecting the suppression/expression of attachment behaviour (see Figure 3.1).[2]

Thus, A1 babies show consistent avoidance, whereas A2 babies show some tendency to approach the mother. B1 and B2 babies are somewhat avoidant whilst B3 and B4 babies are more readily upset by separations and somewhat

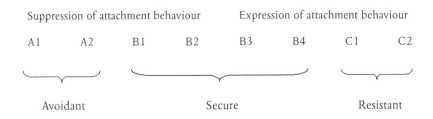

Figure 3.1 Continuum of groups and subgroups reflecting the suppression/expression of attachment behaviour

like resistant babies on reunion. C1 babies are openly angry, while C2 babies express their anger through inappropriate helplessness.

The attachment figure serves both as a haven of safety towards whom the child returns when their attachment system is activated and as a secure base from which the child explores when feeling safe. Main, Hesse and Kaplan (2005) describe the differential attention to these two aspects which children in each of the three attachment groups show. Secure children are flexible in their attention respectively to attachment or exploration, depending on the situation in which they find themselves. Avoidant children maintain their attention inflexibly away from attachment-related experiences. Resistant children are inflexible in maintaining their attention towards attachment-related issues.

Disorganised attachment

Group D: Disorganised/disoriented insecure attachment

It became apparent that some infants did not fit Groups A, B or C. In order to address this problem, Main and Solomon re-examined over 200 strange situation videotapes (Main and Solomon 1986, 1990). They found that the infants did not share a new pattern of behaviour, but instead exhibited odd behaviour which lacked a coherent, organised strategy for dealing with the stress of separation. This led to the introduction of a new category of attachment, namely Group D – disorganised/disoriented insecure attachment. Infants should be considered to meet the criteria for this category if, in the presence of their caregiver in the strange situation, their behaviour falls into one or more of the following behavioural clusters, or indices of disorganisation and disorientation (Main and Solomon 1990):

1. sequential display of contradictory behavioural patterns, such as very strong attachment behaviour suddenly followed by avoidance, freezing or dazed behaviour

2. simultaneous display of contradictory behaviours, such as strong avoidance with strong contact seeking, distress or anger

3. undirected, misdirected, incomplete and interrupted movements and expressions – for example, extensive expressions of distress accompanied by movement away from, rather than towards, the mother

4. stereotypies, asymmetrical movements, mistimed movements and anomalous postures such as stumbling for no apparent reason and only when the parent is present

5. freezing, stilling and slowed 'underwater' movements and expressions

6. direct indices of apprehension regarding the parent, such as hunched shoulders or fearful facial expressions

7. direct indices of disorganisation and disorientation, such as disoriented wandering, confused or dazed expressions, or multiple rapid changes in affect.

Main and Solomon point out that most of the disorganised behaviours do not have even a superficial similarity and are defined 'through exclusion criteria – as *dis*organised and *dis*oriented' (p.152). They propose a simple ordering of the intensity of disorganised behaviour indices, which is presented briefly below. A fuller description of the procedures for identifying infants as disorganised/disoriented, including the full text of this nine-point scale, is found in Main and Solomon (1990).[3]

1. no signs of disorganisation/disorientation

3. slight signs of disorganisation/disorientation

5. moderate indices of disorganisation/disorientation which are not clearly sufficient for a D category placement

7. definite qualification for D attachment status, but D behaviour is not extreme. There is one very strong indicator of disorganisation/ disorientation, or there are several lesser indications

9. definite qualification for D attachment status: in addition, the indices of disorganisation and disorientation are strong, frequent or extreme.

If an infant's behaviour meets the criteria for the disorganised category, an attempt is made to discern the underlying strategy (secure, avoidant or resistant). An infant may therefore be classified as disorganised-secure, disorganised-avoidant or disorganised-resistant. Often just two subgroups are distinguished, namely disorganised-secure (D-secure) and disorganised-insecure (D-insecure), which are sometimes given the more descriptive labels D-approach and D-avoid-resist (e.g. Lyons-Ruth *et al.* 2004). If an underlying strategy cannot be discerned, categorising the infant's attachment status as 'unclassifiable' (U) may be the only option.

It has been pointed out (Lyons-Ruth and Jacobvitz 1999) that disorganisation in infancy was late in recognition because the behaviours are fleeting and often out of context. For example, a child in an apparently good mood may suddenly strike his or her mother. Odd behaviours which lack coherence or apparent sense are easily missed. Well-trained observers, however, are able to pick up on these behaviours, and high inter-rater reliability on the classification of infants as disorganised/disoriented has been established.

The disorganised/disoriented attachment type was not discerned when Bowlby wrote the first volume of *Attachment and Loss* (1969, 1969/1982). However, in that work he describes and explains very similar behaviour: 'Sometimes when two tendencies are present, e.g. to turn to the left and also to the right, they cancel each other out and no behaviour of any sort results' (p.100).

From disorganised to controlling attachment behaviour

Longitudinal studies have shown a shift from disorganised attachment behaviour in infancy to controlling behaviour later in childhood. The classic study is that of Main and Cassidy (1988). In this study of two samples the authors developed a system for classifying attachment organisation at age 6 on the basis of the children's responses to unstructured reunions with parents following a one-hour separation, in a laboratory setting (see Chapter 8). In addition to secure (B), insecure-avoidant (A) and insecure-ambivalent (C) groups, they described and named two new groups, insecure-controlling (D) and insecure-unclassified (the latter being reunion behaviour which does not fit the other groups). A child in the insecure-controlling (D) group is described as seeming 'to attempt to control or direct the parent's attention and behavior and assumes a role that is usually considered more appropriate for a parent with reference to a child' (p.419). Two subgroups are distinguished:

1. *Controlling-punitive.* The child tries to humiliate, or reject the parent, direct, saying to them, for example, e.g. 'I told you to keep quiet!'

2. *Controlling-overbright/caregiving.* The child shows solicitous and protective behaviour toward the parent, or demonstrates care or concern suggestive of a role reversal. The child may show 'an extreme, nervous cheerfullness on reunion' (Main and Cassidy 1988, p.419).

Using this classification system, Main and Cassidy (1988) found that assessments of infant attachment in the strange situation predicted sixth-year reunion responses to mother and, to a lesser extent, to father.[4]

In a meta-analysis of precursors, concomitants and sequelae of disorganised attachment in early childhood (van IJzendoorn, Schuengel and Bakermans-Kranenburg 1999), in the four pertinent studies (including Main and Cassidy 1988) a significant association was found between disorganised infant attachment and later controlling behaviour (n=223, r=0.40, p<0.001).

Despite the organised nature of the controlling children's behaviour, their underlying representations appear by no means organised. Solomon, George and De Jong (1995) addressed this issue in a study of children approximately 6 years old, which assessed both the reunion behaviour of the children using Main and Cassidy's (1988) procedure (see Chapter 8) and their internal representations using a story completion task (see p.113). The majority of the controlling children 'depicted the self and caregivers as both frightening and unpredictable or frightened and helpless' (p.458). The doll-play of controlling children in the story completion task was characterised by 'themes of catastrophe and helplessness or by complete inhibition of play and suggested disorganization of representational processes' (p.447).

These findings indicate that controlling children, although seemingly behaviourally organised, at the representational level continue to be disorganised.

An alternative classification

Crittenden (1995) has developed the Dynamic Maturational Model of attachment, a somewhat different classification of attachment organisation, retaining the A, B and C categories, but substituting A/C for D.

The distribution of attachment patterns

Initial samples in which distribution of attachment patterns was measured did not include the D classification. Following the identification of the disorganised category, a further meta-analysis of disorganised attachment in early childhood was carried out by van IJzendoorn et al. (1999), which included nearly 80 studies[5] on more than 100 samples with 6,282 parent–child dyads and 1,285 disorganised attachment classifications. Table 3.1 shows the distribution of A, B, C and D classifications.

Table 3.1 Distribution of A, B, C and D classifications

	Total N	Classified as A (%)	Classified as B (%)	Classified as C (%)	Classified as D (%)
Ainsworth *et al.* (1978)	106	22	66	12	–
Meta-analysis of 32 samples from 8 countries (van IJzendoorn and Kroonenberg 1988)	1,990	21	65	14	–
Meta-analysis of disorganised attachment in early childhood (van IJzendoorn *et al.* 1999): middle-class, non-clinical groups in North America	2,104	15	62	9	15

In their paper, van IJzendoorn *et al.* (1999) further distinguished their sample of disorganised children into different populations. The distributions of disorganised attachment in these groups is shown in Table 3.2.

Table 3.2 Distribution of D classifications from meta-analysis using Main and Solomon (1990) or other classifications

	% classified D according to Main and Solomon (1990)	% using other classifications of D
Low socio-economic status	34	25
Non-American Western countries	17	18
Maltreating parents	77	48
Depressed[6] mothers	19	21

Retrospective analysis of the high-risk sample in the Minnesota longitudinal study (see Chapter 11) found a rate of attachment disorganisation of 35 per cent at age 12 months (n=122) and 43 per cent at 18 months (n=83) (Carlson 1998).

Stability or predictability of attachment patterns

According to Bowlby (1969/1982, 1973, 1988), the organisation of attachment is labile, that is relatively sensitive to changes of environment, in the early years of life. Evidence shows, he writes, that during the first two or three years, the pattern of attachment is 'a property more of the couple in which the child is a partner than of the behavioural organisation within the child himself' (Bowlby 1969/1982, p.365), and that 'if the parent treats the child differently the pattern will change accordingly' (Bowlby 1988, p.127). As the child grows older, the pattern becomes increasingly a property of the child, becoming more stable and resistant to change (Bowlby 1969/1982).

Bowlby (1988) notes that securely attached children are more able to update their working models of self and parents as a result of the more open communication characteristic of these dyads. For anxiously attached children, however, updating is obstructed by defensive exclusion of discrepant experience and information. Consequently, models and their associated patterns of interaction may persist largely uncorrected and unchanged, even in later interaction with people who may be very different in their interaction.

Another term for stability of attachment pattern is continuity. Discontinuity is deemed 'lawful' if the change follows a change in the caregiving style of an attachment figure (discussed in Chapter 4, p.38) with an increase or a decrease in sensitive responsiveness, or to a change in caregiver. Discontinuity in attachment may also be due to significant intervening trauma (Main *et al.* 2005).

Evidence

(Ages at respective assessments in bold; sample type in italics.)

BELSKY et al.

Belsky *et al.* (1996) report that when the stability rates of A, B and C classifications from five studies of *non-risk* American families were weighted by sample size, a stability rate of 75 per cent was found for 205 **infant**–mother dyads. In the same paper, however, Belsky *et al.* question the design of many of the early studies of stability, pointing to modest sample sizes and a failure to correct for chance associations. In their studies of two infant–mother samples (n=125, n=90) in which attachment was assessed **at 12 and 18 months**, and an infant–father sample (n=120) in which attachment was assessed at **13 and 20 months**, significant stability in attachment security was not found, with rates ranging from 46 per cent to 55 per cent.

VAN IJZENDOORN META-ANALYSIS

In a meta-analysis of disorganised attachment, van IJzendoorn *et al.* (1999) found that the stability of disorganisation **across 1 to 60 months** was significant in both *middle-class* samples and samples with *low socio-economic status* (*p*<0.001 respectively). A significant effect was also found for the association between disorganised infant attachment and later controlling behaviour (n=223; *r* =0.40; *p*<0.001).

THE MINNESOTA STUDY

In 2004, findings were published from the Minnesota longitudinal study (see Chapter 11) regarding continuity of attachment **from infancy to late adolescence** in a *high-risk* sample (Weinfield, Whaley and Egeland 2004). The sample comprised 125 of the original children in the longitudinal study, now aged 19 years, for whom strange situation data scored for disorganisation were available and to whom the Adult Attachment Interview (AAI) was administered at age 19.

Participants who were disorganised in infancy were more likely to be insecure on the AAI and less likely to be autonomous than were participants who were organised in infancy. Eighty-six per cent of participants who were disorganised in infancy were classified as insecure on the AAI. Participants who had a secondary 'secure' classification in infancy were not more likely to be autonomous on the AAI. Disorganisation scores were not related to unresolved loss scores but they were related to unresolved abuse scores on the AAI.

Participants were distinguished into four groups according to stability of attachment. The 'secure–secure' group (n=15) were secure, not disorganised or unresolved, in both infancy and adolescence. The 'secure–insecure' group (n=35) were secure, not disorganised in infancy and insecure or unresolved in adolescence. The 'insecure–insecure' group (n=56) were insecure or disorganised in infancy and insecure or unresolved in adolescence. The 'insecure–secure' group (n=19) were insecure or disorganised in infancy and secure, not unresolved in adolescence.

Findings based on this four-group classification included the following:

- The 'secure–secure' group reported significantly fewer periods of high life-stress than the 'secure–insecure' group.

- The 'secure–secure' group experienced better family functioning in early adolescence (aged 13) than the 'secure–insecure' group.

- The 'insecure–insecure' group was significantly more likely to have experienced early maltreatment than the 'insecure–secure' group.

- When the children were aged 6 years, a safer and more stimulating home environment was provided for the 'insecure–secure' group than for the 'insecure–insecure' group.

The findings of this study of a high-risk sample support the notion of coherent or lawful discontinuity in attachment. However, no single event or characteristic ensured continuity or discontinuity; rather 'attachment relationships continued to evolve in a dynamic fashion' (p.90), suggesting that attachment has 'an adaptive, context sensitive, relational quality' (p.90).

THE WATERS *et al.* SAMPLE

Waters (1978) found a high stability rate of 96 per cent **within infancy** in a *middle-class* sample of children assessed in the strange situation. **Twenty years later**, 50 of the original participants were interviewed using the Adult Attachment Interview (AAI) (Waters *et al.* 2000). Using three classifications (A, B and C) at each age (the insecure disorganised classification was not developed when the infants were assessed), it was found that 64 per cent of participants were assigned to corresponding classifications in infancy and early adulthood ($p<0.005$). Using the secure–insecure dichotomy, 72 per cent of participants received the equivalent classification at both ages ($p<0.001$). 'Stressful life events were significantly related to the likelihood of a secure infant becoming insecure in early adulthood (66.6% if mother reported one or more life events versus 15% if she reported none, $p<0.01$)' (p.687), supporting lawful discontinuity.

FRALEY META-ANALYSIS

In a meta-analysis of attachment stability, Fraley (2002) computed stability coefficients with respect to 27 samples. In all the studies, Time 1 was the assessment of attachment at 12 months in the strange situation. Time 2 ranged **from 13 months to 21 years**, clustering approximately around five temporal periods, namely ages 1, 2, 4, 6 and 19. The stability coefficient from Time 1 to Time 2 was then estimated for each of these five reassessment times.

The correlation for temporal group Age 1–Age 1 was high ($r=1.00$). However, the correlations for the other temporal groups decreased to $r=0.3$ to

0.4 with the exception of the Age 1–Age 6 group where the correlation was $r = 0.67$ (weighted by sample size).

These findings should be treated with some caution, however. First, the meta-analysis included *high-risk* samples, where less continuity would be expected; indeed, unlike any other group, all four studies in temporal group Age 1–Age 6 were of *low-risk* samples. Second, the method for assessing attachment security at the second time point varied. This may have involved some assessment error.

GROSSMANN AND GROSSMANN SAMPLES

Grossmann and Grossmann have carried out two longitudinal studies of *middle-class, low-risk* samples, in Bielefeld and Regensburg, Germany (described in Chapter 11). In the Bielefeld study, attachment to mother **in early childhood** predicted security of attachment at **age 10 years** (Grossmann, Grossmann and Kindler 2005). Neither the Bielefeld nor Regensburg studies found a significant relationship between attachment security at **12 and 18 months** with mother or father and their subsequent own **adult** measures of attachment (Grossmann *et al.* 2005). However, attachment security in **middle childhood** predicted AAI security at age **22 years**.

BERKELEY LONGITUDINAL STUDY

In the Berkeley longitudinal study, carried out by Main and colleagues, attachment was assessed at 12 or 18 months in the strange situation, at age 6 in Main and Cassidy's (1988) reunion procedure and an adapted version of the Separation Anxiety Test (SAT), and at 19 in the Adult Attachment Interview (AAI). The sample comprised 189 *low-risk* families (see Main *et al.* 2005 for a comprehensive account of the study and findings regarding the predictability of attachment behaviour).

Main and Cassidy (1988) found that 84 per cent of children assessed as avoidant, secure or disorganised[7] **in infancy** had the same or equivalent pattern of attachment with respect to their mothers **at age 6**; the figure for fathers was 61 per cent. Disorganised infant strange situation behaviour predicted D-Controlling behaviour at age 6, and also being classified as D-Fearful on the SAT.

With respect to predictability to **young adulthood**, infant security with mother predicted a secure-autonomous versus an insecure AAI. Avoidant infants 'strongly tended to be dismissing of attachment on the AAI, although other insecure children had also become dismissing' (p.279). Children classified as avoidant at 6 years were again very likely to become dismissing on the AAI at 19 years. Again, however, other children had also become dismissing and the association was not therefore significant. Regarding disorganisation, almost all D-Controlling and D-Fearful 6-year-olds were insecure on the AAI. When the Unresolved and Cannot Classify AAI categories were converted to a three-point scale, infant disorganisation and its 6-year-old equivalents (D-Controlling and D-Fearful) 'predicted their "adult" parallel' (Unresolved/Cannot Classify on the AAI) (p.287).

Comment

With the development of the person, the means or modality for assessing attachment must change. In the strange situation and 6-year-old reunion procedure the focus is on the child's behaviour (based on their internal organisation) in relation to their caregiver. In middle childhood, the SAT or narrative stem assessments have been proven as valid means for assessing children's internal working models of attachment. The AAI, with its ingenious method for 'surprising the unconscious', focuses on the linguistic representation of the adult's state of mind with respect to attachment. Thus, non-verbal and verbal modalities are used in the assessment of attachment at different stages of development. With this in mind, Main *et al.*'s (2005) thinking about different forms of predictability, rather than simple stability, offers the opportunity for further advances in our understanding of the long-term trajectories of attachment.

Main *et al.* offer an explanation for these trajectories, describing a secure person as able to attend flexibly to attachment or exploration, depending on the circumstances. By contrast, avoidant/dismissive organisation focuses attention inflexibly towards exploration and away from attachment, while resistant/preoccupied organisation focuses attention inflexibly in the opposite direction. Disorganisation/unresolved status leads to difficulty in constructing a coherent schema with respect to attachment and exploration.

Summary

Based on their cumulative experiences with their attachment figures, infants aged approximately 9 months have developed patterns of attachment specific to these attachment figures. These patterns are measurable by the strange situation procedure between 9 and 18 months. The patterns have been classified into three organised patterns – secure, insecure-avoidant and insecure-resistant/ambivalent – and one insecure-disorganised pattern. The distribution of these patterns is remarkably consistent across different cultures with the majority (approximately 65 per cent) being secure.

After early childhood, these attachment patterns endure into adulthood, although their expression and measurement change with age. Any changes in the patterns follow 'lawful discontinuity' which can be brought about by a change in caregiving, caregiver, significantly traumatic events in the child's life or following therapy in adulthood. The trajectories are more uneven and less predictable in children whose early experiences include adversity and maltreatment.

Notes

1   Ainsworth first studied security theory under the tutorship of William Blatz at the University of Toronto in the late 1930s. She was the first to apply the secure/insecure typology, in her observational study of babies in Uganda. For insights into the development of Ainsworth's work see 'An interview with Mary Ainsworth' (Ainsworth and Marvin 1995).

2   This continuum is sometimes presented as reflecting the threshold for activating attachment behaviour, e.g. Goldberg (2000). This poses two conceptual difficulties. First, as already described, the attachment behavioural system is conceived as continually active, operating in times of absence of threat by continuously monitoring the accessibility of the attachment figure. Second, to quote Main: 'Ainsworth believed that, contrary to appearances, the attachment behavioural system was no doubt activated by the strange situation procedure for avoidant, as for secure, infants, and indeed recordings made during this procedure have pointed to equally strong psychophysiological indices of distress' (Main 1999, p.718). Thus, avoidant infants suppress rather than express the activation. Whilst this may seem a fine point, acknowledging the activation allows acknowledgement of the stress and arousal which is nonetheless experienced by avoidant infants.

3   Main and Solomon define alternate points on this scale, i.e. 1, 3, 5, 7 and 9.

4   There were too few insecure-C children to be included in the study. A, B and D attachment categories with mothers of 84 per cent of the sample were predictive of sixth-year attachments (k=0.76, p<0.001). Of the 12 children who had been insecure-disorganised/disoriented with mother in infancy, 75 per cent were classified as controlling at age 6 years (Table 2, p.420). The predictability for the father–child sample, whilst significant, was relatively weaker, with 61 per cent of sixth-year reunion categories with father predicted from infancy strange situation classifications (k=0.28, p<0.05). Only one child was assessed as controlling with regard to father at age 6 years. Indeed, the authors suggest that the relative weakness of predictability for the father may have been partly attributable to the relatively restricted range of classifications (22 of the 33 father–child dyads were rated as secure in infancy, compared with 12 of the 32 mother–child dyads).

5   The exact number appears not to be stated.

6   As Green and Goldwyn (2002) point out, two studies have shown an association between infant disorganisation and severe or chronic maternal depression or bipolar disorder. It seems likely, they suggest, 'that only severe and/or chronic maternal depression is associated with infant attachment disorganisation and that less severe depression is not' (p.837).

7   Only two infants were classified as ambivalent-resistant (C).

4 What are the Factors Influencing Attachment Organisation (and Disorganisation)?

The contribution of caregiving to attachment organisation

What is caregiving?

Late in his work, Bowlby used the term 'caregiving' *specifically* to describe the caregiver behaviour which is complementary to the child's attachment behaviour. Caregiving, in its pure form, consists of providing protection and comfort so as to deactivate the need for attachment behaviour and restore the threatened person to equanimity and a sense of security. Caregiving is one component of parenting. Other components are, for example, feeding, teaching and playing. In Bowlby's words, however, the 'shared dyadic programme' given 'top priority' is one of attachment–caregiving (1969/1982, p.378).

Whereas the attachment behavioural system in the child functions to *receive* protection, the caregiving behavioural system functions to *provide* protection and thereby, in the parent–child relationship, promote the survival of the child.

Bowlby viewed parenting behaviour, like attachment behaviour, as to some degree pre-programmed with learned detail and thus, in its individual expression, influenced by the parent's own experience:

> Parenting behavior in humans is certainly not the product of some unvarying parenting instinct, but nor is it reasonable to regard it merely as the product of learning. Parenting behavior has strong biological roots,

thus accounting for the very strong emotions associated with it; but the specific form that the behavior takes in each of us turns on our experiences – during childhood especially, during adolescence, before and during marriage, and with each individual child. (Bowlby 1984, p.272)

The caregiving behavioural system is activated when the carer perceives the child's signals of distress, perceives the child to be in a *potential* or *actual* state of discomfort, fear or danger or when the carer becomes aware of natural clues to danger. Having become activated, caregiving begins by enacting carer–child proximity by such behaviours as calling or retrieving the child. This is followed by removing the source of stress or distancing the child from it. There then follow comforting behaviours.

Typically in infants and young children, the child's attachment system and the carer's caregiving system are simultaneously activated, with both child and carer sensing the need for proximity. However, as George and Solomon (1999, p.653) point out, the carer is cognitively more mature than the child and better able to assess real or potential danger. This may result in situations where the carer's caregiving system is activated but the child's attachment system is not. Conflict may ensue, especially involving older children, between the carer's wish to protect and the child's wish for independence. Conversely, situations may occur where the child is frightened but the caregiver knows there is no objective danger. An often-observed example of this is separation between the child and the caregiver, such as when the child is left in the care of a 'baby-sitter', friend or teacher, that is a person who is not an attachment figure. Mere separation is a 'natural clue to danger' for the child, whilst the caregiver knows that the child is safe. Such situations require understanding and a sensitive, reassuring response from the caregiver.

In practice, the term caregiving is used less specifically, to describe the several or overall parenting functions. Ainsworth, working in the 1970s before Bowlby defined the specific meaning of caregiving, did not refer to the term caregiving in her work at that time. She studied and referred extensively to maternal sensitivity, which she regarded both as an overall attribute of the caregiver and a specific scale in her measure of maternal behaviour.

The relationship between caregiving and other domains of parenting
On the final page of the second edition of *Attachment and Loss* (1969/1982), Bowlby emphasises that the parent–child relationship 'contains more than one shared dyadic programme'. Others are a feeding–fed shared programme, a play-mates programme and a learner–teacher (written in this order) programme.

'Thus, a parent–child relationship is by no means exclusively that of attachment–caregiving.' He points out, however, that the shared dyadic programme which is given 'top priority' is the one of attachment–caregiving (1969/1982, p.378).

The association between caregiving and other domains of parenting has received surprisingly little attention. Given the dearth of empirical evidence, in order to provide some answers to this question, the commentaries on this subject by leading attachment scholars are presented.

George and Solomon have studied and written widely on the caregiving behavioural system. In 'Attachment and caregiving' (1999, p.665) they consider whether parental behaviours such as nursing, cleaning and 'affectionate behaviour', which are also central to the child's survival, should be viewed as part of the caregiving repertoire of behaviours. They conclude that a wide variety of parental behaviours are necessary to protect the child, especially the helpless infant.

Main (1999, p.846) emphasises Bowlby's use of the term 'caregiving' to describe the behavioural system which is complementary to infant attachment and reminds us that he was clear that parents do other things to promote their child's development. Examples she gives are teaching, discipline, providing material support, serving as role models and playing. She makes the important point that whilst some children may be disadvantaged by an insecure attachment, they may be advantaged by other aspects of parenting.

Zeanah and Boris (2000) consider which features of the parent–child relationship may be relevant for the child's attachment. They postulate that the caregiver behaviours most salient for the child's attachment are emotional availability, nurturance and warmth, protection and provision of comfort. Less salient for attachment are teaching, play, instrumental care and discipline.

Rutter and O'Connor (1999) reiterate that 'attachment does not constitute the whole of relationships' (p.824). Parent–child relationships also involve 'disciplinary features, the shaping of social experiences, the provision of models of behavior, teaching, conversational interchanges (and hence the development of ideas) and playful interaction' (p.836). They make the important point that effective interventions and parent training methods do not explicitly focus on qualities of attachment or caregiving. Examples given are: high-quality nursery provision, the Perry Preschool Program, and parent training methods pioneered by Patterson and colleagues (1982) and developed further by Webster-Stratton (1996; Webster-Stratton, Hollinsworth and Kolpacoff 1989). They suggest that these broad-based interventions may capture a quality of parenting, for example sensitive responsivity, which is attachment complementary. Our understanding is disadvantaged by a lack of evidence:

> The truth of the matter, however, is that we lack empirical evidence on the connections between attachment and nonattachment components of relationships, and especially on the specific consequences of the different aspects of parenting. Such evidence is greatly needed and requires a coming together of contrasting parenting perspectives in order to test competing hypotheses. (Rutter and O'Connor 1999, p.836)

Increasing attention is being paid to very specific aspects of the caregiver–child relationship within the attachment paradigm. This very focused approach may not be of help to a busy practitioner who may wish to base conclusions about the adequacy of parenting on impressions of overall parent–child interaction. However, caution is required in equating apparently 'good enough' parenting with the specific sensitivity in caregiving required to promote secure attachment (see below).

Empirical evidence for the role of the caregiver in determining organisation (or disorganisation) of attachment security

This section considers the aspects of maternal behaviour which have been found to be central in shaping the infant's attachment organisation or disorganisation.

The association between caregiver behaviour and child security is apparent very early in life:

> Maternal behaviour in both the first and the fourth quarters – and presumably in between also – is significantly associated with the security–anxiety dimension of an infant's attachment relationship with his mother, and…this association is evident even in the first quarter of the first year. (Ainsworth *et al.* 1978, p.152)

The specific antecedents of organised attachments (A, B and C)

In the Baltimore study, Ainsworth and colleagues examined the relationship between the behaviour of infants in the strange situation and the behaviour their mothers displayed when interacting with them at home (Ainsworth, Bell and Stayton 1971; Ainsworth *et al.* 1978).

Measures of maternal behaviour were devised according to the following classes of behaviour: responsiveness to crying, behaviour relevant to separation/reunion, behaviour relevant to close bodily contact, behaviour relevant to face-to-face interaction, behaviour relevant to infant obedience, behaviour relevant to feeding, and general characteristics. Four of the six measures of general maternal characteristics, namely 'sensitivity–insensitivity to signals', 'acceptance–rejection', 'cooperation–interference' and 'accessibility–ignoring', are known as the Maternal Sensitivity Scales (described in Chapter 9).

It is interesting to note that Ainsworth and colleagues considered a wide range of mother–child interactions, of which caregiving (in its specific Bowlby sense) was one aspect.

Ainsworth *et al.* (1978) compared the mean scores for the various maternal behaviours for infant classifications A, B and C.[1] Findings of significant inter-group differences at $p<0.05$ or greater are summarised below.

- Mothers of Group A and Group C infants were significantly more *unresponsive to crying* than mothers of Group B infants.

- Mothers of Group A infants *acknowledged the baby when entering the room* significantly less than mothers of Group B infants.

- Mothers of Group A and Group C infants were *affectionate during bodily contact* significantly less often than mothers of Group B infants.

- Mothers of Group A infants were significantly more frequently *abrupt and interfering when they picked up the baby*.

- Mothers of Group C infants were significantly more often perceived as *inept in their handling of the baby during close physical contact* than mothers of Group B infants.

- Mothers of Group C infants were *occupied with routine activities while holding the baby* significantly more than mothers of Group B infants. This usually involved holding the baby to feed him. The babies in the overall sample seemed eager during the fourth quarter[2] to feed themselves. Thus, continuing to hold infants and resist their efforts to feed themselves tended to cause the infants to rebel and result in unhappy feeding and occasions for struggle.

The sharpest differences between strange situation groups were found in the ratings of general maternal characteristics:

- Mothers of Group A and Group C infants were significantly more *insensitive, rejecting, interfering and ignoring* than mothers of Group B infants.

- Mothers of Group A infants were especially *rejecting* (mothers of Group C infants had on average mid-scale ratings for acceptance–rejection).

Findings regarding the relationship between the four scales of general maternal characteristics and strange situation subgroups are also presented.

SENSITIVE RESPONSIVENESS: THE ANTECEDENT OF ATTACHMENT ORGANISATION

Ainsworth and colleagues concluded that the most important aspect of maternal behaviour associated with infant attachment organisation is *sensitive responsiveness* to infant signals and communications. This is manifested in specific ways in different situations and, the authors believe, pervades the quality of maternal behaviour throughout many specific kinds of interaction. Thus, sensitive responsiveness and other correlated measures of maternal behaviour do not reflect maternal behaviour in absolute terms, but 'they do tap the extent to which a particular mother is able to gear her interaction with a particular baby in accordance with the behavioral signals he gives of his states, needs, and, eventually, of his wishes and plans' (Ainsworth *et al.* 1978, p.152).

Research by Cassidy *et al.* (2005) now suggests that responsiveness *specifically* to the child's attachment behaviour may be the crucial antecedent of attachment organisation, rather than global sensitivity. (This research is more fully described under 'Bridging the transmission gap' on p.53.)

REFLECTIVE FUNCTIONING

Fonagy *et al.* (1998) have used to term 'reflective functioning' or 'mentalisation' to refer to the capacity to understand behaviour by considering one's own underlying mental states and intentions as well as those of the other. The particular concern with respect to attachment is the caregiver's 'capacity to envisage the infant as a mental entity, a human being with intentions, feelings and desires' (Fonagy *et al.* 1994, p.246). Links have been found between maternal reflective functioning and infant attachment classification (Fonagy, Steele and Steele 1991), and parental states of mind with respect to attachment and parental sensitivity (Fonagy *et al.* 1994; Slade *et al.* 2005).

MIND-MINDEDNESS: A FURTHER ASPECT OF MATERNAL SENSITIVE RESPONSIVENESS

There has been a further development in the understanding of the mother's sensitivity to her child, which Meins (1997) has termed mind-mindedness. This concept captures the sensitivity to the child's mental state and the ability to 'read' it. In a prospective study of 65 mother–infant dyads (33 boys and 32 girls all aged 6 months), recruited from local health centres and baby clinics, maternal sensitivity was measured using the Ainsworth *et al.* (1971) scale, as well as measuring mind-mindedness on five measures (Meins *et al.* 2001). The infant's security of attachment was measured at 12 months using the strange situation procedure.

The author found that two categories of the mind-mindedness measure, namely 'maternal responsiveness to change in infant's direction of gaze', and 'appropriate mind-related comments', correlated most strongly with the Ainsworth assessment of maternal sensitivity. The 'appropriate mind-related comments' category accounted for a further 12.7 per cent variance in determining secure attachment at 12 months, beyond the Ainsworth measure of maternal sensitivity. Despite low numbers of insecure infants, it was possible to distinguish that mothers of insecure infants made fewer appropriate mind-related comments than mothers of secure infants, the lowest number of comments being made by mothers of avoidant infants.

EMOTION OR AFFECT REGULATION

The attachment behavioural system provides a context for the development of the infant's affect regulation. When the infant's need for attachment is activated, the infant's feelings are strongly aroused. In the course of a sensitive caregiver's response, the caregiver calms the child and thereby decreases the child's affective arousal. In this way, the caregiver provides the experience and model for the child's acquisition of self-regulation.[3] Emotion regulation is thus a vital by-product of attachment theory. Emotion regulation features in some conceptualisations of attachment disorder, discussed in Part Four.

The specific antecedents of disorganised attachment (D)

Lyons-Ruth and Jacobvitz (1999) point out that an understanding of the central role of fear in attachment theory is crucial to an understanding of attachment disorganisation. They refer to Main and Hesse (1990), who hypothesised that the antecedents of disorganised attachment are frightening or frightened behaviour in the attachment figure. In addition to direct fright to the child caused by parental maltreatment, Main and Hesse (1990) suggest a number of patterns of parental behaviour which seem likely to frighten an infant 'either by being directly threatening or by indicating fright on the part of the parent' (Lyons-Ruth and Jacobvitz 1999, p.175). These include unusual vocal and movement patterns and unusual speech content. These parental behaviours appear to be associated with unresolved loss and mourning.

In her retrospective analysis of disorganised attachment in the Minnesota sample (see Chapter 11), Carlson (1998) found that attachment disorganisation was associated with single parenthood, maternal risk status for parenting difficulties, insensitive/intrusive caregiving and abuse and neglect during the first year of life. Disorganisation was not associated with endogenous variables such as maternal medical history, birth complications or maternal drug/alcohol use. Further, disorganisation was not associated with infant temperament and behaviour ratings at three months.

In a meta-analysis of disorganised attachment in early childhood, van IJzendoorn *et al.* (1999) found that in groups of maltreating parents (n=165), 48 per cent of the children were disorganised. When only Main and Solomon (1990) classifications were used, the figure was 77 per cent. Interestingly, in groups with depressed parents (n=340), the percentage of disorganised children was 21 per cent, and 19 per cent using the Main and Solomon classifications.

Thus, child maltreatment is clearly associated with attachment disorganisation. However, disorganisation is also found in 'normal', non-clinical populations; van IJzendoorn *et al.* (1999) found a rate of 15 per cent in these groups. Researchers have begun to explore in finer detail the process by which frightening or frightened caregiver behaviour is communicated to, and internalised by, the child. For example, in the Atypical Maternal Behavior Instrument for Assessment and Classification (AMBIANCE) Bronfman, Parsons and Lyons-Ruth (1999) have developed a coding system for five broader aspects of disrupted parental affective communication. These are affective communication errors, role/boundary confusion (role reversal), frightened/disoriented behaviour, intrusiveness/negativity and withdrawal. Frequency of these aspects was found to be significantly related to the infant's disorganised attachment behaviours. Their study also led them to identify groups of mothers of disorganised infants whom they termed 'hostile or self-referential regarding attachment' and 'helpless–fearful regarding attachment'. Another area of study concerns the known association between parental unresolved loss or trauma and infant disorganised attachment behaviour.

The role of the child's temperament and genetic factors in influencing attachment organisation

Temperament factors

Infants are recognised as showing different behavioural, emotion-regulation and sociability attributes of temperament, which can be measured reliably (e.g. Infant Temperament Questionnaire – Revised (Carey and McDevitt 1978)). Much of temperament is genetically determined although some of these differences between infants are environmentally determined and acquired in utero. For instance, maternal stress in pregnancy is associated with irritability in infants at 9 months (O'Connor *et al.* 2002, 2003a).

An infant who is perceived as 'difficult' will pose a greater challenge to their caregivers. Moreover, the caregiver may share the infant's 'difficult' temperamental attributes. Temperament may thus constitute a risk factor for insensitive/harsh caregiving and the development of insecure or disorganised attachment for the infant. Beyond this causal association between temperament and attachment organisation, there is little other evidence to link the two. By contrast, several findings point to the lack of a direct and determinative association between temperament and attachment organisation. These are described here.

1. A robust association has been demonstrated between the attachment organisation of mothers and fathers respectively, measured antenatally using the Adult Attachment Interview, and the child's attachment classifications with respect to each of the parents (Steele, Steele and Fonagy 1996). At this age, the child's attachment organisation is still person-specific. These associations could therefore not be genetically determined.

2. An intervention study of low socio-economic mothers and their temperamentally irritable infants found a significant association between an intervention designed to enhance maternal sensitivity and attachment classification at 12 months ($p<0.001$). A significant association ($p<0.001$) was again found between intervention and attachment classification at follow-up at 18 months (van den Boom 1994, 1995) (see Chapter 16).

3. No significant association has been found between infants' proneness to distress, a temperamental attribute, and attachment classification in the strange situation (Nachmias *et al.* 1996).

4.   A study of two samples of same-sex twin pairs (total n=138; monozygotic (MZ) pairs=57; dizygotic (DZ) pairs=81) (Bokhorst *et al.* 2003) found the following:

- Shared environment influences explained 52 per cent of the variance in attachment security; unique environment and measurement error explained the remaining 48 per cent.

- The difference in correlations between temperamental reactivity in MZ and DZ twin pairs ($r=0.77$ and $r=0.44$ respectively) pointed to a genetic component in temperamental reactivity. In further analyses, the model used by the researchers showed 'hardly any influence of shared environment on temperamental reactivity (11%)' (p.1777).

- The association between temperamental reactivity and the four-way attachment classifications (avoidant, secure, resistant and disorganised, assessed in the strange situation) was not significant.

The authors state that 'The current behavioral genetic study found considerable evidence to support the decisive role of environmental factors in the development of (non)secure attachment' (p.1777).

Attachment and autism

A question can be posed as to whether, in view of their difficulties in reciprocal social interactions, children with autism are able to form attachment bonds and develop organised attachment patterns. In a meta-analytic review, Rutgers *et al.* (2004) identified 16 studies looking at attachment in children with autism. These studies confirm that children with autism do form attachments and that, moreover, these attachments are organised and the different patterns can be distinguished. The authors carried out both a quantitative and a narrative review and found that children with autism or within the DSM-IV-TR category of Pervasive Developmental Disorder Not Otherwise Specified (PDD-NOS) were able to form secure attachment and show attachment behaviour. The issues of assessment of attachment organisation, which would be confounded by autistic behaviour, were allowed for in these studies. Across the studies which used the strange situation procedure, 53 per cent of children were securely attached, a lower figure than in the normal population. Children with lower mental development showed more insecurity. For children with higher ability or less severe symptoms of autism, the difference from normal populations disappeared. It was possible to distinguish attachment disorganisation, which was measured in two studies.

Specific genes

In 2000, a group of researchers in Budapest reported a finding which suggested that there may be a genetic contribution to attachment disorganisation (Lakatos *et al.* 2000). Attachment organisation was assessed in the strange situation in a sample of 90 healthy 12- to 13-month-old infants from low-risk families. The infants were also tested for a particular gene (48-bp repeat polymorphism in the third exon of the DRD4 gene), blind to the attachment classification. A particular genetic configuration (7-repeat allele) was found in 12 (71%) of the 17 disorganised children, compared to 21 (29%) of the 73 non-disorganised children; this difference was statistically significant ($p<0.005$). The risk for disorganised attachment among children with the 7-repeat allele was estimated to be 4.15. The authors suggest that 'in non-clinical, low-risk populations, having a 7-repeat allele predisposes infants to attachment disorganization' (p.633).

In 2002, the research group published further findings regarding this link between gene and disorganisation (Lakatos *et al.* 2002). Ninety-five children already genotyped for the dopamine D4 receptor gene were additionally genotyped for the functional -521 C/T single nucleotide polymorphism (SNP). It was found that, whilst the -521 C/T genotype alone had no effect on attachment status, its presence enhanced the association between disorganised attachment and the 7-repeat allele ($p<0.025$). 'In the presence of both risk alleles the odds ratio for disorganized attachment increased tenfold' (pp.27 and 29). The authors conclude that this finding 'supports our previous postulation that the DRD4 gene plays a role in the development of attachment behavior in normal, low-risk populations' (p.29).

In 2004, Bakermans-Kranenburg and van IJzendoorn reported an attempt to replicate the findings of Lakatos and colleagues. In their behavioural-genetic study of 76 same-sex mono- and dizygotic twin pairs, the Lakatos *et al.* findings were not replicated. They did not find an association of disorganised attachment with the 7-repeat DRD4 allele, or with the -521 C/T genotype; nor did the 7-repeat DRD4 allele in the presence of the -521 T variant increase the risk for disorganisation. They had found the role of genetic factors in disorganised attachment to be negligible (see above; Bokhorst *et al.* 2003). Bakermans-Kranenburg and van IJzendoorn state that, whilst 'a modest genetic effect would not be incompatible with an environmental explanation of disorganized attachment', the tenfold increase of the genetic risk reported by Lakatos *et al.* 'might not easily be incorporated in the prevailing Main and Hesse model of disorganized attachment' (2004, p.212). Even when the Budapest and Leiden samples were combined, the absence of an association remained. Bakermans-Kranenburg and van IJzendoorn conclude that 'the empirical evidence to date appears to support variability in parenting or parental factors rather than genetic factors as explanation for the presence or absence of disorganized attachment behaviour' (p.215).

In the same issue, Gervai and Lakatos (2004) provide a riposte to the Bakermans-Kranenburg and van IJzendoorn argument.

A recent paper by the same group (Gervai *et al.* 2005) confirms the previous findings by Lakatos *et al.* (2000, 2002). The mechanism by which this genetic variation in the child exerts its reported effect towards disorganised attachment is not clear. The authors now suggest that not carrying the T.7 haplotype of the DRD4 gene is a resilience factor for the development of early (secure) attachment. The DRD4 gene is thought to be involved in dopamine receptor production in the prefrontal cortex of the brain. Dopamine and the prefrontal cortex probably play a role in functions related to attachment formation. The density of these dopamine receptors increases between 6 and 12 months of life and the T.7 haplotype may reduce the rate of production of the dopamine receptors, doing so at the time of attachment formation.

The debate remains unresolved.

The intergenerational transmission of attachment

The introduction of the Adult Attachment Interview (AAI) protocol (George, Kaplan and Main 1984, 1985, 1996) in the mid-1980s (described in Chapter 8) allowed the assessment of 'state of mind with respect to attachment' in young adulthood and beyond. The AAI coding system is based on the *coherence* of the account of the adult's experiences with their parents, rather than on the *nature* of the experiences or the *content* of the account. Painful childhood experiences with regard to attachment may have become resolved, insecurity in childhood becoming 'earned security' in adulthood. In their classic 1985 paper, Main, Kaplan and Cassidy describe the parents of secure babies as seeming to have considered and integrated unfavourable attachment experiences into a mental process 'long before the interview took place' (p.96). The AAI distinguishes five major categories: autonomous-secure, dismissing-insecure, preoccupied-insecure, unresolved/disorganised and cannot classify.

The link between parental state of mind with respect to attachment and infant security

In their 1985 paper, Main *et al.* found a significant relationship between the security of the mother's working model of attachment, as assessed in the AAI, and her infant's security of attachment ($p<0.001$). A significant relationship was also found for the father ($p<0.05$).

The association between parental state of mind with regard to attachment and the pattern of attachment in the child of that parent has been found in many subsequent studies. In a meta-analysis, van IJzendoorn (1995) found that, based on data from 13 samples (n=661), the correspondence between three-way infant and parental attachment classifications (infant secure/parent autonomous; infant insecure-avoidant/parent dismissing; infant insecure-resistant/parent preoccupied) was 70 per cent. The correspondence between four-way classifications (including infant disorganised/disoriented and parent unresolved/disorganised), based on nine studies, was 63 per cent.

Thus, there is robust evidence for a link between parents' state of mind with respect to attachment (as assessed in the AAI) and infant attachment security (as assessed in the strange situation). Moreover, as previously reported, this association is found when mothers' representations of attachment are assessed antenatally (Steele, Steele and Fonagy 1996). This link is referred to as the transmission of attachment. The question which follows is how the parental state of mind with respect to attachment is transmitted *behaviourally* to the child.

Ainsworth *et al.* in 1978 had advanced from the findings of their research that parental sensitive responsiveness is the key influence on the child's pattern of attachment: 'The most important aspect of maternal behavior commonly associated with the security–anxiety dimension of infant attachment…emerges as sensitive responsiveness to infant signals and communications' (Ainsworth *et al.* 1978, p.152). Thus, following the introduction of the AAI and the demonstrated association between parental representations of attachment and infant attachment organisation, it was hypothesised that sensitive responsiveness constituted the behavioural link. If this was the case, however, two statistical associations needed to be demonstrated. First, there must be a demonstrated link between parental state of mind with respect to attachment and parental sensitive responsiveness. Second, there must be a demonstrated link between parental sensitive responsiveness (parental behaviour) and infant attachment. These links may be presented diagrammatically as in Figure 4.1.

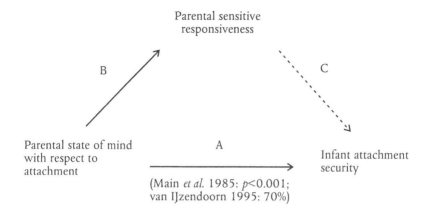

Figure 4.1 Model of the links between parental sensitive responsiveness and infant attachment
Source: This model is based on van IJzendoorn 1995, p.398.

The link between parental state of mind with respect to attachment and parental sensitive responsiveness (B)

In his 1995 meta-analysis, van IJzendoorn also examined the relationship between parental state of mind with respect to attachment and parental sensitive responsiveness. In an analysis of ten studies involving 389 dyads, mostly mother–child pairs, he found an effect size of 0.72, which, according to conventional criteria, is large. This finding is alternatively presented as parental attachment appearing to account for approximately 12 per cent of the variation in parental responsiveness, which, van IJzendoorn states, 'can be considered a confirmation' (p.395) of the hypothesis concerning the association between parental attachment representations and 'parental responsiveness to the child's attachment signals' (p.390).

In their 2005 chapter, Main *et al.* offer a speculative explanation for the insensitive behaviours of parents in insecure-organised states of mind with respect to attachment. Such parents may implicitly seek to maintain a state of '*false* but *felt* security' (p.292) with respect to their childhood primary attachment figures. Thus, infant attachment behaviours may provoke anxiety in insecure-dismissing parents, and infant exploratory behaviours may provoke anxiety in insecure-preoccupied parents, by threatening the parents' state of mind that had been experienced as optimal for continued proximity to their own parents in childhood. Insensitive parental behaviour may be understood, therefore, as maintaining the parent's 'historically desired, and currently "working," state of mind' (p.292).

The link between parental sensitive responsiveness and infant attachment security (C)

In his 1995 meta-analysis van IJzendoorn did not test this link. However, he uses the findings of Goldsmith and Alansky (1987), who conducted a meta-analysis on maternal responsiveness and children's attachment security (link C), and his own findings regarding links A and B in order to calculate effect sizes for sources of influence on children's attachment according to the above model. Goldsmith and Alansky had found a modest effect size of 0.68 for the effects of parental sensitivity on infant security, using Ainsworth's rating scale for sensitive responsiveness. Using this effect size for link C, van IJzendoorn found that 'the influence of parental state of mind on children's attachment through transmission mechanisms other than responsiveness' (p.398) was 0.36. 'In other words, the largest part of the influence would operate through mechanisms other than responsive behaviour as rated by the Ainsworth scales' (p.398). He referred to this failure to account for the transmission of attachment via sensitive responsiveness as the 'transmission gap'.

The transmission gap

In 1997, De Wolff and van IJzendoorn published a meta-analysis of 66 studies involving 4,176 mother–infant pairs on parental antecedents of infant attachment. A moderately small effect size of $r = 0.22$ was found for the association between maternal sensitivity and infant attachment (30 studies, n=1,666). When only studies using Ainsworth's original sensitivity scales were included (16 studies, n=837), the effect size increased to $r = 0.24$. The authors reiterate van IJzendoorn's 1995 conclusion that 'The original concept of sensitivity may not capture the only mechanism through which the development of attachment is shaped' (De Wolff and van IJzendoorn 1997, p.585).

In 2001, the link between maternal responsiveness and infant attachment was further tested (Raval et al. 2001) in a study of 96 mother–infant dyads. The authors concluded that:

> In spite of efforts to explain or reduce the transmission gap by measuring all three components in the same study...only a limited portion of the link between maternal and infant attachment is transmitted via maternal sensitivity/responsiveness. (p.281)

Attachment theorists remained puzzled.

Bridging the transmission gap

The recent work of two research teams has begun to shed some light on this intriguing problem.

Slade *et al.* (2005) report that in a study of 40 mothers and their babies, a significant association ($p<0.001$) was found between adult attachment (assessed in the AAI) and maternal reflective functioning (assessed in the Parent Development Interview, described in Chapter 9). A significant association was also found between maternal reflective functioning and infant attachment (assessed in the strange situation) ($p<0.007$). The authors suggest that reflective functioning may be a 'central mechanism' in the transmission of attachment 'and may well shed light on the "transmission gap"' (p.294).[4]

In a further study of 45 first-time mothers and their infants, Grienenberger, Kelly and Slade (2005) examined the link between maternal reflective functioning and maternal behaviour. Mothers were interviewed using the Parent Development Interview which was scored for reflective functioning (Slade *et al.* 2002). Infant attachment to mother was assessed in the strange situation (see Chapter 8), including Main and Solomon's 1990 coding procedure for disorganisation (see Chapter 3). In addition, maternal behaviour in the strange situation was coded for disrupted affective communication using the Atypical Maternal Behavior Instrument for Assessment and Classification (AMBIANCE) (see Chapter 9). This instrument was originally designed to explore the origins of disorganised infant attachment. As Grienenberger *et al.* acknowledge, in the present study the AMBIANCE was used 'to predict infant secure attachment more broadly, not only disorganized attachment' (p.302).

The study found that:

- disrupted affective communication was inversely correlated with maternal reflective functioning ($p<0.000$)

- mothers with high AMBIANCE scores were significantly more likely to have infants with resistant or disorganised attachment organisation

- maternal behaviour seems to play a mediating role through which maternal reflective functioning is translated in the relationship with the child.

The authors point to the mother's capacity to 'regulate the baby's fear and distress without frightening or otherwise disrupting the baby' (p.306) as the specific aspect of maternal behaviour through which reflective functioning is mediated. Their results 'suggest that aggressive and intrusive, or fearful and withdrawn behaviors, as well as miscommunications and misattunements, may be more likely than maternal sensitivity to be critical in attachment transmission' (p.307).

Like Slade *et al.* (2005) previously reported, this study did not predict insecure-avoidant attachment. Indeed, when the three insecure attachment categories (avoidant, resistant and disorganised) were collapsed, the AMBIANCE predicted infant attachment at only the 0.05 significance level (and much of this effect may have been due to the precision of the AMBIANCE in predicting disorganisation). Thus, the question as to which specific aspects of *sensitively responsive behaviour* influence infant *organised* insecure attachment, and thereby transmit attachment, remains incompletely answered.

A promising solution to the mystery of the transmission gap is offered by Cassidy *et al.* (2005). Their study is in its early stages, and the sample size at the time of this preliminary report is small (n=18). The researchers are particularly focusing on the measurement of maternal sensitivity. Using Ainsworth's conceptualisation of sensitivity, previously described (sensitivity–insensitivity to the infant's signals, acceptance–rejection, cooperation–interference and accessibility–ignoring), each mother was classified as either globally sensitive or globally insensitive. Of the 18 children, 9 who were assessed (in the strange situation) as insecure have mothers who were assessed as insensitive. However, six children assessed as *secure* also have mothers assessed as insensitive (the remaining three mother–child dyads were assessed as sensitive/secure). This finding and the team's observations have led the researchers to suggest that 'although sensitivity is important, insensitivity as it is typically measured is not antithetical to security' (p.41).

In attempting to understand what differentiates insensitive mothers whose babies become secure from those whose babies become insecure, the researchers have focused on the attachment–exploration balance provided by the mother as a secure base. It appears that insensitive mothers whose babies become secure ultimately do respond to the baby's attachment behaviour. Thus, 'a baby may discount much of what a coder might consider *insensitive* – as long as a response to activation of the attachment system comes in the end; and a baby may discount much of what a coder might consider *sensitive* – unless those behaviors serve as a response to activation of the infant's attachment system' (Cassidy *et al.* 2005, p.44).

By specifically focusing on the parental response to attachment behaviour (the provision of a secure base), rather than global sensitivity, Cassidy and colleagues may well have laid the foundations for bridging the transmission gap. They go on to name the other maternal attributes necessary to achieve secure infant attachment as (1) not frightening the child, (2) showing no hostility to the child, (3) not interfering with the child's self-soothing and (4) not interfering with the child's exploration to the extent of alarming the child and thereby precipitating the need for attachment.

Summary

Bowlby referred to the attachment figure's response to the child's proximity-seeking attachment behaviour as caregiving. Attachment organisation is determined by the nature of caregiving which the child receives. While mothers of securely attached infants are sensitively responsive, mothers of insecure-avoidant infants are found to be rejecting and intrusive, and mothers of insecure-resistant infants are under-involved and unpredictable in their responses to the infant. Disorganised attachment has been found to be associated with a frightening or frightened caregiver.

There is no definitive view about the relationship between caregiver sensitivity and other aspects of parenting.

Most parents respond sensitively to children's varied temperaments. Parents who struggle with sensitive responsiveness are likely to find children with a difficult temperament more challenging and this may lead to insecure attachments.

There are clear correlations between parental state of mind with regard to (their own) attachment, the parent's capacity for reflective functioning and their infant's attachment security. It is likely that these adult states of mind are transmitted to the infant through the parent's behaviour towards the child. The formation of a secure attachment requires the infant to know that the attachment figure will (ultimately) respond and do so without frightening the child, showing no hostility to the child, not interfering with the child's self-soothing and not interfering excessively with the child's exploration.

Notes

1   The table presented (p.145) excludes behaviour relevant to face-to-face interaction and feeding.

2   Based on observations at 39, 42, 45 and 48 weeks of age.

3   See Goldberg (2000) for a discussion of attachment and emotion regulation.

4   Limitations of the study are that adult and infant attachment were weakly correlated and the reflective functioning scores of the mothers of secure children could not be distinguished from those of the mothers of avoidant infants. The authors state that the findings are preliminary and require further examination.

5 Affectional Bonds and Attachment Figures

In all but the most exceptional circumstances, children form attachments to their primary carers[1] and typically to others who regularly care for them and with whom they have enduring relationships, such as grandparents. These caregivers are attachment figures. Whether professional caregivers in settings such as day-care centres and nurseries can be defined as attachment figures remains an issue of some debate and the definition of an attachment figure is discussed in this chapter.

An individual can have more than one attachment figure and often has several. Bowlby was clear in his formulation of this. A plurality of attachment figures by 12 months of age, he states, is probably the rule. Given this, the question arises, how are multiple attachment figures internally represented in relation to each other; that is, how are they structured?[2] This is also discussed in this chapter. Before doing so, it is necessary to consider affectional bonds.

What are affectional bonds?

An affectional bond is a social bond which involves intense emotion. According to Bowlby, the term 'social bond' 'is applicable only to those few social relationships to which both parties are committed' (1969/1982, pp. 376–377). Bonds, therefore, are founded on commitment.

> In terms of subjective experience, the formation of a bond is described as falling in love, maintaining a bond as loving someone, and losing a partner as grieving over someone. Similarly, threat of loss arouses anxiety and actual loss causes sorrow; whilst both situations are likely to arouse anger. Finally, the unchallenged maintenance of a bond is experienced as a source of security, and the renewal of a bond as a source of joy. (Bowlby 1979, p.69)

Affectional bonds are not synonymous with relationships. Relationships may be transitory, whereas affectional bonds are enduring. Additionally, relationships refer to the *dyad*, whereas affectional bonds are characteristic of the *individual* and entail representation in the individual's internal organisation. The essential feature of an affectional bond is the desire to maintain closeness to the partner (Ainsworth 1989).

The attachment bond, that is the bond of an individual to an attachment figure, is an affectional bond involving the attachment behavioural system. Other affectional bonds are: the caregiving bond, involving the caregiving behavioural system; the sexual pair bond, involving the reproductive, attachment and caregiving systems; the enduring friendship bond, involving the sociable (sometimes termed affiliative) system and, in some friendships, the attachment and caregiving systems; and sibling and other kinship bonds, involving the sociable, attachment and caregiving systems. The different types of affectional bonds are listed in Table 5.1.

'Bonding'

Some confusion surrounds the terms 'bonds' and 'bonding'. In the non-attachment literature, bonding is often referred to as something that applies almost exclusively to the parent, as pointed out by Schaffer (1990, p.48):

> The term 'bonding' has been widely used to designate the process whereby mothers form emotional relationships with their children… Bonding therefore describes the mother-to-child part of the relationship (as opposed to attachment, which refers to the child-to-mother part).[3]

In attachment theory, an attachment is an affectional bond, as is the caregiving bond. Thus, the child develops an attachment bond with their attachment figure and the caregiver develops a caregiving bond with the child. Being affectional bonds, both involve intense emotion. The difference in the natures of the affectional bonds is, however, crucial. The carer does not form an attachment bond with the child; indeed, Bowlby is repeatedly clear that parental orientation towards the child as an attachment figure 'is almost always not only a sign of pathology in the parent but a cause of it in the child' (1969/1982, p.377).

Caregiving and love

The caregiving affectional bond, therefore, involves a commitment to care for and protect the child and intense emotion, which is typically experienced as love. However, treating the terms 'caregiving' and 'love' as synonymous (for

Table 5.1 The different types of affectional bond

Affectional bond	Subjects	Behavioural system(s)
Attachment bond	Child	Attachment
Caregiving bond	Caregiver	Caregiving
In childhood, these bonds are not symmetrical nor reciprocal, i.e. attachment is directed from the child to the parent and caregiving is directed from the parent to the child. As the child matures into adulthood and the parent ages, some degree of attachment/caregiving reciprocity usually develops.		
Sexual pair bond	Sexual partners	Reproductive
The attachment and caregiving components often accompanying the sexual pair bond tend to be reciprocal. Alternatively, these components may be complementary, with one partner seeking care and protection and the other providing it, much as in the child–parent relationship.		
Enduring friendship bond	Friends	Sociable, attachment, caregiving
The friend must be perceived as a uniquely valued person, i.e. not interchangeable with anyone else. In enduring friendships this perception is invariably mutual and usually involves reciprocal attachment/caregiving.		
Non-parental kinship bond	Family members	Sociable
Typically, in non-parental kinship bonds, one family member is, or is perceived to be, stronger and wiser than the other and a predominantly one-way attachment–caregiving relationship exists, e.g. between siblings, niece/nephew and aunt. This is not, however, inevitable and, especially with the passage of time, attachment/caregiving may become reciprocal or the direction may even reverse.		

example, the child is loved, therefore the child is cared for) is unhelpful and possibly perilous. In childhood, both attachment and caregiving are predicated on the child's need for safety, protection and sense of security. Love typically develops in the formation of these bonds, as Bowlby eloquently describes, but the child's first need is for safety. A loved child who is unsafe is in physical and psychological peril. Love alone is insufficient.

Equally, it may occur that a child is adequately and appropriately protected by their caregiver but the nature of the caregiver's commitment to the child is that of a social bond rather than an affectional bond. Such care, provided in a context devoid of the emotions associated with affectional bonds such as joy, emotional commitment or love, may be termed 'instrumental care' and may be found in some alternative caregiving arrangements.

Love without protection leaves the child vulnerable to physical and psychological harm, whilst instrumental caregiving leaves the child vulnerable to feeling unloved and unworthy. The importance of understanding the attachment and caregiving bonds as affectional bonds, rather than mere arrangements for the child's protection, cannot be overstated.

IS AN ATTACHMENT AN AFFECTIONAL BOND?

Yes, always. This means that insecurely avoidant, resistant or disorganised attachments, being attachments, are affectional bonds and involve intense emotion.

IS THE CAREGIVING BOND AN AFFECTIONAL BOND?

Usually, but not always. In some circumstances, it may be a social bond rather than an affectional bond; that is, it is not always 'a relatively long-enduring tie in which the partner is important as a unique individual and is interchangeable with none other' (Ainsworth 1989, p.711).

IS AN AFFECTIONAL BOND AN ATTACHMENT BOND?

Not necessarily. In particular, the caregiving bond is not an attachment bond. In addition, affectional bonds may be based on sexual (reproductive) or sociable behaviour, without an attachment component. In reality, however, such affectional bonds tend to develop attachment and caregiving components, whether reciprocal or complementary.

How is an attachment figure defined?

Cassidy (1999, p.13) warns against the presumption of an attachment bond when there is attachment behaviour: 'an attachment bond cannot be presumed to exist even though a relationship may contain an attachment component', for example comfort-seeking behaviour. Attachment behaviour can be directed toward three types of figure:

1. a caregiver who *is* an attachment figure

2. a caregiver who is *not yet* an attachment figure but who may *become* an attachment figure

3.   a figure who is not an attachment figure and may *not* become an attachment figure.

Attachment figures are ongoing caregivers. Thus when a child, in the absence of an attachment figure, turns for comfort and protection to a little-known person, or, in desperate circumstances, even a stranger, that person does not become an attachment figure. A stranger may be a 'caregiver' in an emergency.

This leaves the question as to whether temporary relationships, such as with child-care providers or teachers, can be classed as attachments and whether such caregivers can be considered to be attachment figures. Before turning to the research literature, it is worth turning to Ainsworth *et al*. They suggest that temporary relationships are perhaps best considered as 'incipient attachments'. 'Should circumstances permit a continuing relationship, they might well be consolidated as attachments, but when circumstances make the relationship of short duration they do not become sufficiently well consolidated to endure' (Ainsworth *et al*. 1978, p.274).

Are professional child-carers attachment figures?

To test whether infants' relationships with professional (daytime) carers are correctly defined as attachment relationships van IJzendoorn, Sagi and Lambermon (1992) proposed five criteria. These criteria are applicable to groups or samples of children rather than individuals. The five criteria are:

1.   Infant–caregiver samples do not show an overrepresentation of avoidant classifications. (Such an overrepresentation may indicate non-attachment rather than true avoidant attachment.)

2.   Infant–caregiver samples do not show an overrepresentation of unclassifiable cases.

3.   Infant–caregiver classifications are independent of infant–parent classifications.

4.   Caregiver's sensitivity is related to the infant–caregiver strange situation classifications.

5.   Infant–caregiver classifications predict later socio-emotional functioning.

These criteria were tested in studies in Holland and Israel. In the Dutch study, 80 children and their mothers, fathers and professional caregivers were initially involved and 68 children, their parents and professional caregivers participated at follow-up two years later. In the Israeli study 86 infants, their mothers, fathers and metaplot (professional caregivers) were involved in the initial assessment and 59 children, 30 metaplot and 30 kindergarten teachers were involved at follow-up approximately three and a half years later.

On the basis of the findings of these studies the authors tentatively concluded that the infant–(professional) caregiver relationship 'really is an attachment relationship' (van IJzendoorn *et al.* 1992, p.17).

Howes (1999) describes a study of the attachment relationship between the child and their child-care provider, which she and a colleague published following the van IJzendoorn *et al.* analysis. The sample comprised 1,379 children, cared for out of the home. Using Attachment Q-sort scores in a cluster analysis, the children were grouped into profiles consistent with security categories. They found that van IJzendoorn *et al.*'s second and fourth criteria were met, but not the first criterion, with 50 per cent of the children classified as avoidant. Further analysis indicated that older children (preschoolers) 'may sometimes construct a secure attachment relationship with a caregiver in which the child uses the caregiver to organise his or her social and learning environment, but spends little time in close contact with the caregiver' (p.673). This raises the notion of professional caregivers as organisers, rather than comforters, which may particularly apply to teachers.

Howes describes an alternative strategy for ascertaining whether professional carers qualify as attachment figures, this being to focus on the qualities of the carer rather than the child. Three criteria are proposed:

1.   provision of physical and emotional care

2.   continuity or consistency in a child's life

3.   emotional investment in the child.

Howes acknowledges that Ainsworth did not include the first of these criteria in the identification of attachment figures, having found that infants can be attached to adults who do not provide care. Howes also discusses the problem of continuity or consistency of attachment figures over time, clearly an issue in considering professional carers as attachment figures. Howes concludes that the first two criteria (caregiving and consistency) can be identified through network analysis; the third criterion (emotional investment) requires further study.

Howes' position seems to be that 'certain categories of adults frequently available in children's social networks are considered as alternative attachment figures. These categories are fathers, grandparents, child care providers, and teachers' (p.675). Drawing on three additional studies, she further concludes 'the formation of attachment relationships in child care settings appears to be a similar process to that of infant–mother attachment formation' (p.677).

This stance is reinforced in a later work (Howes and Oldham 2001), which opens with the statement, 'It is well documented that children construct attachment relationships with caregivers in the child-care setting' (p.267). The focus of this study was to examine the processes involved in the formation of attachment relationships with alternative caregivers in child-care settings. The study of ten children found that (1) individual variations in attachment behaviours at child-care entry could not predict attachment security six months later, and (2) from the first few days in child-care children began to differentiate between caregivers.

In spite of their conclusions, both van IJzendoorn *et al.* and Howes acknowledge a theoretical difficulty in including professional carers as attachment figures. In their 1992 chapter, van IJzendoorn *et al.* (p.22) point out that 'It remains unclear, however, in what ways the children digest the "loss" of their professional caregivers, who change on a regular basis. This early loss may make the mental representation of the nonparental attachment different from that of the parental attachment.' Howes acknowledges the problem of a lack of continuity or consistency regarding child-care providers and teachers as alternative attachment figures. She suggests that children begin to treat child-care providers as a category of alternative attachment relationships.

Perhaps the last word on this subject should go to Mary Ainsworth. Interviewed in 1994 by Robert Marvin, she was asked the following question:

> If a child is placed in day care for the full day and from a very early age (say 6 weeks) and is with the mother only in the evenings and over the weekends, do you think that baby's mother is still likely to be his primary attachment figure?

Her reply:

> Yes. Group-care situations nearly always include multiple caregivers, and it is much more difficult to form an attachment with one individual out of the several who look after the baby and whose presence is likely to vary day by day. But, if there should be a long-continuing, uninterrupted relationship with some caregiver other than the mother, then, yes indeed, I think you could see the same kind of relationship emerge with that figure as you ordinarily see with the mother. The crucial point is that the relationship be continuing and pretty much uninterrupted – under such conditions, the nonmaternal caregiver can well become an attachment figure closely resembling that which usually evolves in the relationship with the mother. (Ainsworth and Marvin 1995, pp.15–16)

How are the representations of multiple attachment figures structured?

Multiple attachment figures 'are not treated as the equivalents of one another' (Bowlby 1969, p.304). It is usual for infants to show clear discrimination and focus their attachment behaviour on one special person. Bowlby calls this special person the *principal attachment-figure*. He calls other attachment figures *subsidiary attachment-figures*. He termed the child's bias to attach especially to one figure *monotropy*.

The validity of monotropy has more recently been questioned. Rutter (1995, p.551) states that one of the four main changes in attachment theory to have taken place over the years concerns 'abandonment of the notion of "monotropy"'. As Bowlby was clear that children form selective attachments to more than one person, the challenge to the notion of monotropy concerns the extent to which the relationship with the 'special' principal figure differs from that of other attachment figures.

According to Bowlby, the child's selection of their primary and subsidiary attachment figure turns 'in large part on who cares for him' (Bowlby 1969, p.304). In most cultures children are cared for by family members, and very often the child's primary carer is his or her mother. Bowlby is clear, however, that 'the role of a child's principal attachment-figure can be filled by others than the natural mother' (p.304).

In his discussion of subsidiary attachment figures, Bowlby is concerned that an individual perceived as a subsidiary attachment figure should indeed be an attachment figure rather than, for example, a playmate. He is also concerned to correct the misconception that a child with more than one attachment figure will have a 'weak' attachment to his principal attachment figure, and, conversely, a child with a sole attachment figure will have an 'intense' attachment to that figure (1969, p.308). A child does not diffuse his attachment over many figures, but rather has a strong bias to direct attachment behaviour towards one particular person.

Van IJzendoorn *et al.* (1992) refer to the relative influences of multiple attachment relationships as 'the multiple caretaker paradox'. The paradox the authors pose is as follows. The discordance of the quality of attachment relationships with different caretakers is a highly replicated finding. If, for example, the child has a secure attachment to their mother, predicting, for example, positive peer interactions, what is the influence of an insecure attachment relationship with a different carer? It is unlikely that the insecure attachment will have a negative effect on peer interactions, but it is also unlikely that it will have a positive effect.

A hierarchical, integrative or independent structure?

Conceptually, multiple attachment figures may be represented in relation to each other within three possible structures: hierarchical, integrative and independent.[4] A hierarchical structure encompasses the concept of monotropy, that is primary and subsidiary attachment figures in a 'clear order of preference' (Bowlby 1979, p.130). This was clearly Bowlby's view. An integrative structure involves the integration of all attachment relationships into a single representation with no one attachment relationship being more important than another. According to this model, attachment relationships can be viewed as a network within which secure attachments may compensate for insecure attachments. An independent structure considers that attachment representations are independent and differentially influence different developmental domains.

Concordance of attachment classifications

It has been argued (Howes 1999) that the structure of the internal representations of multiple attachments can be empirically examined by investigating the concordance of attachment classifications for different attachment figures. Concordance, it is argued, supports a hierarchical structure: 'The hierarchical organization also suggests that maternal attachment security influences the security of all subsequent attachment relationships' (Howes 1999, p.681). This, however, is a questionable interpretation of a hierarchical structure. A hierarchical structure does not require that all attachments should be similarly classified, but rather that the principal attachment is of the greatest importance and has the greatest influence. Indeed, given that 'attachment is considered a unique reflection of the dyad's history of interactions' (van IJzendoorn et al. 1992, p.9), discordance in attachment classifications is to be expected.

A number of studies have examined the concordance of attachment classifications, in particular the concordance of attachments to mother and father.

In a meta-analysis of 11 studies, Fox, Kimmerly and Schafer (1991) found that 'security of attachment to one parent was dependent upon security to the other parent' and that 'type of insecurity (avoidant/resistant) to one parent was dependent upon type of insecurity to the other' (p.210). The findings, although weak, were significant. This meta-analysis, therefore, indicated that attachment organisation with respect to mother and father was concordant. In a Dutch study carried out in 1990 (reported in van IJzendoorn et al. 1992), the data also pointed to concordance between the infant's attachment classifications to both parents.

A number of other studies which have examined associations between attachment to mother and father and child competence suggest that the respective attachments are independent of each other. For example, Main *et al.* (1985) found that the child's attachment to their mother was more influential. However, child–father attachment has been found to be the best predictor of certain outcomes at certain times. For example, in the Main *et al.* study, friendliness with a stranger was best predicted by child–father attachment when the children were toddlers but not when they were 6 years old.

Howes (1999) reports that a number of mechanisms have been put forward to explain the findings of concordance in child–mother and child–father attachments. The most obvious is that parents select each other on the basis of shared attitudes to child rearing and/or model each other's caregiving strategies. The notion of modelling is supported by a study by Steele *et al.* (1996) who found that infant–mother interaction may influence infant–father interaction, which may then influence infant–father attachment. An alternative explanation of concordance is that child characteristics determine the nature of the attachment irrespective of the caregiver (see discussion of child temperament).

HOW DO THE FINDINGS ON CONCORDANCE CONTRIBUTE TO OUR UNDERSTANDING OF THE STRUCTURING OF MULTIPLE ATTACHMENTS?

It is argued here that a hierarchical structure does not require that attachment relationships should be concordant and that concordance can neither support nor weaken the case that multiple attachments are hierarchically structured. This position differs from that of, for example, Howes (1999), who posits that concordance of attachment relationships supports a hierarchical structure. On this premise, her conclusion is that 'the literature on concordance of attachment relationships provides inconclusive support for the hierarchical model' (Howes 1999, p.682).

As concordance is not predicted in an integrative or independent structure, nor, as argued here, in a hierarchical structure, the findings on concordance, although interesting, do not add to our understanding of the structure of multiple attachments.

The predictability of developmental outcomes from attachment classifications

An alternative approach to the question of the structuring of multiple attachments is to examine the predictability of children's developmental outcomes from attachment classifications. Outcomes which are best predicted by the child's primary attachment relationship support a hierarchical structure and undermine an integrative or independent structure. Outcomes which are best predicted by networks of attachment figures support an integrative structure. Differential outcomes predicted by different attachment relationships support an independent structure.

Howes (1999) reports that 'Studies in which mother– and father–child attachment security are used to predict children's competence have generally found that child–mother attachment security is more influential' (p.682). This lends support to a hierarchical structure.

Studies which include child-care providers and metaplot as attachment figures support an integrative or independent structure rather than a hierarchical structure. Howes (1999) reports two studies which found that preschool children's social competence with peers was better predicted by security of attachment to a child-care provider or metapelet than child–mother attachment security. When networks of caregivers, including child-care providers and teachers as well as parents, are used to predict children's outcomes, 'there is considerable support for an integrative model' (pp.682–683).

Howes (1999) also reports findings from a number of studies which support an independent structure. For example, one study found that toddlers' friendliness with a stranger was best predicted by father–child attachment security. In another, father–child attachment security best predicted negative affect and interpersonal conflict. Two further studies found that problem solving and sibling interaction at age 3 was best predicted by father–child attachment.

Van IJzendoorn *et al.* (1992) found that 'the combination of infant–mother and infant–father attachments, but not the separate relationships, was predictive of later cognitive and socio-emotional functioning' (p.20). The authors suggest that this may be interpreted as support for the integration model. However, these other aspects of functioning do not belong within the attachment paradigm. This finding does not therefore indicate the relative importance of the various *attachment* relationships.

HOW DO THE FINDINGS ON PREDICTABILITY OF DEVELOPMENTAL OUTCOMES CONTRIBUTE TO OUR UNDERSTANDING OF THE STRUCTURING OF MULTIPLE ATTACHMENTS?

Empirical support can be found for all three possible structures, hierarchical, integrative and independent. Evidence for an integrative structure, however, relies on the validity of professional child-carers, as a group of caregivers rather than particular individuals within the group, being attachment figures. This has been questioned on theoretical grounds. The idea of an independent structure is also theoretically questionable, or at least the process through which it may operate is not yet understood. As Howes (1999, p.681) states, 'This process clearly works best when there is a theory to predict why different attachment figures should be more or less influential in a developmental domain.'

Van IJzendoorn *et al.* (1992, p.20) reported from their findings from data gathered in Holland and Israel that 'There was also little support for the hierarchy model. Against the background of our data, it does not make sense to consider nonmaternal caregivers only as subsidiary attachment figures.' They conclude that they found some support for the integration model and advocate a network approach to understand how different internal working models of attachment relationships might integrate and relate to development. They emphasise, however, that a definitive choice between the independence and integration models is difficult to make and conclude that further research is needed.

In his 1994 Bowlby Memorial Lecture, Rutter (1995) questioned the validity of the notion of monotropy, but stated that it is now clear that there are very definite hierarchies in selective attachments.

Is there a principal attachment figure?

Having reviewed salient aspects of attachment theory and relevant empirical studies, the issue regarding the structuring of multiple attachment figures points clearly towards a hierarchy. Central to the notion of a hierarchy of attachment figures is Bowlby's concept of monotropy, that is a preferred attachment figure. The following discussion focuses on this question and, given the contradictory nature of much of the evidence, draws heavily on the thoughts, views and even speculations of leading scholars in the field.

Ainsworth *et al.* (1978, p.272) offered clarification of the meaning of Bowlby's concept of monotropy:

> Bowlby, however, did not mean that there could be only one attachment figure, but implied that there was one principal attachment figure, to whom the others were secondary. This implies a hierarchy of attachment figures.

The authors acknowledge that children use attachment figures other than the mother as a secure base and that the departure of an attachment figure other than the mother can arouse distress. They quote studies in which children showed minimal differences in responses to the departures of mothers and fathers in the strange situation. However, they refer to evidence, particularly the work of Lamb during the 1970s, which indicates that, in highly stressful situations, a preference for the principal attachment figure is shown. This, they point out, is consistent with Bowlby's concept of monotropy and a hierarchy of attachment figures.

It would seem that there are two questions at the heart of this debate. First, in the presence of two or more attachment figures, to whom does the child turn when alarmed? Second, if the child does turn to a preferred attachment figure, is that figure invariably the person who primarily cares for him or her?

Mary Main addresses both issues in her 'Epilogue' to the *Handbook of Attachment* (1999, Item 13, pp.858–861). In her opening remarks on the subject of monotropy and attachment hierarchies she states that questions surrounding both issues remain unsettled. Somewhat humorously, she refers to John Watson's suggestion that monotropy would be favourable in times of emergency:

> For example, debating whom to run to while being rapidly approached by a leopard ('Let's see, X, presently in tree A, holds me nicely, but Y, on rock B, is good at grooming, and Z, on rock C, has the sweetest milk, so, um...') could conceivably be bad for an infant's health. (Main 1999, p.859)

In this situation, an automatic response towards one figure would be viewed as an advantage.

She points out that the issue is important for our understanding of the human mind, because 'a mind that focuses primarily on one other person is by nature a different mind from one that focuses on a set' (p.859). In her view, 'We need a technique for ascertaining favored persons' (p.859), adding that this should be carried out with a rationale that is not personally hurtful. She states that many imaginative techniques have been tried, 'with double swinging doors and parents marching in and taking leave in double step' (p.859). Generally, these studies show a preference for the mother where she is definitely the primary caregiver. However, the issue remains insufficiently explored.

With regard to the second central question, that is on what grounds a principal figure is selected, Bowlby described the selection of principal and subsidiary attachment figures as turning on 'who cares for him'. However, is Bowlby referring to quantity or quality of caregiving? Ainsworth, in her 1994 interview, emphasised that 'It's the *presence* of the caregiving figure rather than the caregiving behaviour that is essential for the attachment to develop' (Ainsworth and Marvin 1995, p.14). Ainsworth continues:

> If two potential attachment figures are concurrently involved, I can't help but think that their relative sensitivity to the baby might well affect the

> growth of the child's attachment – that it would indeed be the more sen-
> sitive of the two who first starts the attachment process going. But I'm not
> sure that this would necessarily be the case. (Ainsworth and Marvin 1995,
> p.15)

Main raises an intriguing puzzle. Early attachment to the mother appears, although is not proven, to have a stronger influence, even when the attachment to the mother is insecure and the attachment to the father secure. (This would seem to contradict Ainsworth's hunch that, given equivalent involvement, it is sensitivity that counts.) Referring to their study using the Separation Anxiety Test or the Kaplan and Main drawing system, Main relates that the overall family representation of a 6-year-old appeared 'influenced almost exclusively by the organization of his or her attachment to the mother rather than the father, during infancy' (Main 1999, p.859). In a follow-up study of 45 of these subjects, security or insecurity with the mother during infancy predicts security/autonomous versus insecure AAI status at age 19. Early attachment to father was not related to AAI status. Both in middle childhood and adolescence, 'the offspring's overall state of mind with respect to attachment…seemed to be chiefly influenced by the mother' (p.859).

Main also reports that studies in Sweden found that mothers were still preferred when the fathers remained at home and mothers went out of the home to work. Main suggests that this 'startling' finding may be related to the infant's earliest experiences with the mother, including prenatal months of hearing her voice. She suggests that this hypothesis may be tested by involving adoptive parents in a similar study, thus ruling out any maternal 'advantage'. She also acknowledges that there may be other explanations for these findings, such as mothers having more parenting practice prior to the baby's birth.

Summary

Attachment and caregiving relationships are one kind of social, affectional bond. Other affectional bonds include kinship bonds, sexual pair bonds and enduring friendship bonds. Two important questions then arise: which of the child's relationships are attachment affectional bonds, and is there a hierarchy between a child's different affectional bonds?

The fact that a child shows attachment behaviour towards a person does not necessarily mean that that person is an attachment figure. An attachment figure will have spent significant time with the child in a capacity which will include caregiving. This could include alternative day-carers as well as parents, providing the relationship is prolonged and emotionally committed, rather than one in which the child is merely looked after. It is likely that there is a hierarchy of attachment bonds, the one with the mother most often being the primary one. The nature of the attachment (secure or insecure) between a child and their attachment person does not strengthen or lessen the child's wish to be with the attachment person or maintain a relationship with them. Longitudinal research has shown that the security (or insecurity) of an infant's attachment to the mother will be reflected in the (later) young adult's state of mind with regard to attachment in the Adult Attachment Interview.

Notes

1   Bowlby was clear that, although in his writing he referred to mothers and not-mother figures, 'it is to be understood that in every case reference is to the person who mothers the child and to whom he becomes attached rather than the natural mother' (Bowlby 1969, pp.177–178).

2   The term 'organised' or 'organisation' is frequently used to describe the arrangement of the internal representations of multiple attachments. The term 'structured' or 'structure' is preferred here, leaving the terms 'organised' and 'organisation' to refer exclusively to the internal representation of a specific attachment to a specific individual.

3   However, Schaffer concludes in answer to the question 'When does maternal bonding occur?' that 'the bonding doctrine, as expressed in its super-glue version, is a gross over-simplification' (p.57).

4   Van IJzendoorn et al. (1992) present monotropy and hierarchy as distinct models, thus these authors distinguish four models. They describe monotropy as implying one important attachment figure, with other caretakers of marginal influence, and hierarchy as a model in which one caretaker is the most important attachment figure, but others may be considered subsidiary attachment figures 'who may serve as a secure base in case the principal attachment figure is not available' (p.10). As Bowlby's writing seems to incorporate monotropy and hierarchy into a single model, this distinction is not made in this discussion.

6 Is Attachment Theory Valid across Cultures?

Culture is an issue of central importance in attachment theory. As previously described, attachment theory is an evolutionary theory, the attachment behavioural system having evolved in the environment of evolutionary adaptedness with the biological function of the protection and survival of the child. It must therefore apply to all humans as a species, irrespective of culture. To suggest that central features of attachment theory do not apply across cultures challenges the universality of the theory and therefore the theory itself.

It is now established that in Western societies the majority of infants are securely attached. This is sometimes referred to as the 'normativity hypothesis', for example van IJzendoorn and Sagi (1999). However, does the preponderance of secure attachment hold in non-Western societies, in particular those societies where early child-care is not based on the nuclear family but instead is shared among wider kinship or social groups? Do attachment studies in non-Western societies support the normativity hypothesis?

Ainsworth's Uganda study

It is often overlooked that one of the first studies to explore attachment in a non-Western, multiple-caregiver society was carried out by Ainsworth in Uganda. Her work there laid the foundation for her later study in Baltimore and her subsequent vast contribution to attachment theory. Whilst her study of Ganda infants was small and exploratory, it was crucially important in the development of the strange situation procedure, and in establishing that in a society in which child-care is more widely shared, infants form attachments to their mothers and use the mother as a secure base.

Bowlby (1969, p.305) reports that Ainsworth found that Ganda children 'tended to focus most of their attachment behaviour on one special person' and quotes Ainsworth's (1964) conclusion: 'there is nothing in my observations to contradict the hypothesis that, given an opportunity to do so, an infant will seek attachment with one figure…even though there are several persons available as caretakers'.

The Gusii of Kenya

Caregiving is shared between mothers and other caregivers, especially older siblings, with a relatively strict apportioning of tasks. Mothers have primary responsibility for the child's physical care and health, whilst child caregivers are more engaged in social and playful activities.

In a study of 26 Gusii infants (Kermoian and Leiderman 1986) 61 per cent were classified as securely attached to their mothers and 54 per cent as securely attached to non-maternal caregivers. (Types of insecurity were not assessed.)

The Dogon of Mali

True, Pisani and Oumar (2001) carried out a study of 27 mother–infant pairs from a rural town and 15 mother–infant pairs from two agrarian villages in Mali. Whilst the infant's primary carer may be their mother, grandmother or other family member, the mother remained nearby during the day and slept with the infant at night. Thus, she was still a central attachment figure.

The assessment in the strange situation included the insecure-disorganised/disoriented category (D) as well secure (B), insecure-avoidant (A) and insecure-resistant/ambivalent (C). The finding regarding infant–mother attachment classification is shown in Table 6.1.

Assigning infants classified as disorganised into a 'best fit' A, B or C classification yielded a distribution of 87 per cent secure, 0 per cent avoidant and 13 per cent resistant.

Whilst these findings support the normativity hypothesis, a question remains concerning the absence of any infants classified as avoidant. Interestingly, True et al. argue that this may be due to the infant's attachment and feeding systems being 'inextricably intertwined' (p.1461). Thus, a mother 'cannot consistently maintain behaviors, such as, aversion to contact or rejection of attachment bids' (p.1462) which are associated with the development of avoidant attachment.

	Town (%)	Village (%)	Total (%)
Secure (B)	68	64	67
Insecure-avoidant (A)	0	0	0
Insecure-resistant (C)	8	7	8
Insecure-disorganised (D)	24	29	25

Table 6.1 Distribution of attachment classifications in two Mali samples

The Israeli Kibbutzim

The website of Kibbutz Ketura[1] describes childrearing on the Israeli kibbutzim as follows:

> The early idealists felt that the nuclear family unit was obsolete, and the entire kibuttz should be one big family unit. Children slept in children's houses with a caretaker to tend to their night needs. While this made for a fascinating experiment (which Bruno Bettelheim analysed in his 'Children of the Dream'), parents and children alike found it distressing.
>
> Today, children on every kibbutz live and sleep with their parents, at least into their teen years, and the children's houses have become day care and activity centers.

The arrangement whereby children and parents slept in separate houses made the Israeli kibbutzim a unique type of communal child-care. In 1977, childrearing on a kibbutz was described by Nathan Fox thus:

> Communal child care begins at the age of 4 days, when the infant is brought home from the hospital. The baby is placed in an infant house under the care of a trained caretaker – a metapelet. The mother, who has a 6-week maternity leave, may care for her child as long as she wishes, though the infant sleeps in the infant house at night.
>
> As the mother gradually resumes her kibbutz duties, the metapelet takes over the major responsibility for the infant's care. At around 3–4 months of age a number of infants are placed under the care of a second metapelet. This woman remains the primary caretaker for the group until the children enter preschool… By the time a child is 1½ years old, its parents see it once a day at 4:00 in the afternoon for 3 hours, when all children return to their parent's home. (Fox 1977, p.1229)

In this early study, Fox examined and compared the kibbutz infant's attachment relationship to his or her primary carer, the metapelet, and to his or her biological mother. His sample comprised 122 children from seven kibbutzim. The experimental design consisted of 13 episodes during which the presence and absence of the mother, metapelet and a stranger were manipulated. The sampling and analysis took account of the infant's ordinal position in their biological family.

In general, Fox found that mothers and metaplot were equivalent as attachment figures. No significant differences were found in separation protest when the mother or metapelet left the child with a stranger. Differences were found, however, in reunion behaviour, and in this regard Fox concluded: 'Children are more attached to their mothers than to their metaplot' (1977, p.1234). Overall, the study found the metapelet to be an 'interchangeable attachment figure' with the mother for most children.

Following this study, Sagi et al. (1985) used the strange situation procedure to assess a sample of 86 infants from 18 kibbutzim and 36 infants living with their families. Fifty nine per cent of kibbutz infants were found to be securely attached to their mothers, compared with 75 per cent of infants attending daycare. The authors suggested that the communal sleeping arrangements of the kibbutz children might account for this finding.

In order to test this hypothesis, in 1994 Sagi and colleagues (reported in van IJzendoorn and Sagi 1999) assessed the attachment security of 23 communally-sleeping kibbutz infants and 25 kibbutz infants sleeping with their families. It was found that 48 per cent of the communally-sleeping infants were securely attached to their mothers, compared to 80 per cent of infants sleeping with their families.

The Hausa of Nigeria

Polygamy among the Hausa of Nigeria facilitates a culture in which several adults share with the mother the care of the child. The child's physical needs, however, are predominantly met by the biological mother.

In a descriptive study of 18 infants, Marvin et al. (1977) observed that, although Hausa infants differ from Western infants in their expression of attachment and exploratory behaviour, they develop attachments to several attachment figures, including their fathers. However, most Hausa infants selected a principal attachment figure, who was usually the person who held and interacted with the infant most frequently. This figure was not necessarily the biological mother. (Security of infant–caregiver attachments was not classified.)

The !Kung San of Botswana

The !Kung San of north-west Botswana is a hunter-gatherer society, and, as van IJzendoorn and Sagi (1999) point out, in this respect resembles the environment (EEA) from which biological systems, including the attachment system, are believed to have evolved. As reported by van IJzendoorn and Sagi, living in small semi-nomadic groups, the !Kung infants studied by Konner (1977) remained in close proximity to their mothers during the day and night and were breastfed on demand. 'In this hunter-gatherer society, the infant–mother bond seems to fulfill a unique function of protection and stimulation, even in the context of a wider social network of caregivers' (van IJzendoorn and Sagi 1999, p.719).

The Efe or Pygmies of Zambia

In this hunter-gatherer society, children are raised in a system of multiple care-givers during the early years. Infants suckle adult females as well as the mother from birth and a large network of caregivers is responsible for childrearing. Morelli and Tronick (1991) reported infants spending 60 per cent of their time with people other than their mother at 18 weeks, and an average of 14.2 care-givers during the first 18 weeks. Despite these child-care arrangements, during the second half of the first year the infants showed a preference for the care of their mothers. Van IJzendoorn and Sagi (1999) report Morelli and Tronick's finding of 'the emergence of a special infant–mother bond, despite the multiple-caregiver context' (p.719).

The academic debate

In October 2000, a challenge to the universality of attachment and therefore the validity of the theory was made in a paper published in *American Psychologist*. This paper caused a flurry of debate, with five Comments from leading scholars in the field subsequently appearing in the October 2001 issue of the same journal, along with the response of the authors of the original paper to the Comments. The assertions made in the original paper, the Comments it provoked and the authors' responses are summarised below.

Rothbaum *et al.*'s (2000) paper begins with the assertion that Western (United States, Canada and Western Europe) theories of achievement are assumed to have universal significance but in fact are deeply rooted in American individual-ism and are ethnocentric. The authors make the same criticism of attachment theory. Conceding that attachment theorists acknowledge cultural influences, the authors nevertheless accuse them of downplaying the role of culture and moreover, when considering culture, focusing on the periphery of the theory, for example specific behaviours or the distribution of secure/insecure attachment, rather than its core. The authors' aim is to shift from a unified theory to indigenous theories (p.1094), later termed psychologies (p.1096), of attachment.

The authors' case focuses on three core hypotheses of attachment theory:

1.   *The sensitivity hypothesis.* Sensitivity in response to the child's signals is the most important antecedent of infant attachment security.

2.   *The competence hypothesis.* Social and emotional competence is a consequence of secure attachment.

3.   *The secure base hypothesis.* Infants explore their environment when they feel protected and comforted by their mother's presence.

The sensitivity hypothesis

The authors question that the criteria used to assess sensitivity are appropriate in all cultures. They suggest that Ainsworth's evaluation of sensitivity, in particular her definitions of *acceptance* and *cooperation*, reflects the value placed on children's autonomy in the United States. In Japan, responsiveness is expressed as 'emotional closeness' and 'helping infants regulate their emotional states' (p.1096). The promotion of exploration and the focus on information in the US compared to the promotion of dependence on mothers and the focus on emotions in Japan lead the authors to conclude that there are 'fundamental differences in the objectives of sensitivity' (p.1097) in the two cultures.

The competence hypothesis

The authors state that attachment theorists define competence in terms of behaviours associated with individuation, such as exploration, independence, self-expression, affect regulation, and positive peer relationships. Whilst such qualities are valued in the West, group-orientated accomplishments, reliance on others and social harmony are valued in Japan. Similarly, emotional openness and sociability are valued in the US, whilst inhibition of expression is encouraged in Japan. Thus, Western measures of competence cannot be expected to be associated with security in Japan.

The secure base hypothesis

The authors refer to five studies in which Japanese babies were observed to engage in less exploratory behaviour than US babies. They argue that the indigenous Japanese concept of *amae*, meaning 'to depend and presume upon another's love or bask in another's indulgence' (p.1100), typifies attachment relationships in Japan, with children showing more dependent behaviours than US children when reunited with their mothers. Behaviours associated with the 'insecure-ambivalent' category are characteristic of the normal *amae* relationship in Japan. This may explain the higher rate of babies so classified in Japan.

The authors' conclusions

Although the authors state at an early stage in the paper that they 'do not deny the biological and evolutionary pre-dispositions that underlie attachment' (p.1095), they conclude that they 'have called into question the universality of attachment theory…by providing evidence that core hypotheses of the theory do not apply in all cultures' (p.1102). They propose 'a new generation of research and theory on attachment' (p.1102). After a thorough process of searching and testing, the authors expect that 'a few attachment universals will remain but that these will be limited to abstract principles, such as the pursuit of proximity and protection, and suffering resulting from loss' (p.1102).

Comments

Posada and Jacobs 2001

Posada and Jacobs comment that Rothbaum *et al.* overlooked evidence from samples in China, Columbia, Germany, Israel, Japan, Norway and the United States, presented in Posada *et al.* (1995), which supports the universality of the secure base phenomenon.

With regard to the sensitivity–security link, 'the issue is not about cultural differences in sensitive behaviour'; differences are expected. 'The key issue is whether sensitivity and security are related' (p.822). Again, Rothbaum *et al.* overlooked evidence from studies in Columbia, Chile and Japan, which supported the sensitivity–security link, although an early study in Japan did not. Furthermore, Rothbaum *et al.* ignored findings that no differences were found between Japanese and US mothers when maternal preferences about interactions, physical proximity and contact were compared. The available evidence supports the universality of the sensitivity–security link.

Attachment theorists would not claim that competence is either a measure of security or a direct consequence of security; security is one of a number of influences on competence and other outcomes. 'The issue is not whether there are cultural differences in definitions of competence but whether security is associated with the socialization outcomes that the theory predicts it should be' (p.822). Findings that secure one-year-old Japanese infants were more compliant with their mothers, curious about objects and socially competent with peers than insecure Japanese infants were overlooked by Rothbaum *et al.*

Chao 2001

Chao accuses Rothbaum *et al.* of a cavalier attitude in defining culture as nation, rather than the values and norms of various social groups. This and their lack of balance between specifics and generality leads them to 'theoretical disaster' (p.823). Culture changes over time and is expressed differently according to gender and class. If attachment theories are developed 'specific to each of the indefinitely numerous and diverse cultures in the world' as Rothbaum *et al.* advocate, 'indefinitely numerous theories of attachment in indefinitely different cultures…will exist'; 'numerous theories amount to no theory' (p.823).

Van IJzendoorn and Sagi 2001

Van IJzendoorn and Sagi point to the irony that individual differences in attachment were first empirically studied in Uganda (Ainsworth 1967), and studies of the universality and cross-cultural validity of attachment theory has continued ever since.

Rothbaum *et al.* were selective in their citation of empirical studies on attachment in Japan. In the main body of their text they cite only two of six relevant studies and rely on circumstantial evidence for much of their argument.

Japan is not a homogeneous culture and attachment studies in different regions have found different results. A study carried out in Tokyo (Durrett, Otaki and Richards 1984), for example, found a similar attachment distribution to that found in Western samples, whereas in a small sample in Sapporo, an overrepresentation of insecure-resistant infants was found. Rothbaum *et al.* cite this study as evidence of many Japanese children being classified as insecurely attached. Van IJzendoorn and Sagi point out, however, that the separations in the strange situation should have been ended when infants were distressed for more than 20 seconds.

Van IJzendoorn and Sagi describe a study in which Japanese mothers were asked to describe their ideal child and compared their descriptions with definitions agreed by experts of the concepts *amae*, attachment and dependence. The mothers clearly favoured the secure child. This study also found a strong association between sensitivity and security.

Van IJzendoorn and Sagi suggest that intracultural differences may be greater than cross-cultural differences. However, in their selective review, Rothbaum *et al.* did not provide new empirical evidence to refute the universality and normativity of attachment.

Kondo-Ikemura 2001

Kondo-Ikemura comments that Rothbaum *et al.* 'overlooked important empirical results that clarify the validity of attachment theory in Japanese samples' (p.825). Moreover, they misunderstood or distorted the meanings of measures.

Studies of Japanese samples not mentioned by Rothbaum *et al.* found significant correlations between attachment security and maternal sensitivity, and maternal and child security.

In the two studies not mentioned by Rothbaum *et al.*, the investigators modified the attachment measures (Attachment Q-sort and the Unresolved scale in the Adult Attachment Interview) for Japanese samples: 'investigators must be culturally biased and well aware of the culture's behavioral repertoire to evaluate concepts adequately. The more carefully the study has been conducted, the more congruent the results are with attachment theory' (p.825).

Rothbaum *et al.* 'failed to present empirical evidence to refute cross-cultural validity in attachment theory'. As a Japanese researcher, Kondo-Ikemura hopes that the paper by Rothbaum *et al.* 'will not be another example of ill-founded foreign (American) pressure to change the Japanese scientific attitude' (p.826).

Gjerde 2001

Whilst agreeing that insufficient attention has been paid to cultural issues in attachment research, Gjerde believes the evidence and conclusions of Rothbaum *et al.* are flawed. Sensitivity and competence may be defined in local terms and variability in the distribution of attachment categories according to context does not challenge the theory.

Gjerde accuses Rothbaum *et al.* of directing an 'exoticising gaze' at attachment theory. Theories about the uniqueness of Japan follow a predictable pattern: all Japanese share a special attribute, for example *amae*, homogeneity is emphasised, the attribute has only marginal relevance to other cultures and is presumed to have prevailed over time. The attributes on which psychologists focus in setting the Japanese apart from the West are usually related to dependency or social harmony. Gjerde comments that such an approach has the potential for excluding other ethnic groups from 'cultural citizenship', adding, 'Rothbaum *et al.* might benefit from a closer examination of the political premises and implications of their review of Japanese culture' (p.826).

Rothbaum et al.'s reply, 2001

With regard to the failure to mention various studies in their original paper, Rothbaum *et al.* reply that their concern with the universality of the sensitivity–security hypothesis 'went far beyond whether correlations among the Western-based measures of these constructs could be found' (pp.827–828). Western ways of assessing sensitivity and secure base are inappropriate because Japanese conceptions of these are so different.

Rothbaum *et al.* disagree with the point made by several commentators concerning the lack of relevance of differences in the expression of parental sensitivity and social competence. 'It is unclear what the hypotheses mean when the constructs with which they are concerned are poorly defined' (p.828).

Rothbaum *et al.* address the criticism made in four of the five Comments that Rothbaum *et al.*'s advocacy in the original paper of indigenous psychologies of attachment 'discards valuable contributions made by Western theories of attachment' (p.828). They suggest that videotaping naturalistic parent–child interactions in stressful situations (as defined by participants in the different cultures studied) may be a particularly effective methodology for exploring indigenous psychologies. They believe that culturally-specific theories of attachment will lead to an enriched theory which would 'describe propensities for sensitivity, competence, and the secure base that are common to all humans' (p.828). Westerners' hegemony in 'the international market of ideas' causes them to be 'prone to apply theories they devise…to people throughout the world' (p.828). Attachment theory will be enriched by a systematic study of cultural variation, especially 'if it is championed by attachment theorists themselves' (p.828).

Recently, Behrens (2005) has revisited the question of attachment classification in Sapporo, Japan. In a study of 45 Japanese mothers and their children aged 6 years, using the Adult Attachment Interview (AAI) and the Main and Cassidy classification criteria for 6-year-olds (Main and Cassidy 1988), Behrens found that insecure Japanese mothers were more likely to have insecure children, and that insecurity was of more than one type (unlike the previous Sapporo study). Although a relatively high proportion of children were classified as 'disorganised' or 'cannot classify', findings indicated that maternal 'unresolved' states of mind correlated with 'disorganised' attachment in the children.

Summary

Commencing with Ainsworth's findings in Uganda and Baltimore, US, studies followed in many different cultures, all of which found attachment theory to be applicable across cultures. This applicability is further supported by the Comments to the Rothbaum *et al.* paper and confirmed by the most recent Behrens study. What may differ across cultures is the expression of maternal sensitivity and the manifestations of secure-base behaviour. These behavioural differences do not invalidate the applicability of the theory.

Note

1   www.ketura.org.il/child.html

Part Two

Assessments[1] *of Attachment and Caregiving*

7 Introduction

Having outlined the nature of attachment and caregiving, it is now necessary to examine how they may be assessed. However convincing the theory may seem, it is unusable unless there is some way to assess or measure its components. Without reliable assessment it is impossible to test the theory, or to apply it in practice as a way of informing intervention.

What follows is not an exhaustive collection of all the assessment instruments available. Those included are classical, widely used or recently developed and show potential clinical usefulness.

Attachment

Assessments of attachment are described in Chapter 8. As previously stated (Chapter 2), attachment is a behavioural system. Children use their experiences with their caregivers to build up a schema or a picture of the responses they expect when they exhibit attachment-related behaviours, which become integrated into internal working models of the attachment figure and the self. Attachment can therefore be assessed through the behaviours observed when the attachment system is aroused, or by accessing the child's working models of attachment. It should be remembered that the distinction between behaviours and internal representations is not as clear as it may appear. The behaviours exhibited by the child are based on internal working models. If the child did not have such models on which to base their behaviour, their behaviours could not be regarded as anything but random. However, in young children, it is only possible to measure the behavioural expression of underlying internal working models. The latter can only be accessed when the child is able to give a direct expression to them.

The most well-known assessment of attachment is the strange situation procedure. This is an assessment of the child's behaviour in response to specific stressors which activate the attachment system. It is the most 'pure' behavioural assessment, although, as discussed above, it allows inferences to be made about the nature of the working model the child has built up because it looks for behavioural organisation.

Observational measures, such as the Q-sort techniques, also assess behaviours (see page 106). These rely on more prolonged observation in a naturalistic setting, and do not introduce specific stressors to activate the attachment system but assume that these will arise naturally over the course of the observation.

The second group of assessment instruments attempts to access the child's working model or internal representation of attachment. They do so in a variety of ways, either by asking direct questions, as in the Child Attachment Interview (CAI), or by assessing the child's responses to general attachment-related themes. The Separation Anxiety Test, and related picture-based attachment assessments, are closer to the 'pure' internal model assessment of the CAI. The narrative or Story Stem techniques assess a combination of internal working models and behaviours, although these are behaviours acted out by the child through doll and animal figures, rather than carried out by the child him- or herself.

In addition to child assessments of attachment, the Adult Attachment Interview (AAI) is described.

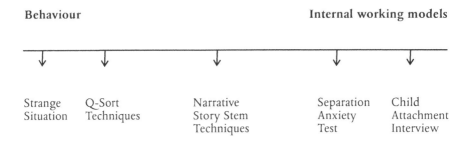

Behaviour   **Internal working models**

| Strange Situation | Q-Sort Techniques | Narrative Story Stem Techniques | Separation Anxiety Test | Child Attachment Interview |

Figure 7.1 Continuum of what is assessed by the major attachment assessments

Caregiving

As described in Chapter 4, the carer's behavioural system which is complementary to attachment is the caregiving behavioural system. In the assessments described in Chapter 9, the focus is on the child's caregiver, assessing either the caregiver's behaviour or their representation of parenting. Whilst this distinction is made, it should be remembered, as with attachment, that behaviours exhibited by caregivers are based on internal representations.

At an early stage in the development of an evidence base for attachment theory, Ainsworth (1969b) explored and described the components and qualities of parenting which are associated with the different patterns of attachment. This gave rise to the *Maternal Sensitivity Scales*, and is the first instrument described. This assessment is based on observations of the caregiver's behaviour. A decade or so later, Crittenden, working with Ainsworth, developed the CARE-Index (Crittenden 1979–2004). This instrument shifts the focus slightly onto parent–child interaction, although caregiver sensitivity remains a central construct. Since then, an assessment of atypical maternal behaviour, which is hypothesised to be an antecedent of attachment disorganisation, has been developed. This is the AMBIANCE (Atypical Maternal Behavior Instrument for Assessment and Classification) (Bronfman, Parsons and Lyons-Ruth 1993, 1999). Although it requires further testing of validity, this seems potentially to be a very useful tool, especially in high-risk populations. The final assessment based on observations of caregiver behaviour described here is the Caregiver Behavior Classification System (Marvin and Britner 1996). This instrument, with its ten caregiver rating scales, of which sensitivity is but one, is likely to be an important aid in furthering our understanding of the complexity of caregiving.

In reviewing the various ways of assessing caregiver behaviour, it becomes clear that each procedure addresses different aspects of caregiver behaviour. Choice of which procedure to use will therefore depend on the particular clinical or research questions.

Two instruments which focus on parental representations are described. The Parent Development Interview (PDI) assesses parents' representations of their children, themselves as parents, and their relationships with their children. The Revised Version includes codings of parental reflective functioning. Finally, the Experiences of Caregiving Interview is described. This intensive clinical-style semi-structured interview, adapted from the PDI, assesses maternal internal working models of caregiving.

Structure for presentation of assessments

An introduction to the theoretical background of each assessment, or group of related assessments, is presented. Each assessment is then described in detail under the following headings:

- *Who designed the assessment and when?* The author(s) and date of the original publication.

- *Any revisions?* This gives details of any revisions and the version currently in use.

- *What does it assess?* This describes what the instrument assesses or measures, according to the continuum model (Figure 7.1), be it behaviours or representations. The type of outcome the assessment yields is also described. This may be a categorical classification (such as Secure, or Avoidant in the strange situation) or a numerical score on a particular relevant dimension (such as Security on the Attachment Q-set (see page 106)).

- *Used with which age group?* This is the age range for which the authors recommend the assessment.

- *Method* This describes how the assessment is delivered and the scoring or rating procedure.

- *Reliability* This gives a summary of data taken from different papers on the reliability of the assessment. The authors and dates of papers are given in the chapter endnotes, with a brief summary of the paper if needed for clarity. There are different types of reliability. These are described in the glossary of research and statistical terms below.

- *Validity* Validity concerns the extent to which the operational definition of a variable actually reflects its true theoretical meaning. An explanation of validity and the various methods used for assessing it is given in the glossary of statistics below.

- *Clinical usefulness* This is a summary of how useful the assessment might be in a clinical setting, based on what has been said about its established reliability and validity, and an assessment of the ease with which it can be administered. This assessment of usefulness takes into account the time and resources needed to train and administer the assessment and the result it yields. If the results are not easily interpretable, or the test is very difficult or costly to administer and score, an assessment is not deemed to be clinically useful.

Glossary of research and statistical terms

Cluster analysis

Cluster analysis is a statistical technique which sorts cases (e.g. people, events) into homogeneous groups (clusters), such that the degree of association is strong between subjects in the same cluster and weak between subjects in different clusters.

Correlation coefficient

There are two main statistics used to assess agreement between two or more scores, whether collected from two different raters or at two different times. For continuous data, this assessment is made using a correlation coefficient. For categorical data, the *kappa statistic* is usually used. A correlation coefficient is a number from 0.00 to 1.00 that describes how closely two variables are related – where 0.00 indicates no relationship and 1.00 indicates the strongest possible relationship. The most common statistic used to describe correlation is the Pearson product–moment correlation coefficient, symbolised as *r*. The value of *r* varies from 0.00 to 1.00. Pearson's *r* also indicates the direction of the

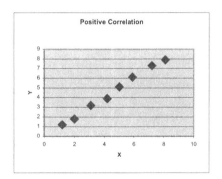
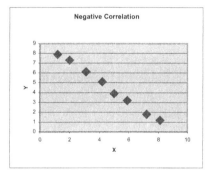

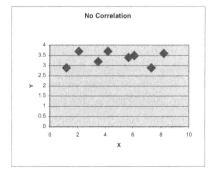

Figure 7.2 Correlation coefficients

relationship, from 0.00 to +1.00 in a positive direction and 0.00 to −1.00 in a negative direction. A positive relationship indicates that as one variable increases, the other increases. A negative relationship indicates that as one variable increases, the other decreases. The nearer r is to 1.00 the stronger the relationship, whether this is plus or minus. Any correlation above 0.50 is considered indicative of a good relationship between two variables. In order for an assessment to be considered *reliable*, correlation coefficients of 0.70 or above are expected. However, in certain circumstances, coefficients lower than 0.50 would still indicate an acceptable degree of *reliability*, particularly if there are large sample sizes.

PARTIAL CORRELATION ANALYSIS

This aims to find the correlation between two variables, after the effect of a third variable has been removed. It can help identify any incorrect correlations, in which two variables appear to be related because of the effect of a third variable, or any hidden correlations that have been masked by a third variable.

Data: two types

Assessments or measures of attachment yield two types of data: categorical, meaning they give a single category rating, and continuous, meaning they give a score on a numerical scale. As an example, height reported as 'very short', 'short', 'average', 'tall' or 'very tall' is categorical data, whilst height measured on a scale from 100 to 200 centimetres is continuous data.

Effect size

In addition to knowing whether there is a statistically significant relationship between two variables it is also useful to know how big the effect size is in order to determine the strength of this relationship.

Factor analysis

This is essentially a data reduction technique designed to identify factors under-lying complicated data sets involving large numbers of variables. It takes a large number of variables and examines the correlations, or relationships, between them to identify certain broader factors which unite them. It investigates where variables 'co-vary', meaning that subjects' answers tend to vary in the same way. For example, a personality research questionnaire is given with a hundred questions. These hundred variables are too unwieldy to examine individually, but factor analysis suggests that the variables tend to cluster into five groups, which are not related to each other. Questions related to sociability might tend to co-vary, as might questions relating to temperament, anxiety, etc. This would therefore have identified five factors, which can be used to describe and explore the data more succinctly. Once a factor has been identified it can be tested to determine its Eigen value. This describes how well that factor explains the variance between the variables. If it has a value of 1 or above the factor is usually assumed to be a good description of the variables.

Kappa statistic

For categorical data the kappa statistic can be used. It is usually used in testing the degree to which two or more raters agree when assigning the same data to categories. The kappa statistic may also be used to test the correspondence between different assessments or measures. In a similar way to *correlation coefficients*, the value of kappa (symbolised by k) ranges from 1.0, indicating complete agreement, to 0.0, indicating no agreement. A negative value of k indicates negative agreement, which would imply that raters tended to avoid making the same categorical assignments as each other. A kappa of 0.70 or higher would usually be considered to be good; however, there are circumstances in which lower kappa values can still indicate a high level of agreement. For more complicated data sets, or for assessments on small sample sizes, the kappa statistic will not reach such high levels but may still indicate a good degree of agreement.

Reliability

Any assessment or measure consists of two elements: (1) the 'true' score, the actual score on the variable, and (2) measurement error. An assessment or measure can be considered reliable if it has a low level of measurement error. It is not possible to observe directly the true score and the error, but we can assess reliability in a number of ways. Reliability describes whether the assessment is able to assess what it claims to assess regardless of other situational influences, such as when it was administered or who administered it. A simple illustration often given to explain this is to imagine a ruler. It is designed to measure length, but if the material from which it was made expanded and contracted greatly with changes in temperature it would not be reliable. The same distance measured on two different occasions might be given different measurements depending on the temperature, not on variations in the distance itself. A ruler is also a standard measure, and ensures that two people using different rulers would get the same measurement. As mentioned above, reliability can be established in a number of ways; there follows a brief description of those referred to in the text.

INTRA-RATER RELIABILITY

This relates to whether the same rater gives a consistent score to a subject on different occasions. It is assessed by asking the same rater to assign a score to a subject twice. The rater either scores one session more than once by using a video or other recording, or scores the same subject on two separate occasions. If the rater gives a consistent score it implies a characteristic of the subject. If, however, the rater does *not* give the same score, it suggests that the score reflects something about the particular conditions during that test session, rather than anything about the subject. This can be reported with a percentage of the number of times the rater made the same judgement, a *correlation coefficient* or a *kappa statistic.*

INTER-RATER RELIABILITY

This relates to whether two different raters give the same subject the same score. It is assessed by asking two or more raters independently to assign a score to a subject, either on the same occasion or on different occasions. If they give the same score it is likely to represent some characteristic of the subject. If they do not give the same score it is likely to have more to do with the rater than the subject. This can be reported using *correlation coefficients, kappa statistics,* or by quoting a percentage. If a percentage is quoted, it refers to the number of occasions that two raters agreed on the rating or score they assigned.

TEST–RETEST RELIABILITY (ALSO KNOWN AS STABILITY)

This relates to whether a subject receives the same rating or score on an assessment or measure given at different points in time. This is appropriate only for variables that would be expected to remain fairly consistent over time, such as intelligence, and not for anything that will vary, such as mood or a developmental attainment. Attachment theory predicts some stability in the child's attachment behaviours, based on their internal working model, unless there are changes in the child's environment. It would not, therefore, be expected to find complete agreement between two administrations of an assessment over a longer period of time, but some level of stability would be expected and would suggest that the instrument is reliable. This is usually reported with a *correlation coefficient* or a *kappa statistic.*

Significance: p value

In some cases reliability and validity will be reported with a *p* value. It stands for probability and reports the likelihood of a given event or result occurring by chance. Probability relates to the chance of a certain event occurring. A p value of 1.0 means that the event will definitely happen, it represents a 100 per cent chance of occurrence. A p value of 0.0 implies no probability that the event will occur by chance, a 0 per cent chance of occurrence. In order to be considered statistically significant the probability that an event has not occurred by chance is normally required to be 5 per cent or lower, such that p is equal to or less than 0.05. The closer the p value is to 0.0 the more significant the event is considered. A p value of 0.05 or lower (written as $p<0.05$) would be reported in order to have confidence in the findings. Sometimes the actual figure for p is not reported, but is described as being 'not statistically significant' and this means it failed to reach a 5 per cent or lower probability.

Validity

Validity is essential if an assessment is to be useful and describes whether the instrument assesses what it claims to. As an example, if a newly devised questionnaire claimed to assess subjects' levels of ambition, establishing validity would require proof that this was really what it assessed. It would need to be proved that it is not actually assessing intelligence, motivation to complete the questionnaire or perhaps even the subject's desire to give the answers they think the interviewer wants to hear. In attachment terms, it is necessary to demonstrate that it is the quality of attachment that is being assessed, not another aspect of the child, the mother or something else entirely. The methods of establishing validity referred to in the text are briefly explained below. It should be noted that validity is rarely established on one occasion by one test, but is established over time.

CONSTRUCT VALIDITY

Construct validity concerns the extent to which the operational definition of an assessment or measure actually reflects its true theoretical meaning.

CONCURRENT VALIDITY (ALSO KNOWN AS CONVERGENT VALIDITY)

This is a way of comparing the results of the instrument with those given by another more established instrument. The instrument is compared to a 'bench mark' or 'gold standard', which is a widely accepted assessment of the same type of behaviour. In attachment research, many of the Story Stem techniques, for example, compared results from the assessment with concurrent parental or observer Q-sorts. If it can be demonstrated that a new assessment gives scores that are consistent with scores given to the same subjects on another well-established model, it suggests that two assessments are tapping the same aspects of the subject. However, a note of caution should be sounded. It does not necessarily prove that the assessment assesses what it claims, merely that it assesses something similar to the original. If this original premise was wrong, then neither instrument may in fact assess what they claim. It is usually tested using percentage of agreement, *kappa statistics* or *correlation coefficients*. It can also be explored using *factor analysis*.

DISCRIMINANT VALIDITY

This is closely related to concurrent validity and concerns whether the instrument may be assessing variables which are theoretically unrelated. If discriminant validity cannot be proven, it is likely that the instrument is tapping a variable(s) other than the one it was designed to assess. This tends to be tested using *kappa statistics, correlation coefficients* or percentages.

PREDICTIVE VALIDITY

This concerns whether the ratings or scores given for a particular assessment predict performance or behaviour in the way that would be expected according to the theory. Using the previous example of a questionnaire to assess ambition, if the theory stated that a subject's level of ambition is related to the position they achieve at work, it would be expected that the ratings or scores subjects gained on the assessment would be related to their career achievement five years later. Attachment theory proposes that a secure attachment allows the child to develop independence (see Chapter 11). It would be expected, therefore, that a child's assessment on an attachment measure aged 18 months would predict their level of independence at school aged 5. If this is demonstrated it suggests that the assessment has predictive validity. This is usually tested using *correlation coefficients*, percentages or *effect sizes*.

Variance: ANOVA

This is a statistical method for comparing three or more samples. It is designed to determine whether there are differences anywhere between any of the samples, or whether they all come from the same population. It tests whether the variance of the scores between groups differ from the variance of scores of individuals within each group. This determines whether the differences among samples could just be caused by chance variation or whether they genuinely differ. It is reported as an F-ratio, with a p value which determines whether the F-ratio calculated is statistically significant. If it is, it implies that the groups do differ from each other significantly. In general the smaller the samples are the greater the F-ratio must be to attain significance. In attachment research, if it was found that a measure gave scores for children classified as secure or insecure that had different means, ANOVA can be used to determine whether the two groups are significantly different. If they are the measure can be said to discriminate between secure and insecure attachment and would therefore be considered valid.

Note

1   The term 'assessment' has been used in preference to the term 'measurement'. This is in the tradition of Mary Ainsworth, who, in her interview with Robert Marvin (Ainsworth and Marvin 1995), pointed out that measurement implies 'assigning numbers that reflect a precise amount or an equal interval ordering'. In her work, she continued, she has 'focused on classifications of patterns or on matching to behavioral descriptions – and that gives you *assessments*' (p.10). This is not to deny that some instruments included in this Part, where numerical scoring is achieved, are more accurately described as measures.

8 Assessments of Attachment

Assessments of attachment based on observation of the child's behaviour

The first assessments of attachment security were developed for use with infants and toddlers and were based on observational assessments of attachment behaviours. These aim to assess the child's attachment security based on the behaviours and reactions that are evoked when the attachment system is aroused. This arousal is achieved in two graded ways, the first being the introduction of a stranger and the second being separation from the caregiver. The behaviours are assumed to be based on the internal working models which the child has developed in relation to particular persons.

Table 8.1 lists the assessments of attachment in child age order.

Separation–reunion procedure

Strange situation

WHO DESIGNED IT AND WHEN?

Ainsworth and Wittig 1969.

ANY REVISIONS?

Ainsworth *et al.* 1978; Main and Solomon 1986, 1990.

WHAT DOES IT ASSESS?

The strange situation procedure assesses the attachment behaviour of young children to their primary carers, although, as outlined above, this behaviour

Table 8.1 Assessments/measures of attachment

Assessment/Measure	Who designed it	When	Child age order (inclusive)	What it assesses
Strange situation	Ainsworth and Wittig	1969	9–18 months	Behaviour
Preschool strange situation	Cassidy, Marvin and the MacArthur Working Group	1987	3–4 years	Behaviour
Attachment Q-set	Waters and Deane	1985	1–5 years	Behaviour
Main and Cassidy attachment classification system for kindergarten-age children	Main and Cassidy	1988	6-year-olds	Behaviour
Separation Anxiety Test (SAT) SAT using four scales SAT using long separation pictures	Klagsbrun and Bowlby Slough and Greenberg Jacobsen, Edelstein and Hofmann	1976 1990 1994	4–7 years	Representation
MacArthur Story Stem Battery	Bretherton, Oppenheim, Buchsbaum, Emde and the MacArthur Narrative Group	1990	3–8 years	Representation
Story Stem Assessment Profile	Hodges	1990	4–8 years	Representation
Manchester Child Attachment Story Task	Green, Stanley, Smith and Goldwyn	2000	4–8 years	Representation
Child Attachment Interview	Target, Fonagy and Shmueli-Goetz	2003	7–12 years	Representation

Continued on next page

Table 8.1 cont.

Assessment/Measure	Who designed it	When	Age range in chronological order	What it assesses
Friends and Family Interview	Steele and Steele	2003	Early adolescence	Representation
Attachment Interview for Childhood and Adolescence	Ammaniti *et al.*	1990	10–14 years	Representation
Separation Anxiety Test (adolescents)	Hansburg	1972	11–17 years	Representation
Adult Attachment Interview	George, Kaplan and Main	1985	Adults	Representation

reflects the nature of their internal working models. It yields a categorical classi-fication in one of four major categories and a set of four seven-point interval scales pertaining to proximity seeking, contact maintaining, avoidance and resistance. A further nine-point scale rating is given for extent of disorganisation as mentioned above.

USED WITH WHICH AGE GROUP?

Young children aged 9 to 18 months inclusive.

METHOD

The strange situation is a structured procedure comprising a series of three-minute-long episodes of increasing stress for the child. These are designed to activate the child's attachment system so that the child's behavioural responses can be observed. The sequence of episodes is outlined in Table 8.2.

The episodes take place in an experimental room, equipped with toys to keep the child occupied. It is usually set up with a one-way mirror so that trained observers can code the interactions, but the procedure must be video recorded too. The interactions are coded according to the level of exploration which the child exhibits, the distress demonstrated by the child on separation and, most crucially, the child's behaviour exhibited on reunion.

Ainsworth *et al.* (1978) identified and named three main patterns of attach-ment, namely secure (B), insecure-avoidant (A) and insecure-resistant (C), as well as eight subgroups. Main and Solomon (1986, 1990) later identified the insecure-disorganised/disoriented-attachment pattern (D). In their procedures for identifying infants as disorganised/disoriented in the strange situation (1990) they define the indices of disorganisation or disorientation under seven thematic headings, along with a nine-point scale for rating the intensity of this behaviour ranging from slight to extremely severe indicators. (See Chapter 3, for a detailed description of the A, B, C and D classification, the indices of dis-organisation/disorientation and the nine-point rating scale.)

RELIABILITY

Inter-rater reliability

Good. High correlation is reported for four joint observations.[1] A strong corre-lation was also reported for classification into major groups.[2]

> These findings suggest that the classificatory system can be used with high satisfactory reliability by experienced judges and with somewhat less agreement among less experienced judges. We suggest that training is necessary before a high degree of classification can be achieved. (Ainsworth *et al.* 1978, p.64)

Table 8.2 Strange situation procedure

Episode number	Persons present	Duration	Brief description of action
1	Mother, young child and observer	30 secs	Observer introduces mother and young child to the experimental room, then leaves.
2	Mother and young child	3 min	Mother is non-participant while the child explores; if necessary play is stimulated after 2 minutes.
3	Stranger, mother and young child	3 min	Stranger enters. First minute: stranger silent. Second minute: stranger converses with mother. Third minute: stranger approaches the child. After 3 minutes mother leaves unobtrusively.
4	Stranger and young child	3 min or less*	First separation episode. Stranger's behaviour is geared to that of the child.
5	Mother and young child	3 min or more**	First reunion episode. Mother greets and/or comforts the child, then tries to settle him or her again in play. Mother then leaves, saying 'bye-bye'.
6	Young child alone	3 min or less*	Second separation episode.
7	Stranger and young child	3 min or less*	Continuation of second separation. Stranger enters and gears behaviour to that of the child.
8	Mother and young child	3 min	Second reunion episode. Mother enters, greets the child, then picks him or her up. Meanwhile stranger leaves unobtrusively.

Notes

* Episode is curtailed if the child is unduly distressed.

**Episode is prolonged if more time is required for the child to become re-involved in play.

Main and Solomon (1990) report inter-rater reliability with new coders working in their laboratory on D/non-D attachment status of 77 per cent to 80 per cent. They also report rates of agreement between Main and coders in two high risk/maltreatment samples of 83 per cent and 94 per cent. Within laboratory agreement across all four strange situation categories (A, B, C and D) in one of these studies was 88 per cent.

VALIDITY
Construct validity

Discriminant function analysis (Ainsworth *et al.* 1978) suggested that the three main patterns of attachment, A, B and C, are distinct and differ significantly from each other. This indicated that a categorical approach to attachment classification was valid and that patterns of attachment can be identified accordingly. The validity of Ainsworth *et al.*'s original tripartite classification and the disorganised/disoriented pattern (D), later identified by Main and Solomon (1986, 1990), has been demonstrated in many subsequent studies.

CLINICAL USEFULNESS

This is a very widely used and well-respected procedure and is clinically useful. It provides useful data, giving a classification that can be used for assessing relationships and providing appropriate intervention. However, it requires trained coders. For many clinical purposes the time and monetary costs of completing it may be too great. It should also be remembered that it can only be used with young children, ideally aged 9–20 months.

Preschool strange situation
WHO DESIGNED IT AND WHEN?
Cassidy, Marvin and the MacArthur Working Group 1987.

ANY REVISIONS?
1990, 1991 and 1992.

WHAT DOES IT ASSESS?
Attachment behaviour.

USED WITH WHICH AGE GROUP?

Preschool children aged 3 and 4 years.

METHOD

The original strange situation procedure may be used, or a modified strange situation procedure involving two three-minute caregiver–child reunions. The classification system yields the following categories:[6]

B Secure

Uses parent as secure base from which to explore. Relaxed, open and smooth, reunion behaviour and communication.

A Avoidant

Detached, neutral communication and physical and affective avoidance of the parent, although does not completely avoid interaction.

C Ambivalent

Strongly protests separation and strongly seeks proximity on reunion. Shows a misture of babyish, coy behaviour and subtle resistance.

D Controlling

Openly tries to control the parent, by using punishing or caregiving behaviour, or both.

> *Controlling-punitive:* angry, punishing humiliating or rejective behaviour directed toward parent.
> *Controlling-caregiving:* caregiving behaviour directed toward the parent, suggestive of a reversal of parental and child roles.
> *Controlling-general:* controlling behaviour that has characteristics of both punitive and caregiving behaviour, or other controlling behaviour that does not resemble either of these types.

IO or U Insecure/other or unclassifiable

Behaviour that does not meet the criteria for any of the other groups.

RELIABILITY

Solomon and George (1999) report that 'the MacArthur Group requires a minimum of 75 per cent agreement for certification' (p.298). Britner, Marvin and Pianta (2005) report high inter-rater reliability, with 84 per cent agreement on the five-category classification and 93 per cent agreement on secure–insecure.

VALIDITY

Teti reports that evidence for construct validity is 'fragmentary at best' (1999, p.215). Some convergence between Cassidy–Marvin classifications and representational measures has been found for the secure–insecure dichotomy. However, in two studies, discrimination of the various insecure categories with representational measures could not be established. In addition, one study found weak relations between the Cassidy and Marvin classifications and the Attachment Q-set.

CLINICAL USEFULNESS

This would seem to be a useful system for the assessment of attachment in pre-school-age children.

Main and Cassidy attachment classification system for kindergarten-age children (sixth-year reunion procedure)

WHO DESIGNED IT AND WHEN?

Main and Cassidy 1988.

WHAT DOES IT ASSESS?

The child's behaviour during a reunion with the parent following an hour-long separation.

USED WITH WHICH AGE GROUP?

Children aged 6 years.

METHOD

'The system is based on a close analysis of the child's response to reunion with the parent during the first 3 to 5 min of reunion following a 1-hr laboratory separation' (Main and Cassidy 1988, p.416). In the two studies described in the original 1988 report, during the hour of separation (which took place after a 'warm-up' period) the child was engaged in free-play and child assessments with the examiner.

The sixth-year classification system is as follows:[7]

Secure

Interacts pleasantly with the parent on reunion, either initiating conversation or responding to the parent's initiations. Remains calm throughout reunion.

Insecure-avoidant
Minimal conversation and interaction with parent on reunion, maintaining affective neutrality and remaining occupied with play. May subtly move away for example, to fetch a toy.

Insecure-ambivalent
Exaggerated intimacy and dependency with the parent. Proximity-seeking characterised by ambivalence or resistance, such as showing discomfort. Subtle hostility toward the parent may be present.

Insecure-controlling
Partially taking parental role towardthe parent; trying to control and direct the parent, either by punitive behaviour such as humiliating the parent or by caregiving behaviour such as trying ot reassure or guide the parent.

Insecure-unclassifiable
Reunion behaviour which does not fit the avoidant, ambivalent or controlling categories. (In their 1988 study of middle-class samples (n=83), Main and Cassidy found that these responses were rare (n=2).)

RELIABILITY
Inter-rater reliability
Main and Cassidy (1988) report inter-rater agreement across all mother–child dyads of 83 per cent (k=0.74) and 77 per cent for father–child dyads (k=0.62). Solomon and George (1999) report a number of studies in which agreement between raters ranged from 70 per cent to 82 per cent, although lesser agreement involving the controlling (D) category is suggested.

Test–retest reliability
Main and Cassidy (1988) report a short-term stability (over a one-month period) of 62 per cent. Stability between one year and six years A, B, C and D classifications with mothers was 82 per cent (k=0.76) and with fathers was 62 per cent.

VALIDITY
Concurrent validity
Solomon *et al.* (1995) report a 79 per cent agreement (k=0.74; $p<0.001$) between doll-play classifications and Main and Cassidy classifications based on

reunion behaviour in a sample of 69 kindergarten children. High agreement was found for children assessed in the reunion procedure as secure (80%) and ambivalent (75%), although lower agreement was found for children assessed as avoidant (55%). However, Solomon *et al.* (1995) report that 'all eight children who had been classified as controlling with mother on reunion were placed in the Frightened doll-play category' (p.455).

Predictive validity
Main and Cassidy (1988) report that 'sixth-year classifications to mother were highly predictable from infant classifications to mother' (p.419). Solomon and George (1999) report a number of studies in which security as assessed by the Main and Cassidy system was related to age-appropriate maternal involvement and support, child social competence, child representations of the feelings of peers, and child self-esteem.

   Solomon *et al.* (1995) found that controlling children showed significantly more behaviour problems and aggressiveness than children assessed as having an organised attachment strategy with mother (*p*<0.04 for both scores). The authors state that their findings 'represent an important step in validating the attachment classification system for 6-year-olds' (p.458).

   Bureau and Moss (2001) assessed the attachment patterns of 103 children using the separation–reunion procedure at ages 5 to 7 years and 102 children using the MacArthur Story-Stem Battery (Bretherton *et al.* 1990b) at ages 8 to 10 years. The results indicated that children with insecure or controlling attachment patterns described their parents as powerless to help them (in situations of fear and distress) and as aggressive (in situations of interpersonal conflict).

CLINICAL USEFULNESS
This would seem to be a useful system for the assessment of attachment in pre-school-age children.

Q-sort methodology

The term Q-sort refers to a descriptive method that has been used in many fields of psychological research, most notably in personality research (see Wittenborn 1961 for a review of early uses). It is a way of defining a set of characteristics thought to be relevant to the area or factor under investigation. These characteristics are then sorted, following set methodology, in order to describe any given individual in those terms. The literature refers to Q-sort methodology to describe the procedure, but usually individual tests are referred to as 'Q-sets'. In the field of attachment literature there are a number of Q-sets, most notably the Attachment Q-set for children and the Adult Attachment Q-set.

Q-sort methodology has three components:

1.   developing a set of descriptive items

2.   ranking items to assign scores applicable to an individual

3.   data reduction and analysis.

The first of these requires the theoretical description of the factor or area being investigated using a number of statements or 'items'. Each 'set' comprises a number of these items written on cards. The second component requires sorting the sets of items into piles according to how much a given item defines the individual being described. The third component is the data reduction and analysis stage.

Q-sorts can also be compared to 'criterion sorts' which are provided by experts in the field of interest who are asked to sort the set of items as if they were describing the ideal exemplar of a certain type of subject. For instance, in attachment literature, this may be to provide a sort for a securely attached child. High correlations between an individual's sort and a criterion sort indicate that the individual closely resembles the exemplar being described. In terms of attachment, this would indicate a secure child.

Factor analyses can also be performed on Q-sort data in order to determine which particular items load onto given factors, or to see if certain items tend to be grouped together, thus indicating a factor.

The Attachment Q-set (AQS)
WHO DESIGNED IT AND WHEN?

Waters and Deane 1985.

ANY REVISIONS?

Attachment Q-set Version 3.0, 1987.

WHAT DOES IT ASSESS?

Behaviour. It yields a description of the child's secure base behaviour and a single score for security along a continuum from secure to insecure when compared with a criterion sort. It does not yield any information about the type of insecure attachment, and does not, therefore, include disorganised attachment.

USED WITH WHICH AGE GROUP?

Children aged 1 to 5 years inclusive. However, the dependency and sociability criterion sorts describe behaviours applicable to 1- to 3-year-olds.

METHOD

The Attachment Q-set consists of 90 items, each on a card with a title and a number of qualifying statements describing it.[8] It can be used to describe secure base behaviour in a number of environments, either at home or in a public place, inside or outside. It is designed to cover the spectrum of attachment-relevant behaviours, with items concerning a broad range of secure base and exploratory behaviour, affective response and social cognition. The observer spends a set amount of time observing the child (Waters recommends at least two sessions each of one-and-a-half to two hours) (Waters undated).

RELIABILITY: OBSERVER-COMPLETED SORTS

Inter-rater reliability

Good. Raters appear to obtain similar results when rating the same child on different occasions.[9]

RELIABILITY: PARENTAL-COMPLETED SORTS

The mothers of the children observed were trained in the Q-set technique and were asked to observe their child for one week and then complete the Q-set at the end of that time. They were asked to repeat the exercise the following week. These two scores were then combined to give a maternal composite score.[10]

Inter-rater reliability

Moderately good correlations between mother-completed and observer-completed sorts.[11]

Test–retest reliability

Good. Mothers tended to give similar scores on both occasions.[12]

VALIDITY: PARENTAL-COMPLETED SORTS

Concurrent validity

Poor. Comparison was made between the strange situation scores and Q-set scores but results failed to reach significance.[13]

VALIDITY: OBSERVER-COMPLETED SORTS

Concurrent validity

Good. When observer-completed Q-sorts were compared with ratings on the strange situation they were able to distinguish secure from insecurely attached children.[14]

Predictive validity

Poor. Unable to demonstrate predictive power of the Q-set, although several suggestions are made by the authors as to why this may be the case.[15]

CLINICAL USEFULNESS

It can be used with a wider age range and in a number of settings, which may improve its ecological validity. The Attachment Q-set may have another advantage over other attachment assessments because it ensures that every rater, be they observer or parent, is rating the child based on the same set of behaviours. This may reduce the chance for rater bias to affect the scoring. It appears that experienced observers can provide reliable descriptions of children's attachment, but parents may not be able to do so. If a child is insecurely attached and parental insensitivity is one factor influencing this, parental ratings are unlikely to be as objective as an outside observer's. However, parental ratings of their children on this Q-set may give clinically useful information, certainly in assessing how the parent sees the relationship.

The Attachment Q-set may be a useful tool but it can only identify secure versus insecure attachment, and cannot provide discrimination between types of insecure attachment. It is one-dimensional and this limits its clinical usefulness.

Moreover, it relies on the likelihood of stressful occurrences for the child during the period of observation, leading to proximity-seeking behaviour, but this cannot be ensured. Q-sorts are time consuming.

Assessments of attachment based on the child's internal working model/representation

Early in the preschool years children begin to move from encoding their knowledge about attachment relationships in sensorimotor representation to encoding it using mental representation. Techniques that tap these mental representations can provide a way of investigating the development of attachment representations from infancy, through childhood and into adult life.

There have been three main approaches to accessing children's internal representations of attachment relationships: (1) asking children to respond to pictures; (2) asking children to describe and enact Story Stem completion tasks, using doll and animal figures; (3) asking children questions regarding their actual attachment relationships.

Picture response tasks

Theoretical background

Picture completion tasks are designed to allow access to children's representations, or internal working models, of attachment relationships and the child's beliefs and feelings about these. The intention of the tasks is to present children with an attachment-related picture and then rate their response. Providing the child with a picture allows an indirect way of assessing the child's representations. It is also an acceptable approach for children who are used to adults asking them to talk about pictures in storybooks. Children's responses cannot be taken as evidence of their actual experiences, since an element of fantasy or storytelling is usually invoked by asking the child about a character in a picture. It should not be inferred that what a child describes in response to a picture has actually happened to them, although of course autobiographical detail may be revealed. What is being assessed is the child's generic representation of attachment figures and relationships.

Method

Picture response tasks involve the presentation of an attachment-related picture, which is introduced by the adult interviewer. The child is then asked to describe how the child in the picture feels and what the child will do.

The tasks vary in the number and type of pictures used, particularly the severity of the separation depicted. They also vary in the degree of emotional arousal engendered in the child by the interviewer.

Separation Anxiety Test (SAT)

WHO DESIGNED IT AND WHEN?

Hansburg 1972 (for adolescents aged 11 to 17 years inclusive).

ANY REVISIONS?

Revised for 4- to 7-year-olds (Klagsbrun and Bowlby 1976). Revised 1994 (Jacobsen, Edelstein and Hofmann). Revised with four scales (Slough and Greenberg 1990). Kaplan (1987) has developed a revised version of the SAT (described in Main *et al.* 2005).

WHAT DOES IT ASSESS?

Representation.

USED WITH WHICH AGE GROUP?

Versions for children aged 4 to 7 years and adolescents aged 11 to 17 years inclusive.

METHOD

The child is introduced to six photographs of separation-related scenes, ranging from mild (a parent says goodnight to a child in bed), to more stressful (a child watches parents going away for two weeks). The original Hansburg version contained 12 pen and ink drawings, and the six pictures excluded from the version for younger children contained more severe separation-related scenes, such as a child watching a mother being taken away in an ambulance, or a child and father standing by the mother's coffin. It was felt these would be too distressing for younger children. Once the interviewee has been shown the picture he or she is then asked how the child in the picture feels and what that child will do. If the child cannot suggest how the child might feel a list of possible responses is given such as lonely, sad or angry, but the child is told they do not have to choose one of these.

Solomon and George (1999) report that Kaplan 'developed a classification system for children's responses to the pictures that differentiates attachment groups on the basis of the children's emotional openness and ability to envision constructive solutions to feelings engendered by separation' (p.303). This yields four classifications, which are very similar to those seen in the strange situation:

> B *Resourceful*: child was open about feelings of vulnerability and was able to discuss coping with separation constructively. They did not become disorganised or disorientated.
>
> A *Inactive*: child was able to talk about vulnerability or anxiety but not generate constructive suggestions for coping.
>
> C *Ambivalent*: child often demonstrated contradictory responses, e.g. shifting between being angry with the parent and wanting to please the parent.
>
> D *Fearful*: child demonstrated inexplicable fear, a lack of constructive suggestions for dealing with separation, or disorganised or disoriented thought.

RELIABILITY

Inter-rater reliability
Good but limited information.[16]

VALIDITY

Concurrent validity
Moderately good but limited information.[17]

CLINICAL USEFULNESS

This instrument has been used fairly extensively and several adaptations have been made. Reliability and validity figures look good but there is limited information.

Adaptation of the Separation Anxiety Test using long separation pictures

Solomon and George (1999) report that, in 1994, Jacobsen *et al.* adapted the Separation Anxiety Test by using a series of pictures which illustrate a long separation from parents. Inter-rater reliability was good,[18] as was test–retest reliability,[19] concurrent validity[20] and predictive validity. The measure is reported to have successfully predicted variables for children aged 7 to 15 on cognitive-developmental tasks, self-esteem, teacher-reported attention and participation in class, insecurity about themselves and grade point average, even when the effects of IQ were controlled for.

Revised Separation Anxiety Test with four scales

In 1990, Slough and Greenberg revised the SAT for 4- to 7-year-olds using six pictures describing a child in various separation situations, ranging from mild (parents tuck child in bed and leave room) to more stressful (parents go away for two weeks). The pictures represent the same scenarios as in the Klagsbrun and Bowlby (1976) version, but were updated and modified to show only the back of the child's head in each photograph so that any emotional expression was removed. The child was asked what they thought the child in the picture might feel and why, and what that child might do. The child was then asked more directly what they themselves would do in the same situation. Three SAT summary rating scales were developed:

1. *Attachment*: four-point scale (4=high, 1=low) rates expression of vulnerability and need; an acknowledgement of separation-related affect for the three severe separation scenarios

2. *Self-reliance*: four-point scale (4=high, 1=low) rates statements of well-being and ability to cope in response to three mild separation scenarios

3. *Avoidance*: three-point scale (3=high, 1=low) rates refusal to discuss emotionally significant issues; inability or refusal to answer questions or suggest feelings, in response to all six scenarios.

In addition, a scale of *Emotional Openness* was developed. This was a nine-point scale (9=high, 1=low) which rated the child's ability to express feelings of vulnerability without losing self-control. Emotional openness scores were given for the child's own responses to the six separations and for the responses attributed to the child in the picture.

Inter-rater reliability was moderately good. Agreement on the emotional openness scale for interviewees' descriptions of the child in the picture was 50 per cent exact and 74 per cent within one scale point. Agreement for the interviewees' descriptions of themselves was 50 per cent exact with 71 per cent within one scale point. Concurrent validity was poor, although the limited reported results are ambiguous.[21]

CLINICAL USEFULNESS

The limited reliability data and fairly poor validity data make clinical use of this measure difficult. However, as an updated version of the SAT it seems preferable to the original in terms of the pictures it uses. The findings suggest that children may respond differently when asked about another child (i.e. the child in the picture) than when asked about themselves.

Narrative Story Stem techniques (NSSTs)

Why use narrative techniques?

The doll play techniques used in NSSTs are a development of earlier picture tasks. They are designed to access the same information as the picture tasks, tapping children's representations of attachment relationships. They are designed as a way of engaging the child with the subject matter in a relatively non-threatening manner. Children are used to being asked to tell stories or to talk through scenarios with adults and are therefore unlikely to be disturbed by the process. It is a much less challenging assessment measure than asking children direct questions. Unlike adults, who can be asked to reflect on their feelings and cognitions, children often find this difficult and giving them a narrative format allows some structure to be placed on their answers without restricting the information they can give. The stems/scenarios presented to the child include a number of different stressors, not confined to separation.

Why use dolls?

Using dolls in the narrative also allows the interview to take on more of the characteristics of play. Play is the area of children's lives where they can explore both their fantasies and their realities. Story Stem techniques are not attempting to elicit direct representations of specific events in the child's life, although it is possible these may come out. What the technique aims to do is access the child's generic expectations of attachment figures and the child's relationships to these. The techniques may be less daunting for children, especially maltreated children, if presented in this play format.

Method

Most Story Stem completion tasks follow a basic method. The child is presented with a set of figures with varying numbers of family members, including a child of the same gender as the interviewee. Animals may also be included in some of the techniques. The adult interviewer uses the figures to enact the beginning of a story. The adult then says 'Show me and tell me what happens next' and the child takes over control of both the figures and the narrative. Prompts or probe questions may be used in order to elicit a clearer response, or clarify the child's intentions in a particular story.

The techniques vary in the number of stems presented, the degree of anxiety evoked in the child and in a number of other particulars of methodology. The degree of identification between the child interviewee and the doll figures also varies from one technique to another.

The MacArthur Story Stem Battery (MSSB) is initially described. Other Story Stem batteries have also been developed in relation to the MSSB. Story Stems have proved to be very useful and there is now a consortium of some 50 researchers, most of them clinicians, using Story Stem assessments in about ten countries.

MacArthur Story Stem Battery (MSSB)[22]
WHO DESIGNED IT AND WHEN?

Bretherton *et al.* 1990b.

The basic framework for the development of the MacArthur Story Stem Battery was provided by three sets of collaborators, originally working independently on narrative techniques. Bretherton and Ridgeway (1990), who had developed the Attachment Story Completion Task, began working with Buchsbaum and Emde and they were later joined by Oppenheim. (For Attachment Doll-play Interview, see Oppenheim 1997.)

Some of the stories in the MSSB are used in the story sets of other narrative stem instruments.

WHAT DOES IT ASSESS?

Attachment representations and perceptions of parenting.

USED WITH WHICH AGE GROUP?

Children aged 3 to 8 years inclusive.

METHOD

The stems are presented in an animated fashion in order to engage the child. Neutral prompts such as 'Does anything else happen in the story?' are used to encourage the child, and certain specific probes are also used. For instance, during the stem related to the child being injured, if the child does not mention this, the interviewer asks 'Does anybody do anything about the hurt hand?' The procedure lasts approximately 40 minutes and is videotaped for the purpose of coding.

The battery comprises 14 stems relating to conflicts and emotional events in the context of parent–child relationships:

Warm-up: Birthday

1. Spilled juice (attachment/authority)

2. Lost dog/reunion (attachment)

3. Mum's headache (moral dilemma)

4. Gift for Mum or Dad (oedipal)

5. Three's a crowd (peer conflict)

6. Hot gravy (attachment/authority)

7. Lost keys (family conflict)

8. Stealing candy (moral)

9. Departure (attachment)

10. Reunion (attachment)

11. Bathroom shelf (moral dilemma)

12. Climbing a rock at the park (mastery, attachment)

13. Child exclusion by parents (oedipal)

14. The cookie jar (moral dilemma)

End: Family fun

Coding systems

A coding system was developed by Robinson and colleagues (1992) which is based on common themes probed by the various stems: moral rules, prosocial behaviour, empathy, exclusion, attachment, parental nurturance and non-nurturance and conflict/aggression (see also Robinson and Mantz-Simmons 2003).

Other coding systems have also been developed. Bretherton and Oppenheim (2003) suggest that 'the choice of coding method be governed by

the specific aims of each particular study, as well as the age of the child participants and the size of the sample' (p.69).

RELIABILITY
Inter-rater reliability
Oppenheim, Emde and Warren (1997) report good inter-rater reliability.[23]

Waters, Rodrigues and Ridgeway (1998) report significant although
moderate correlations between assessments at 3 and 4 years with a precursor of
the MSSB.

Test–retest reliability
Test–retest reliability was good to moderate.[24]

VALIDITY

Oppenheim *et al.* (1997) report moderately good predictive validity with
respect to the Child Behavior Checklist (CBCL) (Achenbach 1991).[25]

A study has examined possible links across generations in the emotion narratives of parents and their children (Steele *et al.* 2003b). Mothers' attachment
narratives as assessed in the AAI during pregnancy were compared to the narratives of their 5-year-old children, assessed using a subset of 11 Story Stems from
the MSSB. It was found that the 'children's use of limit-setting themes was significantly more likely if their mothers' attachment interviews had been scored
autonomous-secure ($p<0.01$, two-tailed)' (p.172).

CLINICAL USEFULNESS
Widely used.

Story Stem Assessment Profile (SSAP)
(Formerly known as the 'Little Pig' Story Stem Assessment)

WHO DESIGNED IT AND WHEN?
Hodges 1990.

ANY REVISIONS?
Rating manual revised 2002 and Hodges *et al.* 2004.

WHAT DOES IT ASSESS?

Representation. It assesses the child's expectations of the parent–child relationship in various domains, and also allows assessment of aspects of defence and avoidance, related to emotional regulation. Ratings can then be combined so as to yield scores for global constructs, such as security of attachment.

USED WITH WHICH AGE GROUP?

Children aged 4 to 8 years inclusive.

METHOD

The battery consists of 13 stems, five with a preliminary rating scheme, devised on the basis of clinical experience in the assessment of abused children, and eight selected from the MacArthur Story Stem Battery. The stems are presented in a standard order using the MSSB standard doll family (child of the same sex as the interviewee, a same sex younger sibling, a mother and a father). The child is asked to give names to the two children, which are not actual names of the child interviewee and his or her siblings. Animal figures are also used in two stories. The stems are as follows:

1. *Crying outside*: doll family at home, child figure goes outside and behind house, sound of crying.

2. *Little pig*: little pig leaves the other pigs and goes on a long walk past all the other animals, then exclaims he is lost, can't see the other pigs and doesn't know how to get back.

3. *Stamping elephant*: animals and doll family are outside the house. Elephant comes and stamps around loudly ('sometimes this elephant gets a bit fierce'), scaring the children and the animals.

4. *Bikes*: child and friend ask Mum if they can go out on their bikes, Mum says 'yes, but be careful'. The children go really fast on their bikes and then the child falls off.

5. *Picture from school*: child makes picture in school and thinks 'this is really good, I'm going to take it home when I go home from school'; after school he or she takes picture and goes home, knocks at the door.

Stems selected from MSSB

1. *Spilt juice*: family seated at the table drinking juice, child reaches across the table for more and spills the jug of juice over the floor.

2. *Mum's headache*: Mum and child watching TV, Mum says she has a headache and must turn the TV off and lie down for a while, asks child to do something quietly meanwhile. Friend comes to door and wants to come in to watch TV programme with child.

3. *Three's a crowd*: child and friend are playing ball in garden, while parents are talking to neighbours over fence. Little sib wants to play too but friend refuses, saying he or she won't be child's friend any more if he or she lets sib play.

4. *Burnt hand*: family is waiting for dinner, Mum is cooking at stove and warns child to be careful, pan is hot. Child can't wait, reaches for pan, spilling the dinner on the floor and burning hand.

5. *Lost keys*: child enters room to find parents angrily quarrelling over who lost the keys.

6. *Bathroom shelf*: mother briefly goes next door to neighbour, warning children not to touch anything on the bathroom shelf while she is gone; younger sib cuts finger and needs a plaster.

7. *Monster (or burglar) in the dark*: child in bed, parents sitting on sofa. Child hears noise, lights go out, child fears it is a monster (or burglar).

8. *Exclusion story*: parents on sofa, father tells child they want some time alone and asks child to play in own room for a while; as child leaves, mother and father hug.

The basic methodology is much the same as for the other NSSTs. The interviewer introduces each stem by enlisting the child's help to 'set the scene' with the correct characters. The interviewer then shows and tells the child the Story Stem, dramatising the affect and the dilemma presented in the stem so as to engage the child emotionally. The interviewer then invites the child to 'Show me and tell me what happens next'. There are certain required probes depending on the response, and the interviewer may also ask certain neutral prompt questions, for clarification. Administration usually takes about an hour.

Each interview is videotaped and the recordings are transcribed to give both the verbal and non-verbal narrative responses. Both are given equal weight in the rating of the child's responses, on the basis that many of the mental representations of caregiving which the technique aims to access are not retrievable verbally.

The SSAP rating system gives a three-point rating to each story for the presence or absence of about 40 themes or characteristics. These include representations of parents (e.g. aware when child is distressed; rejecting; providing comfort); representations of children (e.g. seeking adult help when appropriate; endangered; parenting adults); indicators of defence and avoidance of anxiety (e.g. disengagement from task, altering given parameters of stem); and indicators of disorganisation (e.g. unexplained shifts from portrayal of an adult as a good to a bad figure or vice versa, catastrophic fantasies, extreme aggression). There is a manual (Hodges *et al.* 2004) detailing criteria and examples for each.

Ratings on individual themes are used for detailed clinical assessment, and can also be treated as components of attachment classifications and used to generate global constructs such as attachment security, insecurity, defensive avoidance and disorganisation, and positive and negative representations of adults and of children can be generated. For example, attachment security would include ratings of parents in the narratives as aware when children are distressed or in need of help; offering practical help; offering emotional comfort and affection; setting limits; not being punitive; not rejecting the child; and not being aggressive toward the child. It would also include ratings of children as seeking help when appropriate from parents; acknowledging distress (rather than trying to make out that there is no distress or need for help or comfort); able to cope with difficulties by their own efforts or by actively enlisting help, when this is realistic; not unduly aggressive or in danger themselves; and not being either overcompliant to the parents or controlling (or parenting) the parents.

RELIABILITY

Inter-rater reliabilities for raters trained on the rating system average 87 per cent.

Construct scores have high alphas indicating strong internal consistency (Hodges *et al.* 2003a).

VALIDITY

Ratings on individual themes and on global construct scores are significantly correlated with total and subscale scores on the Strengths and Difficulties Questionnaire and the Child Behavior Checklist in a sample of 111 adopted children aged between 4 and 8. Forty-eight of these children were non-maltreated and were adopted in infancy, and 63 were maltreated and subsequently placed for adoption after the age of 4.

In the same sample, ratings on individual themes and on global construct scores were significantly related to whether or not the child had suffered maltreatment. The technique thus demonstrates good discrimination between children who have and have not been maltreated. Among the maltreated group, the degree of adversity prior to placement was also significantly related to differences in Story Stem responses, indicating that the measure can discriminate more and less severe levels of abuse. Significant changes in the direction of greater security were shown when the assessment was repeated after one and again after two years, indicating that the measure can be used to reflect changes as the children settled into their new families (Hodges *et al.* 2003b, 2003c).

Importantly, SSAP responses of late-adopted maltreated children have been shown to have concurrent validity with Adult Attachment Interview responses of their adoptive parents (Steele *et al.* 2003a). Remarkably, these associations appeared within three months of placement, highlighting the immediate impact adoptive parents have upon their late-placed children. Specifically, children adopted by autonomous-secure and resolved parents showed more optimal profiles or less troubled profiles on the SSAP.

Standardisation data on non-adopted children are so far lacking.

Small, unpublished studies of clinical series of children have demonstrated meaningful and statistically significant differences between sexually abused children and comparisons, and between children subject to factitious or induced illness and comparisons. These findings have been presented at numerous meetings on attachment and adoption since 2000.

CLINICAL USEFULNESS

Useful, especially with maltreated or vulnerable children, due to its indirect, non-threatening style. At no point is the child asked directly about themselves or their experiences, thus minimising distress or avoidance. The use of two stems with animals allows an even greater step of displacement. The authors report that children usually tolerate the assessment well and even initially reluctant children often become engaged and enjoy the process.

The administration of 13 stems allows more anxious children a longer time to become at ease with the task. The diverse starting points of the stems also allow the child the opportunity to present and develop different themes. This means that recurrence of a theme in the child's response is more likely to represent a significant underlying pattern of representation in the child. The detail of the rating scheme allows a greater level of analysis which can be clinically helpful.

The Manchester Child Attachment Story Task (MCAST)
WHO DESIGNED IT AND WHEN?

Green *et al.* 2000.

ANY REVISIONS?

A computerised version is currently being tested.

Manual revision (2004) includes a structured baseline assessment to distinguish between characteristic developmental variables in the child from those specifically shown in the attachment scenarios. The original number of six vignettes was reduced to four. The opening and closure non-attachment vignettes were retained.

WHAT DOES IT ASSESS?

Attachment representation in the early school years. It yields a numerical score on four continuous scales: Mentalising, Metacognition, Disorganised and Narrative coherence. It also gives an overall categorical rating for 'strategy of assuagement'.

USED WITH WHICH AGE GROUP?

Young school-age children (approximately 4½ to 8½ years).

METHOD

The MCAST comprises a series of six Story Stems. Before the test begins the child is shown a doll's house and various objects and is asked to choose a doll character to represent themselves and another to represent the primary carer in whom the interviewer is interested. The MCAST has a number of features which differ from other NSSTs. It focuses on a single dyad, rather than on a larger family. It emphasises child identification with the doll figures, specifically asking the child to identify one of the dolls as themselves. It also induces a higher degree of anxiety and distress in order to arouse attachment-related thoughts and behaviours in a similar fashion to the strange situation.

Vignettes

1. breakfast routine

2. child awakes at home alone with a nightmare

3. child is playing outside and falls over and hurts a knee, causing pain and bleeding

4.   child develops acute abdominal pain

5.   the child becomes lost in a crowd whilst shopping with the carer

6.   family trip.

Story Stem 1 is designed as a non-attachment-related comparison (baseline) vignette; Stories 2, 3, 4 and 5 are attachment-related 'distress' vignettes; Stem 6 is a non-attachment closure vignette.

The general method is the same as for other NSSTs but for each of the 'distress' vignettes there is an induction phase in which the interviewer emphasises the distress represented in the child figure to the point where the interviewee is clearly involved and sympathetically aroused. For each vignette the child plays out a story completion and is then asked a series of questions to clarify the intention behind the play and asked a number of mental state attribution questions, for example 'How is the child doll feeling now?', 'What would the parent doll like to do now?' The interview ends with a period of free play in which the child is asked to play out something the family like doing together. This is designed as a 'winding down' period before the interview finishes.

Coding scheme

The coding scheme is unique in combining strange situation coding procedures with adult attachment coding procedures on the basis that at this developmental age both are relevant to the child's narrative representations. It produces full categorical attachment classification outcome codings similar to the strange situation procedure. It additionally produces continuous scores for security, meta-cognition, mentalising, disorganisation and narrative coherence.

RELIABILITY

Inter-rater reliability
Good. Raters tended to agree in their classifications.[26]

Test–retest reliability
Good, although stability was higher for those rated as secure.[27]

VALIDITY

Studies have shown that for children under the age of 4½ years the instrument overcodes disorganisation and over 8½ tends to overcode security.

Construct validity

Green *et al.* (2000) report that the content validity of the MCAST is supported by a factor analysis of its items, with the strongest factor containing 'items (proximity seeking, assuagement and progression to exploratory play) that are central to the attachment behavioural cycle and the outcome coding of attachment security' (p.60). Discriminate validity of individual vignettes was also found, suggesting to the authors that a method using fewer vignettes might be satisfactory for general use. Subsequent versions have reduced the vignettes to the most discriminating vignettes.

Concurrent validity

Goldwyn *et al.* (2000) found that overall agreement between the MCAST and the Separation Anxiety Test in a non-clinical sample of 34 young school-age children was 80 per cent (k=0.41, $p<0.01$). This study also reports a significant association between categorical disorganisation coding on the MCAST and unresolved status on the concurrently assessed maternal Adult Attachment Interview (AAI) (n=30, 77 per cent agreement, k=0.49, $p<0.10$).[28] Given the strong association between unresolved maternal representations and disorganised child attachment at various ages, it is reasonable to conclude this as a concurrent validity measure.

Validation on low risk samples showed association between disorganisation and symptom scores. In clinical groups there is validation data (Green and Goldwyn 2002; Green *et al.* 2001) with strong association between disorganisation and parent-rated symptomatology, ADHD, maternal expressed emotion and child language.

The MCAST is currently being used in ten developmental and intervention qualitative studies in the UK and Europe.

CLINICAL USEFULNESS

The MCAST is easy to administer, although coding and analysis of response requires more specialised training. It is relatively short, but requires video recording facilities.

The deliberate emotional engagement of the child by the interviewer during the 'induction phase' may cause a degree of distress. Green *et al.* address this point and argue that the degree of anxiety or distress that may be aroused is no greater than a child would normally experience in everyday life and is so short lived that it should not cause the child any undue harm and is thus ethical.

Interview techniques

Child Attachment Interview (CAI)

WHO DESIGNED IT AND WHEN?

Target, Fonagy and Shmueli-Goetz 2003.[29]

ANY REVISIONS?

This is the most recent edition, the previous edition (Revised Edition III, 1997) having been extensively modified following piloting.

WHAT DOES IT ASSESS?

Representations of attachment security with each parent and the overall state of mind with respect to attachment.

USED WITH WHICH AGE GROUP?

Children aged 7 to 12 years.

METHOD

The CAI consists of a semi-structured interview that lasts between 20 minutes and an hour. Interviews are usually audio or videotaped. The interview protocol is based on the Adult Attachment Interview (AAI; described below) but, unlike the AAI, the CAI focuses on recent attachment-related events and how the current relationships with each parent are represented.

The interview comprises 14 questions and probes:

1. Who is in your family (lives with you in your house)?

2. Tell me three words that describe yourself (examples)?

3. Can you tell me three words that describe what it's like to be with your mum (examples)?

4. What happens when Mum gets upset with you?

5. Can you tell me three words that describe what it's like to be with your dad (examples)?

6. What happens when Dad gets upset with you?

7. Can you tell me about a time when you were upset and wanted help?

8. What happens when you are ill?

9. What happens when you hurt yourself?

10. Has anyone close to you ever died?

11. Is there anyone that you cared about who isn't around any more?

12. Have you ever been away from your parents for the night or for longer than a day?

13. Do your parents sometimes argue? Can you tell me about a time when that happened?

14. In what ways do you want/not want to be like your mum/dad?

The CAI is scored according to both what the child says and their non-verbal communication. Children's responses are rated on eight scales, three of which, namely 'preoccupied anger', 'idealisation' and 'dismissal', are rated separately for mother and father. Scores range from 1, as the lowest score, to 9 as the highest score.

- *Emotional openness*: assesses the child's ability to express and label emotions and to ground them in descriptions of interactions with attachment figures.[30]

- *Preoccupied anger*: this was adapted from the Involving Anger scale of the AAI[31] but unlike the AAI includes involving denigration or contempt, as well as anger itself.

- *Idealisation*: measures the extent to which the child presents an unsupported picture of an 'ideal' parent.

- *Dismissal*: measures active denial of attachment and the presentation of parents and attachment experiences as unimportant.

- *Self-organisation*: measures the child's internal representation of self-efficacy, related to whether the child can identify or suggest self-initiated and constructive conflict resolutions.[32]

- *Balance of positive/negative references to attachment figures*: this scale was based on the assumption that secure children would more readily recognise and integrate positive and negative aspects of parental figures. It therefore measures how balanced the child's description is of attachment figures.

- *Use of examples*: measures the child's ability to provide relevant and elaborated examples.

- *Resolution of conflicts*: rates the child's ability to describe constructive resolutions to conflicts.[33]

A score is also given relating to the overall qualities of consistency, development and reflection shown in the child's answers. Besides the linguistic analysis, a behavioural analysis of children's responses to the interview situation and questions is also completed, taking account of eye contact, changes in tone of voice, marked anxiety, changes of posture in relation to the interviewer and contradictions between verbal and non-verbal expression.

To obtain a secure classification, the child must have a rating of approximately five or above on all CAI scales, except for Idealisation, Dismissal and Preoccupied Anger scales where a score of three is required. A level of security (Secure, Very Secure, Insecure, Very Insecure) is then assigned with respect to both mother and father.

RELIABILITY

Inter-rater reliability for CAI main classification
Information limited.

Test–retest reliability
Good. The classification across three months was quite stable across 46 cases. The median was 0.63. The security classification for representation of mother was 0.75 or above, and for father was 0.65 or above. All children coded disorganised on one occasion were coded the same three months later. There was a considerable variability in the stability of the scales.[34] Thirty-three children were retested one year later. The stability of the scale scores was moderate. The median correlation was 0.40. Once again, there was a considerable spread in the stability of the scales.[35]

VALIDITY

Discriminant validity
Moderately good. There was no statistically significant difference between the mean age of children classified as secure or insecure with each parent. Neither gender nor social class predicted security of attachment, and the prevalence of Black or Asian children were comparable in the secure and insecure groups. In this non-clinical sample, the number of children living with both parents was not higher in the secure than in the insecure group. Verbal IQ was almost identical among children with secure vs. insecure representations of attachment security with each parent. This is noteworthy because of the importance given

to linguistic coherence in the coding of attachment representations. Expressive language scores were also collected on a sub-sample of 88 children. There was a slight, statistically non-significant superiority of expressive language for the secure children both with their mothers and fathers.

Predictive validity

Good predictive validity between mothers' current state of mind with respect to attachment as assessed by the AAI and their children's attachment status as assessed by the CAI.[36]

CLINICAL USEFULNESS

Information from this measure may yield interesting and important information about the child. However, caution needs to be exercised in using the CAI with children who are living with parents who are or may be emotionally or physically abusive or neglectful. This instrument invites the child to reflect on their relationships with their parents in a way which could challenge the child's defences and coping mechanisms when the child may not be protected. This test requires training for its administration and rating.

Friends and Family Interview (FFI)

WHO DESIGNED IT AND WHEN?

Steele and Steele 2003.

ANY REVISIONS?

None found.

WHAT DOES IT ASSESS?

Representations of attachment, in particular coherence concerning attachment relationships.

USED WITH WHICH AGE GROUP?

This interview was developed for use with children at the end of middle childhood and the beginning of adolescence. It is based on the assumption that the central developmental issues of young people of this age are peer relationships, their changing sense of self and emerging capacities for reflecting (on things they like best, things they like least, and more generally their ambivalent feelings about themselves, friends and family).

METHOD

The interview opens with the following invitation:

> I want to get an idea about you, what sort of person you are, what you like to do, and most of all how you think and feel about your relationships with friends and family. One thing we sort of take to be true about all people and relationships is that there are things we like best in ourselves and in other people (things we might like to keep the same), and other things that we like least (or not very much at all) in ourselves and other people (things we might like to change). So this might be something we talk about as I ask you the following questions.

The interview comprises 26 questions which focus on self, peers (best friend), siblings and parents. Respondents are asked to describe the most and least liked aspects of the way things are with regard to each of these domains. Specific probes are included, for example concerning disagreements that arise and how they are negotiated. Throughout, respondents are asked to illustrate their stories with examples from daily life. Questions that might be 'most taxing upon these young people's capacity for coherent speech' (Steele and Steele 2005, p.147) are placed at the end of the interview. For example, Question 25:

> Now, could you think back and tell me if you think your relationship with your parents has changed since you were little?

The interviews are tape-recorded (for later transcription) and video-filmed.

Coding

The coding system applies a four-point rating scale to a number of dimensions within the following categories:

1. Coherence

2. Metacognition or reflective functioning

3. Evidence of secure-base availability

4. Evidence of self-esteem

5. Peer relations

6. Anxiety and defence.

RELIABILITY

Inter-rater reliability and test–retest reliability are not reported in the 2005 paper.

The 2005 paper reports that the four sets of ratings for coherence, that is truth, economy, relation and manner, were examined for internal consistency using Chronbach alpha coefficients. Each alpha computed was greater than 0.74 (range=0.74 to 0.88), indicating strong internal consistency.

VALIDITY

Discriminant validity

The authors state that the discriminant validity of the AAI, namely that a highly educated person may be low in coherence on the AAI while an unskilled may be high, 'sets the goalpost for any proposed interview-based measure of attachment security in middle childhood' (p.141). In the sample of 57 11-year-old children reported in the 2005 chapter, using the 'Vocabulary' and 'Similarities' sub-scales of the WISC-III^{UK}, correlations between the children's verbal intelligence and their observed attachment-based coherence were non-significant.

Predictive validity

In the sample reported in the 2005 chapter, at the age 11-year follow-up, age was positively and significantly correlated with over all coherence (r=0.26; p<0.05 one-tailed), suggesting that maturation 'enhances the child's potential for demonstrating meta-representational capacities' (p.149).

FFI assessments of secure base availability of both mother and father correlated positively and significantly with each of the five ratings of coherence. The authors point out that these correlations, in the r=0.40 to 0.60 range, nevertheless indicate that 'the children's levels of coherence cannot be attributed directly to their experiences of warmth and support from their parents' (p.149). They suggest that coherence seems to be operating in the FFI much like it is presumed to operate in the AAI, that is 'as an organizer of experience, including reflections, evaluations, and re-descriptions of experience at a meta-representational level within the mind' (p.154).

For both daughters and sons, the coherence sub-scale of quality or truthfulness in the FFI was consistently and significantly higher if mother's AAI was classified autonomous-secure. Other findings point to the particular influence of fathers' AAIs on the coherence of sons. Further gender-specific findings are reported in other correlation and regression analyses.

In the findings reported in the 2005 chapter, correlations between attachment security with mother at 12 months and coherence at 11 years in the FFI were not found (according to Table 7.2). However, in further analyses some links to infant–mother attachment security, in particular with respect to non-verbal ease in the FFI, have been found (H. Steele, personal communication, 2005).

CLINICAL USEFULNESS

The FFI is a relatively recently developed instrument. With wider use and the demonstration of inter-rater reliability, this interview may prove to be a useful instrument towards assessing attachment in children older than 11 years. However, although not a long interview, the 26 items with probes may be too time-consuming in most clinical settings. In addition, training is required for administration and coding. Nevertheless, familiarity with the FFI and its constructs is likely to be useful for clinical practice.

Attachment Interview for Childhood and Adolescence (AICA)

WHO DESIGNED IT AND WHEN?

Ammaniti *et al.* 1990.

ANY REVISIONS?

None found.

WHAT DOES IT ASSESS?

Mental representations of attachment relationships in late childhood and early adolescence.

USED WITH WHICH AGE GROUP?

Children and young adolescents aged 10 to 14 years.

METHOD

The AICA is a revised version of the AAI (described below) for participants in late childhood and early adolescence. The structure of the interview and the sequence of the questions are unchanged, but the language has been simplified and made age appropriate. It is a semi-structured interview, which is usually audio or videotaped.

The coding system of the AAI is used to classify adolescents into one of four categories for overall state of mind with respect to attachment:

1. Dismissing of attachment relationships

2. Secure, freely valuing of attachment

3.   Preoccupied with attachment relationships

4.   Unresolved with respect to past loss or trauma.

In addition, the interview transcripts are scored on 12 nine-point scales. Five scales assess 'probable childhood experience' and childhood relationship to each parent (loving, rejecting, neglecting, involving, pushing to achieve), and seven 'representational' scales assess the present mental representation of attachment (idealisation, anger, derogation, passivity, coherence of transcript, lack of memory, and meta-cognition). Idealisation, anger and derogation are scored separately for mothers and fathers.

Responses to the AICA are coded following Main and Goldwyn's (1998) coding system for the AAI. The coherence scale must be assessed very carefully in order to take into account the developmental stage of the child. What may be rated as incoherence for an adult might simply reflect a developmentally normal lack of sophisticated thought for a 10-year-old.

RELIABILITY
Inter-rate reliability
A high degree of inter-coder agreement can be reached with well-trained AAI coders.

VALIDITY
Concurrent validity
Results showed that the distribution of attachment categories in the 10- and 14-year-old participants are not significantly different from those collected in other studies using the AAI with adolescent and young adult samples. The AAI coding system appears to be reliably adaptable to the AICA material.

CLINICAL USEFULNESS

Good, but as with the AAI it is time-consuming and costly to administer and score. It yields useful information and may prove a more child-friendly approach than the more formidable AAI. It appears to be able to tap underlying attachment factors without being influenced by normal adolescent fluctuations in mood and relationships to parents, which is a risk with this population. However, it remains unpublished and may therefore be difficult for clinicians to access.

Adult Attachment Interview (AAI)

Although the AAI is for use with adults, it is included here because the validation of some measures described in this section includes association with the AAI. Furthermore, the AAI contibuted to the burgeoning interest in narrative measures, previously described.

WHO DESIGNED IT AND WHEN?

George, Kaplan and Main 1984.

ANY REVISIONS?

1985, 1996.

WHAT DOES IT ASSESS?

Representation. It yields a categorical classification similar to the strange situation across five categories: Autonomous, Dismissing, Preoccupied, Unresolved/Disorganised and Cannot Classify.

USED WITH WHICH AGE GROUP?

Adults.

METHOD

It takes the form of a semi-structured interview which is usually audio or video tape recorded. Adults are asked to recall memories from childhood and evaluate them from their current perspective. It probes alternately for general descriptions of relationships, specific autobiographical supportive or contradictory memories, and descriptions of current relationships with parents. The interview consists of 15 standard questions, which are asked in a fixed order, and each question has a set of standardised probes. The questions cover the following areas:

- an initial 'warm-up' question asking for a description of family composition
- five adjectives or phrases which describe the interviewee's relationship with each parent with memories or experiences of each descriptor and why they had chosen them
- which parent they had felt closest to as a child and why

- what they had done as a child when they were upset, hurt or ill, with examples

- what they remembered about their first separation from their parents

- whether they had ever felt rejected by their parents

- whether they had ever felt threatened by their parents

- how they thought their adult personalities were affected by their childhood experiences

- why their parents had behaved as they did

- how the relationship with their parents had changed over time

- how the experience of being parented may have affected their responses to their own children.

In addition, the interviewee is asked to decide:

(a)   specific losses through death of significant persons in their lives

(b)   traumatic experiences (including significant abuse).

The interview lasts approximately an hour. It is transcribed verbatim to allow for coding. The coding is based not on the content of autobiographical memories, but on the way experiences and their effects are evaluated and reported. The nature of the interviewee's attachment is manifested in their coherence during the interview. Only content that directly contradicts the interviewee's evaluations affects the coding.

The AAI coding system (Main and Goldwyn 1984, 1998) yields the following classifications for overall state of mind with respect to attachment:

Autonomous–secure
Presentation is coherent and consistent and responses are clear, relevant and do not get tangled or run on and on. A classification of autonomous is not reliant on having had a secure or stable childhood, but requires the adult to be able to reflect and discuss experiences coherently.

Dismissing–insecure
Descriptions of parents are highly positive but are unsupported or later contradicted by recalled events. Interviewees often insist that they are unable to

remember childhood attachment experiences. They seem to minimise their attention to attachment-related information.

Preoccupied–insecure
Interviewees show confused, angry or passive preoccupations with attachment figures. Their interviews often contain long, tangled sentences. The interview seems to generate excessive attention to attachment-related information.

Unresolved–disorganised
Interviewees so classified show disorganised discourse in relation to a specific loss or trauma, such as abuse. A substantial loss of monitoring or reasoning must occur during discussion of a particular event.

Cannot classify
This is a more recent classification category (Hesse 1996) and was developed to classify subjects whose discourse shows a combination of contradictory patterns.

RELIABILITY
Test–retest
Good to moderate. High levels of agreement between two test administrations are reported, although unresolved classifications have less stability, possibly reflecting the grieving process.[3]

VALIDITY
Discriminant validity
Moderately good.[4]

Predictive validity
Good predictive validity between parental rating on AAI and their infant's classification on the strange situation.[5]

CLINICAL USEFULNESS
It appears to show good reliability and validity and therefore could be useful in predicting infant attachment and targeting intervention. Its use is limited due to the lengthy interview and rating procedure. Training to both carry out and rate the AAI is also specialised and expensive and this may rule it out as an option for most clinicians.

Notes

1   Ainsworth *et al.* (1978): frequency measures showed high correlations for features such as exploratory behaviour or crying ($r=0.93$). Measures of interactive behaviour again showed high correlations, with a range from $r=0.75$ for avoidance to $r=0.94$ for resistance.

2   Ainsworth *et al.* (1978): 96 per cent agreement for Group A; 92 per cent for Group B; 75 per cent for Group C. Less agreement was found for subgroups, with most discrepancy involving A1 and A2.

3   Bakermans-Kranenburg and van IJzendoorn (1993): study of 83 mothers, interviewed twice by different interviewers with a two-month interval between interviews; 78 per cent (k=0.63) of subjects were given the same classification for both interviews; 83 per cent of autonomous subjects remained in the same classification. However, when the unresolved classification was taken into account fewer classifications (61%) remained unchanged. This may reflect the changing nature of the grieving process to which many unresolved classifications may be attributable. When subjects who had experienced recent loss were removed from this category, the test–retest reliability was higher.

4   Waters *et al.* (1993) coded interviews related to job experience, using a similar protocol to the AAI, and found that discourse style during this was not related to discourse style during AAI. Bakermans-Kranenburg and van IJzendoorn (1993) found no effect of memory for non-attachment-related autobiographical recall, intelligence, or social desirability of responding style was reported.

5   Van IJzendoorn (1995): in a meta-analysis of 18 samples (n=854), an ability to predict categories of insecure and secure child attachment was shown. When the 'unresolved' classification was excluded, AAI 'dismissing' classification predicted 'avoidant' strange situation classification (combined $r=0.45$) and AAI 'preoccupied' classification predicted 'ambivalent' strange situation classification (combined $r=0.42$). The 'unresolved' classification showed correspondence with the 'disorientated/disorganised' strange situation classification (combined $r=0.31$). If the 'unresolved' category is included, the 'preoccupied' AAI classification has the weakest predictive power, but this may be related to the very small numbers of 'preoccupied' adults and 'ambivalent' children that are reported.

6   Descriptions of the categories are taken from Solomon and George (1999) and Teti (1999).

7   Based on Main and Cassidy 1988.

8   The complete set of 90 items with explanations is available from the Measurement Library on the Stony Brook website (www.psychology.sunysb.edu/attachment).

9   Waters and Deane (1985) report a previous study involving two observers making three- to four-hour visits, once alone and once as a pair. After both visits each observer completed the Q-set. Correlations between the two Q-set descriptions of each child were highly reliable (from $r=0.75$ to $r=0.95$).

10 Van Dam and van IJzendoorn (1988): used simple parental version with 75 items in Dutch translation. Study with 39 families with a mean age of 18 months (±2 weeks). Mothers sorted cards twice, once before and once after their lab visit to take part in the

strange situation, helped by research assistants who provided basic training in the procedure. Q-set outcomes were correlated with criterion sorts for Security, Dependency, Sociability and Desirability (Waters and Deane 1985) for 12-month-olds.

11   Ibid. The correlation between mothers' composites and observers' composites ranged from $r=0.59$ to 0.93; the mean correlation was $r=0.80$.

12   Ibid. Reliability scores over about ten days: Security $r=0.75$, Dependency $r=0.86$, Sociability $r=0.78$, Desirability $r=0.82$.

13   Comparison of security scores on the Q-set was made between anxious and secure groups, A/C and B on the strange situation. Secure children tended to have lower scores (mean -0.429) than the anxious children (-0.377) but an ANOVA did not show this to be statistically significant ($F=1.4$, $p=$ns), and it did not reach significance when desirability was accounted for ($F=1.96$, $p=$ns). There were no significant partial correlations between security measured by Q-set and resistance, avoidance and proximity seeking/contact maintaining as measured by the strange situation.

14   Ibid.

15   Van Dam and van IJzendoorn (1988) were not able to establish validity, but suggest a number of possible reasons (e.g. cultural validity, small sample size) and report that it cannot be concluded the instrument is not valid. The strange situation may tap slightly different aspects of attachment than the Q-set. If so, total convergence would not be expected. Whilst this may be true, their findings do cast doubt on the validity of maternal Q-sorts.

16   Klagsbrun and Bowlby (1976) in a study of 61 children in their first term at primary school. Klagsbrun and Bowlby did not carry out tests of reliability for their original pilot study, but report that they believed agreement between raters to be high.
    Kaplan (1987) in a study with 38 children who had been tested using the strange situation at 12 months: 76 per cent reliability for category.

17   Klagsbrun and Bowlby (1976). Correspondence between strange situation classifications and SAT classifications was 68 per cent for the four groups ($k=0.55$). Correlations between teacher's assessments of child's settling into school and their SAT classification was $r=5.57$, $p<0.001$.

18   Jacobsen et al. (1994): $k=0.80$ to 0.87.

19   Ibid.: $k=0.78$.

20   Ibid. Agreement between classifications on the representational test and concurrent classification according to Main and Cassidy's (1988) reunion behaviour test was 89 per cent for the secure versus insecure classification, and 80 per cent for the three groups B, A, D. There was also agreement between classifications and earlier strange situation classifications given when the children were 18 months old, with agreement on the main groups at 82 per cent.

21   Slough and Greenberg (1990). For 5-year-olds the attachment scale scores were positively related to security ratings on the Main and Cassidy (1988) measure following a 3-minute separation from their mothers. Scores on the avoidance scores for self descriptions had the highest correlation ($r=-0.46$, $p<0.001$). However, the ratings were unrelated to ratings of reunion behaviour after a longer 90-minute separation.

Children did differ in their scores depending on whether they were talking about themselves or the child in the picture. The emotional openness score significantly differed for children whose attachment scale scores for descriptions of themselves differed from their descriptions of the child in the picture. Children who received the same scores for themselves and the other child had higher emotional openness scores than children who received higher scores for the other child than for themselves (F=3.28, p<0.05).

22   For a full description of the MSSB, see Emde, Wolf and Oppenheim (2003).

23   Oppenheim et al. (1997) used the battery to assess children's representations of their mothers for a group of 51 children at 55 months and 66 months of age: k=0.85.

24   Oppenheim et al. (1997). A coding system was developed to assess children's expectations and representations of interactions with mothers. Factor analysis was completed and gave three factors with eigenvalues greater than one: positive representation of mother, negative representation of mother and discipline. Over the year reliability between test and retest was high: positive – r=0.52, p<0.001; negative – r=0.39, p<0.01; discipline – r=0.37, p<0.01.

25   Oppenheim et al. (1997). Correlations between ratings on the three factors and scores on CBCL Externalising behaviour problem scores were moderate and statistically reliable. Correlations between Positive representations of mother and Externalising scores were negative, thus children who had more positive ratings of their mothers at age 4 were rated by their mothers as having fewer externalising behaviour problems at both 4 (r=–0.20, p<0.10) and 5 (r=–0.25, p<0.05).

26   Green et al. (2000). For categorical classification: secure vs. insecure (B vs A/C/CC) 94 per cent, K=0.88; categorical D vs. non-D classification 82 per cent, K=0.41. Agreement on categories of attachment (A/B/C/CC) excluding primarily disorganised 91 per cent, K=0.74. When forced ABC classifications were made for primarily disorganised subjects, agreement was 80 per cent (K=0.622).

27   The repeat interviews took place after a median of 5.5 months; 76.5 per cent of ABC categories remained stable. Those rated secure were more likely to be stable than those rated insecure. There was a relationship between number of secure vignettes and stability. There was a bias towards security for participants who consented to the second stage, with 76 per cent of those consenting to the repeat rated as secure and 47 per cent rated as insecure. This should be borne in mind as it may bias the findings.

28   Agreement between three-way attachment categories on the MCAST and AAI was not significant; nor was agreement on security/insecurity. Given the different natures of these assessments, however, this comparison is less appropriately viewed as an indication of concurrent validity.

29   Cicchetti and colleagues have developed independently a similar protocol which they have been administering for ten years, but without a coding system.

30   The authors were influenced by Sroufe's affect-regulation model (Sroufe and Fleeson 1986), and studies which have identified emotional openness as an important aspect of children's attachment-related narratives and a marker of security of attachment (Oppenheim 1997; Slough and Greenberg 1990).

31   Main and Goldwyn 1994.

32   Cassidy 1988; Oppenheim 1997; Sroufe, Fox and Pancake 1983.

33   Oppenheim 1997.

34   Anger with mother appeared to be stable across three months, but was not the case regarding Anger with the father. Idealisation for both parents was quite unstable. Nevertheless, Emotional Openness, the Use of examples and Coherence seemed highly consistent across the three months. On the parent-specific scales, only Dismissing was highly stable for both mother and father.

35   Emotional Openness, Use of example and particularly Coherence and Anger with father were quite stable. On the contrary, parent-specific scales, particularly Idealisation and Anger with father, were quite unstable.

36   The correspondence between main attachment classifications for mother–child dyads were highly significant (64 per cent agreement; k=0.29, $p<0.01$). However, none of the seven children classified as Preoccupied, and only one of the six children classified as Disorganised, had mothers with AAI classified as Secure. The association between mothers' AAIs and the child's attachment security for the father (65 per cent agreement; k=0.29, $p<0.01$) was as strong as for the mother. None of the eight children classified as Preoccupied regarding their father, and only one of the six classified as Disorganised, had mothers with AAIs classified as Secure. As such, it seemed that Preoccupied and Secure classifications were more predictive of the child's security. Of secure/autonomous mothers 66 per cent had children whose CAIs were secure with respect to mother, and 66 per cent had children who were secure with their father. Of 25 preoccupied mothers 18 had children with Insecure classifications with respect to mother (72%), and 82 per cent were insecure regarding their father. Unresolved classification on the AAI did not predict child insecurity regarding either mother or father. Atypical (Disorganised) classifications in the CAI regarding both mother and father were only found in cases where the mother's AAI had been classified as Unresolved.

9 Assessments of Caregiving

Assessments based on observations of caregiving

Table 9.1 lists the assessments of caregiving in child age order.

Maternal Sensitivity Scales

Who designed it and when?

Ainsworth (1969b), during the early stages of the Baltimore study (Ainsworth, Bell and Stayton 1971; Ainsworth *et al.* 1978).

Any revisions?

None found.

What does it assess?

General maternal characteristics.

Used with which age group?

Mothers of young children.

Method

Observations of maternal characteristics are rated on four nine-point, scales:

SCALE 1: SENSITIVITY VS. INSENSITIVITY TO THE BABY'S SIGNALS[1]

This scale deals with the mother's ability to *perceive* and interpret accurately the signals and communications implicit in her infant's behaviour, and given this understanding, *respond* to them appropriately and promptly. Thus, the mother's sensitivity has four essential components:

Table 9.1 Assessments of caregiving

Assessment/Measure	Who designed it	When	Child age order (inclusive)	What it assesses
AMBIANCE (Atypical Maternal Behavior Instrument for Assessment and Classification)	Bronfman, Parsons and Lyons-Ruth	1993	Infants	Atypical maternal behaviour
Maternal Sensitivity Scales	Ainsworth	1969	Infants and young children	General maternal characteristics
CARE-Index Toddler CARE-Index	Crittenden	1979	0–15 months 15 months–3 years	Mother–infant interaction
Parent Development Interview: Infant, Toddler, Revised and Brief Versions	Aber et al.	1985	Infants and toddlers	Parent's representation of relationship with child
Caregiver Behavior Classification System	Marvin and Britner	1996	Preschool children	Caregiver behaviour
Experiences of Caregiving Interview	George and Solomon	1996	Young school-age children	Maternal internal working models of caregiving

(a)   her awareness of the signals

(b)   an accurate interpretation of them

(c)   an appropriate response to them

(d)   a prompt response to them.

The scale ranges from 1 to 9 and is defined on alternative points as follows:

9. Highly sensitive

7. Sensitive

5. Inconsistently sensitive

3. Insensitive

1. Highly insensitive.

A 'highly sensitive' mother is exquisitely attuned to the baby's signals and responds to them promptly and appropriately. She is able to see things from her baby's point of view.

A 'highly insensitive' mother seems geared almost exclusively to her own wishes, moods and activity and her interventions are shaped largely by signals within herself. She routinely ignores or distorts the meaning of the baby's behaviour and her response is inappropriate in kind or fragmented and incomplete.

SCALE 2: COOPERATION VS. INTERFERENCE WITH BABY'S ONGOING BEHAVIOUR

The central issue of this scale is the extent to which the mother's interventions break into, interrupt or cut across the baby's ongoing activity rather than being geared in both timing and quality to the baby's state, mood and current interests. The degree of interference may be assessed in accordance with two considerations:

(a)   the extent of actual physical interference with the baby's activity

(b)   the sheer frequency of interruptions.

Again, the scale ranges from 1 to 9 and is defined on alternative points as follows:

9. Conspicuously cooperative

7. Cooperative

5. Mildly interfering

3. Interfering

1. Highly interfering.

A 'conspicuously cooperative' mother views her baby as a separate, active, autonomous person, whose wishes and activities have validity of their own. Respecting the child's autonomy, she arranges the environment in such a way as to minimise the need for interference and direct control.

A 'highly interfering' mother has no respect for her baby as a separate, active and autonomous person, whose wishes and feelings have a validity of their own. She seems to assume that the baby is hers and that she has a right to do with him what she wishes, imposing her will on his, or shaping him to her standards, or merely following her own whims without regard to his moods, wishes or activities.

SCALE 3: ACCEPTANCE VS. REJECTION[2]

This scale concerns the balance between the mother's positive and negative feelings about her baby and the extent to which she has been able to integrate or resolve her conflicting feelings.

A highly accepting mother accepts her infant even when he is angry or unresponsive. She may occasionally feel irritated by his behaviour, but she does not cast him in the role of opponent.

A highly rejecting mother frequently feels angry and resentful towards her baby. She may grumble that he interferes unduly with her life, or she may show her rejection by constantly opposing his wishes or by a generally pervasive mood of scolding and irritation.

SCALE 4: ACCESSIBILITY VS. IGNORING

This scale concerns the mother's psychological accessibility to her infant when she is at home and in this sense physically accessible to him.

The accessible mother seems able to attend to her baby's signals and communications, despite distraction and other demands on her attention.

The inaccessible or ignoring mother is often so preoccupied with her own thoughts and activities that she does not even notice her baby, let alone acknowledge his signals.

Reliability
INTER-RATER
Good.[3]

Validity

Maternal Sensitivity Scales mean scores significantly distinguished Group A and Group C patterns of attachment from Group B (Ainsworth *et al.* 1978). Indeed, the authors report that it was in the rated general characteristics (Maternal Sensitivity Scales) that the sharpest inter-group differences emerged. The usefulness of the Maternal Sensitivity Scales in assessing maternal sensitive responsiveness has been demonstrated in its wide use since the 1978 publication. In some studies two of the scales have been used, rather than all four.

Clinical usefulness

The Maternal Sensitivity Scales are clinically useful and quite possibly underused. In particular, they may be helpful in understanding the emotional abuse and neglect of children.

The CARE-Index

Who designed it and when?

Crittenden 1979. First published in Crittenden 1981.

Any revisions?

Several revisions 1979–2004.

What does it assess?

The quality of adult–infant interaction. The author describes that 'Although the adult is most often the mother, the procedure can be used with fathers, other relatives, health visitors, daycare providers, and infant intervention personnel' (Crittenden 2005, p.1 of English version on website).

The CARE-Index assesses adult overall sensitivity in a dyadic context. Crittenden emphasises that 'sensitivity as assessed by the CARE-Index is not an individual characteristic; it is a characteristic of a specific relationship. Thus, the same adult could display different degrees of sensitivity with different children' (Crittenden 2005, p.1 of English version on website). The CARE-Index therefore assesses both adult and child characteristics.

Used with which age group?

From birth to 15 months. The Toddler CARE-Index is used for children aged 15 months to 3 years.

Method

The assessment is based on a short, videotaped play interaction of three to five minutes, occurring under non-threatening conditions. The videotaping may be done at home, in a clinic setting or in a research laboratory.

The coding system is structured around the central construct of adult sensitivity to infant signals. Crittenden stresses that although this appears to be an individual characteristic, as it is operationalised in this procedure, sensitivity is a *dyadic* construct.

Seven aspects of interactional behaviour are coded:

1.   facial expression

2.   verbal expression

3.   position and body contact

4.   affection

5.   turn-taking contingencies

6.   control

7.   choice of activity.

The first four aspects are assessments of affect within the dyad; the last three refer to temporal contingencies. In the Coding Manual for the CARE-Index (Crittenden 1979–2004), the author points out that although the CARE-Index was developed many years before the formulation of her Dynamic-Maturational approach to attachment theory, 'its two most basic constructs are embedded within the CARE-Index' (p.4).

The seven aspects of interactional behaviour contribute to one of seven scales:

- *three types of adult descriptors*: sensitive, controlling and unresponsive

- *four types of infant items*: cooperative, difficult, compulsive and passive.

Crittenden points out that the CARE-Index does not directly assess the attachment pattern, as the procedure does not introduce a stressful condition 'that will elicit individuals' self-protective strategies' (Crittenden 2005, p.2 of English version on website). Rather, it assesses dyadic characteristics that are associated with attachment.

Reliability

Coders are tested for reliability following training which takes approximately eight days. A further five days' training is required for the Toddler CARE-Index, plus practice and a reliability test. In order to prevent pairs of coders becoming highly attuned with one another and drifting away from the international standard, it is essential that coders consult with other skilled coders and periodically work with the original teaching tapes. 'For this reason, initial reliability is given for only one year and must be updated with evidence of further work and continued competence. Later reliability extends for longer spans of time, but must be supported by periodic attendance at advanced CARE-Index seminars with other skilled coders' (Crittenden 2005, p.4 of English version on website).

Validity

CONCURRENT VALIDITY

Crittenden points out (2004) that, although the CARE-Index assesses sensitivity in interaction, it differs from other procedures in several ways. Amongst these differences, the CARE-Index alone assesses the 'compulsive' or inhibitory patterns of infant adaptation. Thus, the CARE-Index is a relatively unique instrument yet to be compared with other systems of rating caregiver behaviour and infant adaptation, and correspondingly tested.

PREDICTIVE VALIDITY

Crittenden reports in the Coding Manual for the CARE-Index (Crittenden 2004, p.8) that Crittenden and Bonvillian (1984) found 'differential outcomes using the measure for middle-class, low-risk mothers, deaf mothers, low income mothers, mothers with mental retardation, abusive mothers, and neglectful mothers'.

Atypical Maternal Behavior Instrument for Assessment and Classification (AMBIANCE)

Who designed it and when?

Bronfman, Parsons and Lyons-Ruth 1993.

Any revisions?

1999.

What does it assess?

Atypical maternal behaviour, specifically aspects of disrupted parental affective communication with the infant. Benoit *et al.* (2001) point out that the AMBIANCE 'was originally designed as a research tool for the purpose of tracing the origins of infant disorganized attachment and its links to emotional and behavioral problems' (p.622). However, they state that their present pilot study 'demonstrates its applicability to clinical studies particularly those designed to assess treatment efficacy and effectiveness' (p.622).

Used with which age group?

Infants.

Method

The initial coding system was based on maternal behaviour observed in all episodes of the strange situation (Lyons-Ruth, Bronfman and Parsons 1999). The AMBIANCE has also been used to code atypical maternal behaviour during a five-minute play interaction (Benoit *et al.* 2001).

The AMBIANCE yields scores for the following:[4]

(a)   a total score for five separate dimensions of disrupted parental affective communication:

- *affective communication errors*, e.g. invites approach verbally then distances

- *role/boundary confusion (role reversal)*, e.g. elicits reassurance from infant

- *frightened/disoriented behaviour*, e.g. exhibits frightened expression; quavering voice or high, tense voice

- *intrusiveness/negativity*, e.g. pulls infant by the wrist; bared teeth; looming into infant's face; attack-like posture

- *withdrawal*, e.g. holds infant away from body with stiff arms

(b)   a summary score obtained by adding scores for each of the five dimensions

(c)   a qualitative seven-point scale for level of disrupted communication

(d)   a bivariate classification for disrupted or not disrupted
       communication.

Reliability
INTER-RATER

Lyons-Ruth *et al.* (1999) report high levels of inter-rater reliability.[5] Benoit *et al.*
(2001) also report high inter-rater agreement,[6] although the authors note that
their reliability for some scales was marginally acceptable. This suggests, they
write, 'that more intensive training or further articulation in the manual may be
required in preparing this tool for broad use' (p.622).

Validity
CONCURRENT VALIDITY

For those dimensions where equivalent behaviour was assessed, AMBIANCE
subscores were significantly correlated with maternal behaviour observed at
home (Lyons-Ruth *et al.* 1999, 2004).

PREDICTIVE VALIDITY

As predicted, the frequency of atypical maternal behaviour was significantly
correlated ($r = 0.39$, $p < 0.01$) with the extent of the infant's disorganised attachment behaviour (assessed on the nine-point scale for level of disorganised
attachment behaviour) (Lyons-Ruth *et al.* 1999). Affective communication
errors, disorientation and negative-intrusion behaviour were also significantly
related to level of infant disorganisation.

In their intervention study, Benoit *et al.* (2001) used the AMBIANCE 'as an
indicator of the efficacy of two brief interventions in reducing atypical behaviors and disrupted communication during play interactions' (p.611). The
authors report that findings confirmed their prediction that AMBIANCE scores
would reflect effects of caregiver training aimed at enhancing caregiver sensitivity. The authors state that their data further indicate that 'the AMBIANCE is
highly sensitive to differences in caregiver behavior associated with clinical
problems and their treatment' (p.622).

Caregiver Behavior Classification System
Who designed it and when?
Marvin and Britner 1996.

Any revisions?

None found.

What does it assess?

Parents' patterns of behaviour in a separation–reunion procedure.

USED WITH WHICH AGE GROUP?

Preschool-age children.

Method

This parental classification system is coded from observations of parent–child interaction in the strange situation and other separation–reunion procedures. Attention is given to parental behaviour across the entire situation, but especially during leave-taking and reunion. In addition, special attention is given to five dimensions of caregiver behaviour: gaze, organisation of proximity and contact, quality of discourse, affect regulation and discipline or structuring of the child's behaviour.

The rating scales distinguish ten dimensions of patterns of parental patterns which 'represent qualities of caregiver behavior in attachment–caregiving contexts that have been theoretically and/or empirically linked to child attachment strategies' (Britner *et al.* 2005, p.88). Each of the following ten dimensions is rated on a nine-point scale:

1. affection

2. over-involving with respect to attachment

3. role-reversing

4. rejecting

5. neglecting

6. pressuring to achieve

7. negative affect

8. sensitivity

9. parental delight

10. support for competent exploration.

A Caregiver Behavior Classification System is constructed as follows:[7]

ORDERED-SECURE: BETA

Parents show a relaxed and intimate behaviour pattern with their children in the strange situation. They are comfortable monitoring their children's play and offering them comfort when needed.

ORDERED-INSECURE: ALPHA

Parents avoid or dismiss intimate, caregiving interactions, either minimising interactions with their children or restricting interactions to non-caregiving domains such as exploration.

ORDERED-INSECURE: GAMMA

Parents over-encourage their children's attachment behaviour, intimacy and dependency, while at the same time, tending to resent the consequent burden.

DISORDERED-INSECURE: DELTA

Parents show some disorganisation and abdication in their caregiving role with their children: they seem not to take the 'executive' role. A best-fitting second-ary Alpha, Beta or Gamma classification is also made.

IOTA

Parents show a pattern which is distinct from the Alpha, Gamma or Delta groups, or a combination of these patterns. A number of sub-patterns have been identified.

Reliability
INTER-RATER

Britner *et al.* (2005) report high inter-rater reliability. The mean for exact agree-ment on the nine-point scales was 78 per cent, and for agreement within one point, 89 per cent. Exact agreement on the five Caregiver Behaviour categories was 86 per cent, and on Caregiver Behaviour secure–insecure, agreement was 90 per cent.

Validity

A highly significant level of concordance was found between the five-category caregiver classification and child classifications in the preschool strange situation ($p<0.01$). Exact agreement between Beta/non-Beta mothers and their secure/insecure children was 85 per cent. The authors point out that the use of this system in other parent–child interactional contexts is required for the establishment of external validity.

Clinical usefulness

This instrument is potentially very useful; as the authors point out, further tests of validity are required, some of which are already underway. The assessment has two very important features. First, the instrument assesses parental caregiving behaviours in a stressful procedure (i.e. the strange situation). As the authors point out, this enables the instrument to 'tap into caregiving system behaviors that might not be observed in less stressful situations' (Britner *et al.* 2005, p.96). Second, the instrument moves beyond the assessment of sensitivity (which is included) to rate nine other dimensions of caregiving. This instrument may therefore facilitate a broadening of our understanding of the antecedents of attachment patterns.

Assessments/measures of caregiving based on the caregiver's internal working model/representation of caregiving or relationship with the child

Parent Development Interview (PDI)

Who designed it and when?

Aber *et al.* 1985.

Any revisions?

Several revisions. 2004 version: Parent Development Interview–Revised (PDI-R) (Slade *et al.* 2004). The PDI-R can be used to score parental reflective functioning (Slade *et al.* 2002). The interview has been adapted for use with different populations. There is an infancy version, a toddler version, a revised version and a brief version.

What does it assess?

Parents' representations of their children, themselves as parents and their relationships with their children.

Following Fonagy *et al.* (1998) and collaborative work with Fonagy and colleagues at the London Parent–Child Project, the PDI-R (Slade *et al.* 2004) has been adapted to enhance its suitability for coding reflective functioning.

Used with which age group?
Different versions can be used with parents of infants or toddlers.

Method
The PDI is a 45-item semi-structured interview. Like the AAI, it is intended to assess internal working models of relationships. Thus, in a similar approach to the AAI, parents are asked to choose five adjectives to describe their relationship with the child. The interview seeks to explore parents' understanding of their child's behaviour, thoughts and feelings. In addition, the interview asks parents to describe the internal affective experience of parenting. Similarly, parents are asked to describe their child's internal experience in a range of situations. The interview takes between one-and-a-half and two hours to administer.

The PDI coding system (Slade *et al.* 1993) is divided into three sections:

PARENTAL AFFECTIVE EXPERIENCE CODES
The first section aims to assess features of the parent's representation of the affective experience of parenting. The authors stress that these codes are not aimed at assessing the parent's representation of the child, although their thoughts and feelings will be important considerations in coding decisions. The six Affective Experience Codes are Anger, Neediness, Separation Distress, Guilt/Shame, Joy/Pleasure and Competence/Efficacy.

CHILD AFFECTIVE EXPERIENCE CODES
The second section of the code assesses the parent's representation of the affective experience of the child. These four Affective Experience Codes are Anger, Dependence/Independence, Separation Distress and Joy/Pleasure.

QUALITY OF REPRESENTATION
The third section of the code assesses the 'overall quality of the representation as manifested in the coherence of the representation of the child, and in the richness of perception of parental representations' (Slade *et al.* 1993, p.3).

Most of the scales are scored on a nine-point continuum, with very low scores indicating efforts to avoid, deny or downplay emotional experience and very high scores indicating more disruptive and intense levels of emotion. Some scales are scored on a three-point scale and coherence and richness of perception are scored on a five-point scale.

Reliability
INTER-RATER

High inter-rater reliability scores have been reported. For example, Aber *et al.* (1999) reported inter-rater reliability coefficients ranging from 0.80 to 0.95, with a mean of 0.87, for four trained raters.

Validity
CONSTRUCT AND PREDICTIVE VALIDITY

Slade *et al.* (1999) found that parental representations of the child were linked to adult attachment and mothering variables. Aber *et al.* (1999) reported that changes in mothers' affective experience of parenting were predicted by positive mothering and 'daily hassles'. Slade (2005) reports that Hermelin-Kuttner (1998) found that 'mothers' ego flexibility during pregnancy predicted to low levels of anger and high levels of separation distress on the PDI when infants were 10 months old' (Slade 2005, p.277).

Clinical usefulness
This is a clinically useful instrument which explores in some depth parents' representations of their children, themselves as parents and their relationships with their children and parental reflective functioning.

Experiences of Caregiving Interview
Who designed it and when?
George and Solomon 1996.

Any revisions?
None found.

What does it assess?
Maternal internal working models of caregiving.

Used with which age group?

Young school-age children.

Method

This is an intensive clinical-style semi-structured interview adapted from the PDI. Mothers are asked to describe themselves as parents, to describe their relationship with their child and to describe how they managed attachment-related issues such as separations and starting school. The responses given are rated on the content and the process of thought expressed. They are rated on four scales:

> *Secure Base*: assesses the degree to which the caregiving representation reflects maternal commitment and ability to provide physical and psychological safety and protection.
>
> *Rejection*: assesses the degree to which the caregiving representation reflects the child and themselves as unwilling to participate in the caregiving relationship.
>
> *Uncertainty*: assesses the degree to which the caregiving representation reflects questioning, doubt, confusion or vacillation in opinion regarding themselves as the carer, the child and the relationship.
>
> *Helplessness*: assesses the degree to which the representation of caregiving reflects evaluations of the self, child and relationship as being out of control.

Each scale has seven points. Any score at or above the midpoint is considered characteristic of the representation being measured. Therefore, a rating of four or above on the Secure Base scale indicates a mother whose maternal representation is of caregiving security.

Of most interest are maternal evaluations of feelings, thoughts and behaviour in situations posing real and psychological threats to the young school aged-child (e.g. separations, safety, stress), even if these differed from reality. Maternal evaluations of events and child behaviours are of interest for rating purposes, even if these differ from the raters' evaluations.

Reliability

INTER-RATER

Good. Agreement between raters was high for all four dimensions.[8]

Validity
CONCURRENT

Good. There is a strong concordance between ratings of maternal representations of caregiving and child attachment.[9]

Maternal representations were converted into classifications according to the highest score on the profile. Thus, for example, if the 'Secure Base' dimension was the highest, the classification 'Secure Base' was given. These maternal classifications were then compared with the child's classification and concordance was found for 26 of 32 cases.[10]

Concordance between the Experience of Caregiving Interview and the Adult Attachment Interview is also high.[11]

Clinical usefulness
Good.

Notes

1 The descriptions of Scales 1 and 2 are taken from Ainsworth's 'Maternal Sensitivity Scales', mimeograph, JHU, Baltimore, Revised 1969, accessed July 2006 from the Stony Brook website (www.psychology.sunysb.edu/attachment/measures/content/ainsworth_scales.html).

2 The descriptions of Scales 3 and 4 are taken from Ainsworth *et al.* 1978, pp.142–143.

3 Ainsworth *et al.* (1978): the four scales were rated on home visits at 39, 42, 45, 48, 54 and (when possible) 51 weeks. Two of the five judges unavoidably had knowledge of other assessments. (Steps were taken to eliminate possibility of halo effect.) Mean inter-rater correlation coefficients: sensitivity–insensitivity 0.89; cooperation–interference 0.86; acceptance–rejection 0.88; accessibility–ignoring 0.87.

4 Described in Benoit *et al.* 2001 and Lyons-Ruth *et al.* 2004.

5 Total Atypical Behavior Score $r=0.67$; Affective Communication Errors Subscore $r=0.75$; Role Confusion Subscore $r=0.76$; Disorientation Subscore $r=0.73$; Withdrawal Subscore $r=0.73$; Disrupted Communication Classification Agreement = 87 per cent, k=0.73.

6 For total number of disruptive behaviours, r between pairs of coders ranged from 0.74 to 0.91. For level of disruption, the range was 0.60 to 0.72. For the bivariate classification of disrupted versus not disrupted, two coders agreed on 100 per cent of cases, and the third agreed on all but one case, yielding an overall kappa of 0.77.

7 Taken from Britner *et al.* (2005), Table II.

8 George and Solomon (1996): study using 32 mother–child dyads with kindergarten-aged children. Correlations were calculated on 24 interviews by two raters. Secure Base $r=0.77$, Rejection $r=0.81$, Uncertainty $r=0.90$ and Helplessness $r=0.85$.

9   Ibid. ANOVAs indicate a significant difference in scores on the maternal dimensions in line with child classifications of attachment security. Secure Base $F=11.04$, $p<0.000$, Rejection $F=9.59$, $p<0.000$, Uncertainty $F=4.45$, $p<0.01$, Helplessness $F=8.97$, $p<0.000$.

10   Ibid. 81 per cent, $k=0.75$, $p<0.000$.

11   69 per cent, $k=0.58$, $p<0.000$.

Part Three

Correlates of Attachment Organisation with Functioning

10 Which Domains of Functioning are Hypothesised to be Correlated with Attachment and What are the Possible Pathways of its Influence?

There is a substantial evidence base showing clear associations between different patterns of attachment and children's psychological and behavioural functioning. What remains less clear is an explanation of the mechanisms involved. Thus, this chapter considers two central theoretical questions concerning the relationship between attachment and functioning, before moving on to research issues and the evidence base for this relationship, which are presented in Chapter 11.

The two central theoretical questions concerning the relationship between attachment and functioning are:

1. Which domains of functioning, precisely, are hypothesised to be correlated with attachment?

2. If attachment security is found to be associated with functioning in other behavioural systems, what are the pathways of its influence? Five possible models are presented.

Each of these questions will be considered in turn.

Which domains of functioning are hypothesised to be correlated with attachment?

A broad range of associations has been studied in relation to attachment security. As Belsky and Cassidy (1994) point out, 'there is no shortage of developmental phenomena to which attachment security has been linked'. They are led to the conclusion that 'Bowlby's and Ainsworth's theorizing has been the springboard for a broad continuum of implicit, if not explicit, theories of attachment' (p.381). Similarly, Thompson (1999) writes, 'clearly attachment is not expected to foreshadow *every* important subsequent accomplishment in a child's life' (p.272).

Table 10.1 (based on Belsky and Cassidy 1994 and Thompson 1999) summarises the domains of functioning which are hypothesised to be associated with attachment security according to a range of views, from 'narrow', to 'broad' and 'very broad'. These views may be conceptualised as on a continuum.

Table 10.1 Different views of the domains of functioning associated with attachment security	
	Domains of functioning hypothesised to be associated with attachment security
Narrow view	Trust, confidence and harmony in relationship with parent and significant others
	Emotion regulation
	Self-reliance (versus dependency), ego-resilience, personal efficacy
	Relational intimacy
	Interpersonal (social) competence
	Relationship-based developmental disorders
Broad view	The above plus:
	Sociability with unfamiliar adults and peers
	Understanding of and orientation towards others
Very broad view	The above plus:
	Language and cognitive competence
	Play competence, exploratory skill
	Communication style
	Other outcomes influenced by self-confidence and ego functioning

The answer as to which of these views is most supported by the evidence requires consideration of the next theoretical question.

What are the possible pathways of the influence of attachment?

Five possible models are presented.

There is little disagreement among attachment theorists that attachment security influences the domain of functioning concerned with relational intimacy (narrow view); these are the 'within system' or 'domain specific' consequences anticipated by the theory. However, if and when an association is found between attachment security and functioning in another behavioural system, for example play competence (very broad view), what is the pathway of its influence? Does attachment security exert a direct influence on this functioning (*Model 1*) or does it share an influence with another factor (*Model 2*)? Is the perceived influence of attachment security real or spurious? Perhaps both attachment security and play competence, for example, are separately influenced by a third, independent factor (*Model 3*). These three possibilities may be represented diagrammatically as in Models 1, 2 and 3 (see Figures 10.1–10.3).

As shown in Figure 10.3, the observed association between attachment security and functioning in another behavioural system is spurious, as both attachment security and for example self-confidence in play are separately influenced by a third, independent factor, in particular a common parenting style.

This third possible model begs an important question, namely what is the evidence regarding the association between sensitivity/competence in caregiving and sensitivity in other domains of parenting? As discussed in Chapter 4, there is scant evidence on this subject. This question and the validity of this model is, therefore, currently unanswered. The conceptual distinction, however, between caregiving and other domains of parenting remains of the utmost importance for both researchers and practitioners alike.

Model 4: Attachment security influences functioning in another behavioural system by influencing the feeling state associated with that system

Bowlby's conclusion regarding the 'top priority' of attachment–caregiving in the dyadic parent–child programme suggests that the safety of the child is paramount. As described in Chapter 3, safety refers to the objective condition; security refers to the feeling state. If so, it is possible that attachment security influences functioning in other behavioural systems by influencing the feeling

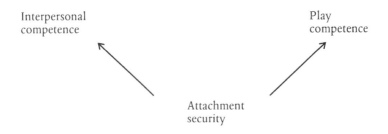

Figure 10.1 Model 1: Attachment security influences functioning in another behavioural system (very broad view)

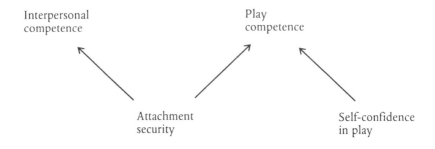

Figure 10.2 Model 2: Attachment security shares its influence on functioning in another behavioural system with another factor, e.g. self-confidence

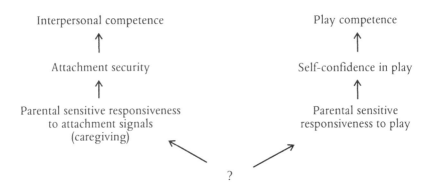

Figure 10.3 Model 3: Attachment security does not influence functioning in another behavioural system

state associated with those systems, rather than by directly influencing competencies. Thus, attachment security may influence self-confidence in, for example, play competence, exploratory skills or cognitive competence, that is functioning included in the 'broad view'. Moreover, attachment security may exert an influence in this way irrespective of parental sensitivity in the non-attachment–caregiving domain.

This can be represented diagrammatically by making a slight adjustment to the previous model (see Figure 10.4).

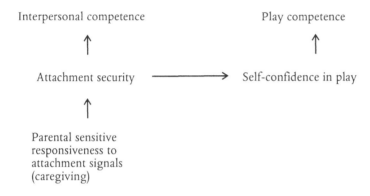

Figure 10.4 Model 4: Attachment security influences functioning in another bahavioural sustem by influencing the feeling state associated with that system

This model would seem to be supported by Ainsworth and Bell (1974). According to their third definition of competence, the infant's ability to influence his environment by influencing his carer fosters a general 'sense of competence' and this influences the development of increased competence in other domains, whether viewed in absolute or age-appropriate terms. Their finding that maternal responsiveness to signals supported the development of social competence adds empirical weight to this proposition.

There is yet a further possibility (*Model 5*). As Greenberg (1999), echoing Bowlby, explains, 'when a secure and trusting bond forms between parent and child, the parent reciprocally develops a favorable working model of the child – one that includes attributions of responsiveness, warmth, and trust, and thus sets the stage for reciprocal and cooperative interactions' (p.482). Thus, there may be a feed-back loop within the caregiving–attachment relationship. A secure child relates to the caregiver in such a way (positively, trusting) that the caregiver *responds* with greater sensitivity. As well as reinforcing the caregiving affectional bond, this may generate sensitivity in other (non-caregiving) domains of parenting. This idea may be represented diagrammatically in a fifth and final model (see Figure 10.5).

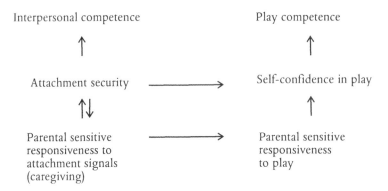

Figure 10.5 Model 5: A feed-back loop may operate in which attachment security enhances caregiver sensitivity in another parenting domain, e.g. play, which promotes greater child competence in that domain

Conclusion

It is very difficult to establish from the available data which of these models, as heuristic devices, is the most helpful in understanding the pathways between attachment security and functioning. One thing, however, is clear: the finding of a correlation between two variables does not inform us of the direction or pathway of the effect. In order to test the pathway, each of the variables in the model must be measured and their respective influences calculated. For longitudinal research, intervening variables, including a possible change in attachment security, must also be assessed. This requires theoretically informed and methodologically rigorous research (see beginning of Chapter 11) and reliable measures of the variables on all three tiers in the model, that is parenting sensitivity, child feeling states and child competencies, in various domains and, for longitudinal research, repeated measures over time. The link between caregiving sensitivity and attachment security is already established; the link between parental sensitivity and child feeling states and competencies in other domains is greatly in need of study. Although much important work has been done, the 'boundaries of attachment' and the 'derivative conundrums' (Belsky and Cassidy 1994, pp.381–383) with respect to domains of functioning are not yet unravelled.

It is important to appreciate that the need to understand the pathways to competent functioning is of more than academic interest; it has crucial implications for treatment. Treatment which seeks to address a lack of competency in the child, in whatever domain of functioning, must take account of the factors and pathways that influence that competency. Treatment approaches which do otherwise may be ineffective.

Summary

Security or insecurity of attachment is accepted as a probabilistic indicator of a child's functioning in a number of domains. What is less clear is which domains are associated with attachment security and what the mechanisms are for these associations. Both direct and indirect influences may operate and, indeed, caregiving sensitivity and other associated aspects of parenting may influence the child's functioning.

11 Evidence for Correlations between Attachment Security/Insecurity and the Child's Functioning

Research issues

Cross-sectional or longitudinal studies?

The question 'What is the influence of attachment security on functioning?' can be posed in two ways:

1. What is the influence of attachment security on contemporaneous or concurrent functioning? (Cross-sectional studies)

2. What is the influence of attachment security on later functioning? (Longitudinal studies)

'Later' refers to a period of time of any duration between the assessment of attachment and the subsequent assessment of functioning.

A particular difficulty exists regarding the inclusion of disorganised attachment in ongoing longitudinal studies. The identification and assessment of the disorganised/disoriented category is a relatively recent development in attachment theory and research and was not included in longitudinal studies which commenced some time ago. The Minnesota Parent–Child Project is one such study. However, researchers on this project have revisited, where available, videotapes of the original attachment assessments and reclassified the children's attachments to include the disorganised category. (Many of the findings of the Minnesota Parent–Child Project are reported in the review of studies below.)

Normative or non-normative samples?

Normal or normative samples comprise populations in which the extremes are represented in very small numbers. Thus, a normative sample is appropriate when investigating the normal features of a population, but less helpful when investigating abnormal features, which are likely to be represented in very small numbers at the extreme ends of the distribution.

Much research in attachment has been carried out using normative samples. It is now well established that the distribution of attachment patterns in normal populations is approximately two-thirds secure and one-third insecure, including approximately 15 per cent disorganised-insecure (described in Chapter 3). This raises a research issue concerning sample size. In a normative sample of, for example, 60 participants, it would be expected that approximately 40 participants would have a secure attachment organisation (B), approximately 11 participants would have an insecure organisation (A or C) and approximately nine participants would have an insecure disorganised attachment (D). Distinguishing two groups, of secure and insecure attachment, with numbers of 40 and 20 respectively, allows analyses of some power. (Many studies with normative samples do, in fact, distinguish only secure and insecure attachment, as can be seen in the review of studies.) However, analyses of the disorganised group of nine participants are problematic.

It is known that the prevalence of disorganised attachment is much higher in particular social groups and clinical populations. For example, in a meta-analysis of disorganised attachment in early childhood (van IJzendoorn *et al.* 1999) it was found that in populations of low socio-economic status (SES) 24 per cent of infants were classified as disorganised, in groups of mothers with alcohol or drugs abuse the percentage of disorganised infants was 43 per cent, and in groups of maltreating parents 48 per cent of the children were found to be disorganised.

Moreover, disorganised attachment has been found to be associated with a range of contemporaneous and later difficulty, including problems in non-relational as well as relational domains of functioning (findings are reported in the review of studies below).

Studies of normative samples are appropriate and useful in exploring the consequences of secure and insecure organised attachments but are not helpful in understanding the consequences of disorganised attachment. In order to advance our understanding of disorganised attachment, samples are required in which there is an expected high rate of (1) disorganised attachment, and/or (2) difficulties in child functioning including difficulties which meet the threshold for a disorder. Such samples may be specific in their inclusion criteria, for example children of parents with known difficulties, or children known to have been maltreated, or high-risk samples, for example children in families of low socio-economic status. In contrast, samples in which a low rate of difficulty is anticipated, for example middle-class families, are referred to as low-risk samples. Clinical samples comprise children who have been referred to a clinic or who have been diagnosed as having a disorder.

Thus, high-risk or clinical samples are more appropriate for the study of children with severe difficulties or psychopathology. There is, however, an important exception to this general rule. Normative samples of exceptionally large size would be expected to include sufficient numbers of children with severe difficulties to allow analyses of sufficient power. For these studies, however, the issue is whether the data collection is sufficiently fine in its detail.

In conclusion, the research issues outlined certainly present a challenge for researchers. Greenberg (1999) considers that the following types of studies are unlikely to increase our understanding of the link between attachment and externalising pathology:

- *studies of low-risk populations*: a low base rate of psychopathology is to be expected

- *studies based on non-random samples*: easily obtainable volunteers may include a low proportion of insecure children

- *studies with small sample sizes*: such studies have little power to detect significant relationships

- *studies based on a single-cause model*: this is too simplistic a model; often even moderator or mediator variables are not considered.

'Such studies,' Greenberg writes (p.474), 'neither prove nor disprove the effects of attachment, unless one expects strong main effects.'

The evidence

There is considerable evidence, much of it emanating from the Minnesota Longitudinal Study of Parents and Children,[1] of statistically significant associations between (a) secure attachment in early childhood and later good functioning, and (b) early insecure attachment and later emotional and behavioural difficulties.

Commencing in 1975, the Minnesota longitudinal study sample comprised 267[2] first-time mothers in their third trimester of pregnancy, recruited through the Minneapolis Public Health Department. All the women were from a background of poverty, a majority were single, most had a relatively low level of education and many were young (the youngest was 12). Many of the mothers experienced significant stressful life events, including a high incidence of family conflict, substance abuse and frequent moves. The study sample, therefore, is a high-risk sample.

A major objective of the Parent–Child Project was to identify factors which account for good parenting and healthy parent–child relationships, even in the face of high-risk circumstances. Attachment theory was a framework for the research.

Wide-ranging assessments of the mothers' characteristics, circumstances, parent expectations and prenatal care were carried out when mothers were recruited into the study. Assessments of the mothers and children continued after the birth of the child. In infancy, assessments of parents, children's temperament, and observations of parent–child interactions were carried out at birth (days 1–3), 3, 6 (twice), and 12 (twice) months. Thereafter assessments were conducted every 6 months until age 2½ years, yearly through the third grade, three times between 9 and 13, and at ages 16, 17½, 19, 23, 26 and 28. Data collection included teacher reports of behaviour and emotional health. Currently the researchers are assessing adaptation of participants in their late 20s, to link adaptation during this period to assessments from infancy onwards and to identify factors that account for stability and change across development.

As the study began prior to the development of a coding system for disorganised/disoriented attachment, the initial assessments of attachment in the strange situation at 12 and 18 months used A, B and C classifications only. However, disorganisation/disorientation was subsequently coded for 157 of the original participants whose videotaped strange situation had survived (Carlson 1998) and analyses incorporating this classification were conducted.

The Minnesota study created an index of psychopathology from interviews with the Kiddie Schedule for Affective Disorders and Schizophrenia (K-SADS), administered at age 17½ years (Carlson 1998). Weinfield and colleagues (1999) report that avoidant and disorganised attachment assessed at 12 to 18 months accounted for 16 per cent of the variance using this index of psychopathology. They describe this as a 'highly significant result, and particularly impressive over this length of time' (Weinfield *et al.* 1999, p.81). Carlson (1998) reports that attachment disorganisation ratings significantly predicted psychopathology ratings controlling for avoidant attachment and other variables

($p<0.05$). According to Weinfield *et al.*'s summary of Carlson's findings, 'Attachment history remained significant after other variables were accounted for, and early measures based on competing hypotheses, such as infant temperament, did not predict outcome significantly' (p.81).

In their 2005 book devoted to the Minnesota study, *The Development of the Person*, Sroufe *et al.* state that with regard to global pathology at 17½ years, the strongest single predictor from the first six years of life was disorganised attachment ($r = 0.34$). 'Thus, severe dysregulation in the caregiver–infant dyad is associated with more extreme disturbance at the end of adolescence' (p.246). Avoidant attachment was less strongly but significantly correlated ($r = 0.25$); resistant attachment was not.

Grossmann and Grossmann's two longitudinal studies, the Bielefeld Project and the Regensburg Project, have also produced important findings regarding the correlates of attachment. The Bielefeld Project began in 1976/7, the original sample comprising 49 middle-class families living in northern Germany. At age 21–22 years 78 per cent of the original sample participated. A comprehensive battery of assessments was administered at different time points, including the strange situation in the first year and at 24 and 36 months, the Separation Anxiety Test and Adult Attachment Interview with both parents when the children were 6 and 10 years old, the AAI at 16 years and again at 22 years.

The Regensburg Project commenced in 1989. The sample comprised 51 non-risk families. The participation rate at age 21–22 years was 75 per cent. In a slightly altered battery of assessments, a reunion situation with mother was included at 4½, 6 and 8 years. Findings from these studies are described below.

Secure attachment and good functioning

- In a sample of 25 boys and 23 girls, it was found that children securely attached at 18 months were at 24 months higher on *positive affect* ($p<0.01$) and lower on saying 'no', crying or whining, negative affect (all $p<0.05$), and engaging in aggression toward mother ($p<0.01$) (Matas, Arend and Sroufe 1978).

- Thompson (1999) cites a number of studies which found that, during shared tasks with their mothers in follow-up assessments during the second year of life, securely attached children showed greater *enthusiasm, compliance, positive affect* and *affective sharing* (and less frustration and aggression) during free play with their mothers.

He concludes, 'Securely attached infants tend to maintain more harmonious relations with parents in the second year' (p.274).

- In the Bielefeld Project, in a videotaped family interaction task involving 10-year-olds, it was found that a composite index security of attachment to mother was significantly related to *fewer disagreements* during the task and to 'a relative priority of *connectedness* over separateness' (Grossmann, Grossmann and Zimmermann 1999, p.778).

- Thompson (1999) describes a study by Slade (1987), which found that securely attached infants displayed longer and *more complex symbolic play* in the second year than insecurely attached infants, especially in experiments where mothers contributed to the children's play. Thompson quotes Slade's conclusion, 'secure dyads "work" better' together (p.275).

- Attachment organisation and dependency on preschool teachers was examined in a sample of 40 children attending two classes at the University of Minnesota nursery school (Sroufe *et al.* 1983). The children's ages ranged from 47 to 60 months, with a mean age of 52 months. The children's attachments were largely stable at 12 and 18 months. The definition of 'dependency' included extreme reliance on the teacher for help and seeking attention from the teacher at the expense of peer relations. The study found that children who were securely attached as infants showed significantly *less emotional dependence* on their preschool teachers and significantly *more seeking attention in positive ways.* The authors conclude:

  > The high dependency of both anxiously attached groups, despite their differences in manifest behaviour in the attachment assessments, suggests that the roots of overdependency lie in the quality of the early infant–caregiver relationship. (p.1615)

- At age 10 in summer camp it was found that children with histories of a secure attachment sought less contact with adults and both avoidant and resistant children were rated as more dependent. Differences in dependency have continued to be found in the follow-up at age 15 (Sroufe, Carlson and Shulman 1993).

- Weinfield *et al.* (1999) report three studies which found associations between secure attachment histories and *persistence in tool use* in toddlers, *goal-direction* and *achievement-orientation* in children age 5, and *greater effort playing a competitive game* with an unfamiliar experimenter. Weinfield *et al.* conclude that the findings on *dependency, self-reliance* and *efficacy* suggest that early attachment history contributes to 'a child's growing effectiveness in the world' (p.77).

- Weinfield and colleagues (1999) report that in the Minnesota Parent–Child Project, using a composite rating of *empathy* based on Q-sort descriptions such as 'shows concern for others', preschool teachers' ratings significantly distinguished children with secure and anxious attachment histories. In the same research empathetic responses to distressed peers were rated in preschool children's free-play. It was found that children with secure histories showed greater empathy than children with avoidant histories. No significant differences were found for resistant children, although they tended to become distressed when witnessing the distress of others. The authors conclude that attachment appears to contribute to the prediction of empathy in childhood.

- Weinfield and colleagues (1999) report that the data from their longitudinal research uphold the hypothesised relationship between attachment security and *interpersonal competence*. Using teacher ratings of social proficiency, it was found that preschool children with secure histories were 'dramatically more competent' (p.80).

  Greater interpersonal competence in the more intricate social world of middle childhood was also found among children with secure histories. A closer study of 47 children showed that compared to children with anxious attachment histories, children with secure histories formed more friendships in summer camp, were more accepted by the group and better coordinated their various relationships. Weinfield *et al.* (1999) report that these findings held in adolescence. Moreover, adolescents with secure histories were rated as more socially competent in a variety of ways including leadership abilities and, for girls but not boys, friendship intimacy. Weinfield *et al.* conclude that their data on social competence strongly support attachment theory.

- *Greater sibling harmony* was found among children securely attached to their parents than insecurely attached (Teti and Ablard 1989). However, the promotion of sibling harmony may be an aspect of sensitive parenting that is independent of the children's attachments.

- In the Regensburg Project, secure adolescents showed significantly more indications of *positive defences*, such as *reflectivity, altruism* and *humour* in their views of negative experiences with attachment figures than insecure adolescents (Grossmann *et al.* 2005).

Attachment and the stress response

One aspect of the body's necessary coping response to acute stress is an elevation of serum cortisol, which commences in early infancy. Cortisol secretion is part of the hypothalamic-pituitary-adrenal (HPA) axis. There are individual variations, likely to be enduring, in the response to stress, which are based on differences in temperament (Boyce, Barr and Zeltzer 1992) as well as on prior experience. Prior experience can affect responses to stress by sensitisation and by shaping the child's perception of an experience as stressful or not. In his paper entitled 'Why stress is bad for your brain', Sapolsky (1996) has succinctly summarised evidence indicating a significant correlation between sustained stress, excess cortisol and damage to the hippocampus. The hippocampus is integrally concerned with memory (Squire 1992). Prolonged high levels of cortisol lead to hippocampal cell death. Long-term elevated, but not toxic, cortisol levels make the hippocampal neurons susceptible to the effects of commonly-encountered threats to the brain, namely hypoxia, epileptic seizures, hypoglycaemia, physical trauma and toxic chemicals. It is possible that some other brain regions (the cingulate gyrus and the frontal lobes) may be adversely affected by excess cortisol levels early in life (Gunnar 1998).

Gunnar (1998) postulates that security of attachment constitutes a buffer to the HPA axis stress response in human infants. For example, Nachmias *et al.* (1996) have shown that 18-month-old securely attached children showed no elevation of cortisol when responding fearfully to the approach of a stranger (a clown), in their mother's presence. This finding held whether or not the children were rated as constitutionally inhibited in new social situations. By contrast, constitutionally inhibited *and* insecurely attached children showed a significant elevation in salivary cortisol when approached by the clown. It was also shown that, for these latter infants, maternal intrusiveness and insensitive encouragement of the infant towards the clown contributed to the elevated cortisol response. Infants who showed a disorganised/disoriented attachment were found to have higher cortisol levels *during* the strange situation (Hertsgaard *et al.* 1995). As the strange situation is a mild stressor compared to most experiences of child abuse and neglect, these results reflect the extent of these children's vulnerability to stress.

Early insecure attachment and later emotional and behavioural difficulties

An overall picture emerges of an association between insecure-avoidant attachment and behaviour problems and negative affect on the one hand, and insecure-ambivalent/resistant attachment and anxiety and social withdrawal on the other hand. The greatest difficulties are, however, encountered in children who were found to have a disorganised attachment. These will be considered later.

INSECURE-AVOIDANT ATTACHMENT

- Lyons-Ruth, Alpern and Repacholi (1993) found that the best predictor of teacher ratings of *hostile* behaviour in children aged 5 years was disorganised attachment in infancy. However, a high percentage of this group were considered to have an underlying avoidant strategy.

- The Minnesota Parent–Child Project found that, for boys, an early history of avoidant attachment was related to *aggression* in childhood, based on teacher ratings of aggression in grades 1, 2 and 3 ($p<0.05$) (reported in Egeland and Carlson 2004).

- In another study of the Minnesota data (reported in Egeland and Carlson 2004), adolescents whose *antisocial behaviour* had a childhood-onset (compared to adolescent-onset and 'never antisocial' groups) were more likely to have been avoidantly attached at 12 and 18 months compared to the 'never antisocial' group.

- Weinfield *et al.* (1999) report findings from the Minnesota Parent–Child Project that teachers in both preschool and elementary school (unaware of the children's attachment histories) assessed more *negative affect, anger* and *aggression* in children with anxious attachment histories than secure histories. Differences were also found in the interactions between children in play pairs. Weinfield *et al.* cite findings that avoidant children were significantly more likely to *victimise their play partners*, secure children were never victimisers nor victims, and resistant children were likely to be victims if paired with avoidant children.

- In the Regensburg Project, it was found that avoidant children were more *hostile* and *scapegoating of peers* than secure children in their peer-interaction in preschool (Suess, Grossmann and Sroufe 1992).

INSECURE-AMBIVALENT/RESISTANT ATTACHMENT

- Weinfield *et al.* (1999) report that children with resistant histories have been found to be generally more anxious, and less forceful and confident, than children with secure or avoidant histories. They describe the findings of two studies as examples. In one study it was found that children aged 4½ years with resistant attachment histories were more *hesitant* about engaging a novel object than avoidant or secure children. In another study resistant children were identified by their elementary school teachers as more *passive* and *withdrawn* than secure or avoidant children.

- Greenberg (1999) reports findings of the Minnesota Parent–Child Project (Warren *et al.* 1997) regarding attachment security and *anxiety disorders.* A current diagnosis or history of an anxiety disorder was found in 15 per cent of 172 young people aged 17 who received a psychiatric interview. A current or past anxiety disorder was found in 12 per cent of those assessed as secure in infancy, 16 per cent of those assessed as avoidant in infancy and 28 per cent of those assessed as ambivalent in infancy. Controlling for infant temperament and maternal anxiety, ambivalent attachment in infancy modestly but significantly predicted anxiety disorder. Greenberg points out, however, that individuals secure in infancy did not show a lower rate of overall disorder than ambivalent infants.

INSECURE-DISORGANISED ATTACHMENT

These attachments are associated with the greatest difficulties in later childhood and adolescence.

- Greenberg (1999) reports findings of a longitudinal study in Cambridge, Massachusetts, in which teachers independently rated hostility and hyperactivity in a sample of 64 preschool children (80 per cent of the original sample). It was found that children rated as *hostile* with peers and adults were significantly more likely to have been assessed as insecure in infancy, especially disorganised/ disoriented (71 per cent disorganised compared to 12 per cent secure), and to have caregivers with chronic depressive symptoms.

- Greenberg (1999) further reports the findings of a follow-up study of a high-risk sample in Pittsburgh in which infant attachment security modestly predicted preschool behaviour problems at age 3 years. At follow-up at age 5 it was found that insecure attachment at 12 months uniquely predicted behaviour problems as rated by parents using the Child Behavior Checklist. Clinically elevated levels of *aggression* were found in 17 per cent of children assessed as securely attached in infancy, 28 per cent assessed as ambivalent, 31 per cent assessed as avoidant and 60 per cent assessed as disorganised. A disorganised attachment in infancy *and* a parental rating of difficult temperament at age 2 years strongly predicted aggression at age 5, children with both factors being in the ninety-ninth percentile for aggression.

- Greenberg (1999) reports three studies, in each of which he is a co-author, which have examined attachment security in samples of clinic-referred children who met criteria for *oppositional defiant disorder* (ODD). In two of the studies, approximately 80 per cent of the clinic children showed insecure attachments, compared to 30 per cent of the comparison children. The clinic children showed a disproportionately high rate of the *controlling* classification, hypothesised to be a developmental transformation of disorganised/disoriented attachment.

- The Minnesota longitudinal study found that both avoidant and disorganised attachment in infancy predicted *dissociation* at age 17 years. At age 19 years, infant disorganisation was significantly related to dissociative symptoms. Weinfield *et al.* (1999) report that 'the relation between disorganized attachment and dissociation remained after childhood trauma was partialed out' (p.82).

Studies of children disorganised in infancy draw a picture of later childhood as being characterised by controlling, angry, hostile and oppositional behaviours. Alongside this external expression of difficulty, however, the studies also indicate that the children are low in self-confidence and social competence, struggling in their academic performance and, in assessments of internal representations, depict the self and caregivers as both frightening and unpredictable or frightened and helpless. As Solomon *et al.* (1995) report, 'The doll-play of controlling children was characterized by themes of catastrophe and helplessness' (p.447) or by complete inhibition of play, which the authors describe as a 'brittle strategy' (p.460). The distress, vulnerability and 'brittleness' of these children needs to be considered again in the following discussion regarding attachment disorder.

Discussion

There are speculative explanations for the clear associations between insecure attachments and later difficulties.

For example, Dozier, Stovall and Albus (1999) explain the rationale for the avoidant-externalising, resistant-internalising link thus. An avoidant-insecure attachment strategy involves the minimisation of the expression of attachment needs. In this strategy, the individual defensively turns attention *away from* the anticipated unavailability of the attachment figure(s) and the accompanying distress. This defensive exclusion of experience and information causes the individual to inhibit or be out of touch with the reality of their feeling state[3] and its antecedents. With attention turned away from the self, and the lack of resolution of negative representations, distress is expressed externally. Thus, minimising strategies predispose the individual to *externalising* disorders.

Conversely, a resistant strategy involves the maximisation of expression of attachment needs. In this strategy, the individual turns their attention *towards* their distress and the availability of the attachment figure(s). Distress is therefore more likely to be expressed internally, with heightened awareness of negative representations. Thus, maximising strategies predispose the individual to internalising disorders.

Egeland and Carlson (2004) suggest how dissociation is theoretically and empirically linked to disorganised/disoriented attachment and a history of trauma. As described in Chapter 4, the antecedents of disorganised attachments in infancy are thought to be frightening or confusing parental behaviour, the attachment figure who should be a haven of safety being instead the source of threat and fear. The child is then caught in an irresolvable conflict, unable to simultaneously approach and flee. Feelings and experience may then be 'put aside' or separated from awareness. Faced with later trauma, these children are likely to respond by 'disconnecting disturbing stimuli from normal cognitive and emotional processing' (p.43). This suggests a model in which early disorganisation renders the individual vulnerable to the effects of later trauma. Egeland and Carlson suggest that these findings may help to explain why trauma is not always associated with dissociation. It is the prior disorganised attachment which renders the child or adolescent doubly vulnerable to the effects of trauma.

However, the associations are not entirely linear or straightforward. Thompson (1999) references several follow-up studies which failed to find a straightforward association between attachment and problematic behaviour in the preschool years. In some studies, intervening experiences, such as environmental stress or difficulty in the parent–child relationship or other factors, were found to mediate the association between attachment and later problematic behaviour.

As Egeland and Carlson (2004) state:

> In summary, early disturbances in attachment relations, not generally viewed as pathology or directly causing pathology, lay the foundation for disturbances in developmental processes that can lead to psychopathology. Understanding the processes that begin as relationship disturbance and that may lead in time to individual disorder through their impact on neurophysiological and affective regulation is a central task for the field of developmental psychopathology. (p.31)

POSTULATED MECHANISMS FOR LINKS BETWEEN EARLY ATTACHMENT AND LATER FUNCTIONING

There is increasing evidence for incremental and interactive models in understanding the link between early attachment and later social functioning. For example, the Minnesota longitudinal study found that attachment security in infancy accounted for 13 per cent of the variance in middle childhood friendship competence nine years later. However, when assessments of attachment were combined with assessments of appropriate stimulation and guidance between the ages of 2 to 3½ years, the variance accounted for in the middle childhood friendship score doubled (Sroufe *et al.* 2005b). 'In a parallel manner,' the authors report, 'our assessments of support for emerging autonomy in early adolescence also supplement infant attachment in predicting later adolescent peer competence, and so forth' (Sroufe *et al.* 2005b, p.58).

In other recent analyses of the Minnesota data (Carlson, Sroufe and Egeland 2004), structural equation modelling was used to examine the influence of early experience on adolescent functioning and the relations between changing representational quality and behaviour over time. Early experience was reflected in attachment quality assessed at 12 and 18 months and toddler experience based on the quality of the mother–child relationship assessed in a laboratory problem-solving procedure at 24 months. The results suggested an indirect link between early experience and adolescent social functioning. They report: 'A model representing interactive contributions of representational and behavioral experience represented that data significantly better than a model representing noninteractive contributions' (Carlson *et al.* 2004, p.66). This finding is elaborated in a diagrammatic depiction of the pathways via which early experience influences social functioning in adolescence. The importance in these pathways of relationship representation during early and middle childhood and early adolescence lends support to the hypothesis that 'representation is a carrier of experience' (Carlson *et al.* 2004, p.78).

As the original infant participants grow into adulthood, longitudinal research is shedding light on the long-term effects of early attachment. As Sroufe *et al.* (2005b, p.59) describe, 'The picture that is emerging…is one of developmental complexity.' The authors also report, however, that 'Almost always…when attachment history is combined with other variables, including peer experience at various ages and later experiences with parents, predictions of outcomes are enhanced' (p.62). These findings indicate that, directly or indirectly, infant attachment has an enduring effect.

Summary

Clear findings from both cross-sectional and longitudinal studies show an association between secure attachment and good functioning in a number of domains. Security of attachment also appears to be a buffer to the physiological stress response. There are strong associations between early insecure-avoidant attachment and later aggression, anti-social behaviour and negative affect; and between early insecure-resistant attachment and later anxiety and passive withdrawn behaviour. Insecure-disorganised attachment is strongly associated with later hostile and aggressive behaviour as well as with dissociation. Postulated mechanisms have been discussed in this chapter.

Notes

1   Also known as the Minnesota Parent–Child Project. Information about the study may be found on the University of Minnesota website (http://education.umn.edu/icd/Parent-Child). Details of the study and its findings have been published in *The Development of the Person* (Sroufe *et al.* 2005a).

2   The sample size may vary in published reports. This is due to the availability of the relevant data for specific research questions.

3   As previously described, avoidant persons nevertheless experience psycho-physiologically measured distress during heightened activation of the attachment behavioural system.

Part Four

What is Attachment Disorder?

12 Two Versions of Attachment Disorder

There are two discourses on attachment disorder. One is based on disciplined scientific enquiry which seeks to understand disturbances of attachment with careful reference to theory, international classifications and evidence. This discourse is found in academic journals and books and the references given to support the statements made are those of respected attachment theorists and researchers. As well as Bowlby and Ainsworth, these include Tizard, Hodges, Chisholm, O'Connor, Zeanah and colleagues in their various research teams. This work is reviewed in the following chapter.

An alternative discourse is found in some clinical practice, non-academic literature and on the Internet. This discourse often makes passing reference to Bowlby and the academic literature, and then proceeds to make claims which have no basis in attachment theory and for which there is no empirical evidence. In particular, and most worryingly, quite unfounded claims are made for the efficacy of alternative 'attachment' therapies.

International classifications

Attachment disorders are described, with diagnostic guidelines, in the two major international classifications, ICD-10 and DSM-IV-TR. These are summarised below.

ICD-10 and DSM-IV-TR classifications of attachment disorder

ICD-10 (The Classification of Mental and Behavioural Disorders in the *International Statistical Classification of Diseases and Related Health Problems, Tenth Revision* (World Health Organization 1992)) describes two distinct attachment disorders, namely Reactive Attachment Disorder of Childhood (RAD) and Disinhibited Attachment Disorder of Childhood (DAD).

DSM-IV-TR (*The Diagnostic and Statistical Manual of Mental Disorders, Fourth Edition, Text Revision* (American Psychiatric Association 2000)) describes Reactive Attachment Disorder of Infancy or Early Childhood (RAD) which takes the form of one of two subtypes: Inhibited Type and Disinhibited Type.

Both ICD-10 and DSM-IV-TR stipulate that RAD should be differentiated from pervasive developmental disorders. Both state that RAD is likely to occur in relation to abusive or impoverished child-care. However, both warn against automatic diagnosis in the presence of abuse or neglect; 'not all abused or neglected children manifest the disorder' (World Health Organization 1992, p.281); 'some children may form stable attachments and social relationships even in the face of marked abuse and neglect' (American Psychiatric Association 2000, p.128).

The frequency with which many clinicians use this 'diagnosis' overlooks the cautionary note in ICD-10 which states that in relation to disorders of social functioning 'there is uncertainty regarding the defining diagnostic criteria, and also disagreement regarding the most appropriate subdivision and classification' (World Health Organization 1992, p.277).

Figure 12.1 illustrates the core features and associated symptomatology of the two variations of attachment disorder according to DSM-IV-TR and ICD-10.

The ICD-10 includes a number of descriptors which are not included in DSM-IV-TR:

- types of abuse as well as neglect in describing the antecedents of RAD, i.e. *commission* as well as *omission*

- associated emotional disturbance in RAD and the possibility in middle and later childhood of emotional disturbance in DAD

- poor social interaction with peers in both RAD and DAD.

Another version

The 'diagnosis' of 'attachment disorder' has exploded over recent years, such that, at 18 July 2006, an entry of the term in the website search engine 'Google' produces a staggering response of 4,990,000 items[1]. Sadly, this abundance of usage of the term appears not to be matched by an abundance of understanding as to what it means. Children with 'attachment disorder' are described as liars, thieves, lacking in conscience and as having various other negative attributes.

- Markedly disturbed and developmentally inappropriate social relatedness in most contexts.

- The disturbance is not accounted for solely by developmental delay and does not meet criteria for a Pervasive Developmental Disorder.

- Onset before age 5 years.

- Requires a history of significant neglect.

- (Implicit) lack of identifiable preferred attachment figure.

DSM-IV-TR Reactive Attachment Disorder (RAD)

Disinhibited Type

Diffuse attachments as manifest by indiscriminate sociability with marked inability to exhibit appropriate selective attachments (e.g. excessive familiarity with relative strangers or lack of selectivity in choice of attachment figures).

Inhibited Type

Persistent failure to initiate or respond in a developmentally appropriate way to most social interactions, as manifest by excessively inhibited, hypervigilant, or highly ambivalent and contradictory responses (e.g. the child may respond to caregivers with a mixture of approach, avoidance and resistance to comforting, or may exhibit frozen watchfulness).

ICD-10 Disinhibited Attachment Disorder (DAD)

- Diffuseness in selective attachments.

- Generally clinging behaviour in infancy and/or indiscriminately friendly.

- Difficulty in forming close, confiding relationships with peers.

- Possible associated emotional or behavioural disturbance.

ICD-10 Reactive Attachment disorder (RAD)

- Strongly contradictory or ambivalent social responses especially at partings and reunions.

- Infant may approach with averted look, gaze strongly away while being held, or respond with a mixture of approach, avoidance and resistance to comforting.

- Possible emotional disturbance with apparent misery, unresponsiveness and withdrawal, and/or aggressive responses to own and others' distress.

- Fearfulness and hypervigilance in some cases.

- Social play impeded by negative emotional responses.

- Possible impaired physical growth.

Figure 12.1 Core features of attachment disorder

The demonising tone of the attributes and descriptions of these very troubled and troubling children is not always offset by an acknowledgement of their past abusive and neglectful experiences.

There appears to be licence to produce limitless items to characterise this apparent entity. Lists of attachment disorder 'symptoms' are easily found on the Internet and not infrequently include:

- avoids making eye contact – especially with parents, yet will look into your eyes when lying

- asks persistent nonsense questions and chatters incessantly

- is fascinated with fire, blood, gore, weapons and evil

- engages in food-related issues – hoarding, gorging, refusing to eat, eating strange things

- displays cruelty to animals

- displays no conscience – shows complete lack of remorse.

As a further example, the website of the Evergreen Consultants in Human Behavior (2006) in the United States offers a 45-item 'symptom checklist'. Items can be marked 'none', 'mild', 'moderate' or 'severe', 'as it pertains to your child'. In addition to the items listed above, this checklist includes: victimises others (perpetrator, bully), exploitive (manipulative, controlling), bossy, stealing, enuresis, encopresis, lack of cause-and-effect thinking, learning disorders, language disorders, grandiose sense of self-importance.

In the *Handbook of Attachment Interventions* (Levy 2000), Thomas (2000, p.72) writes: 'Attachment-Disordered children act worse when given information about what is going to occur. They use it to manipulate their environment and everyone in it.' In their report, the APSAC Task Force on Attachment Therapy, Reactive Attachment Disorder, and Attachment Problems (Chaffin *et al.* 2006) refer to a number of websites of proponents of controversial theories of attachment disorder.

These loose, if not wildly inclusive, lists do not accord with ICD-10 or DSM-IV-TR and are in part based on unsubstantiated views of Zaslow and Menta (1975) and Cline (1991), (see Chapter 18). Attachment organisation is rarely, if ever, mentioned. Past harmful experiences are often acknowledged and many of these behaviours are likely to be consequences of child abuse and neglect rather than being located within the attachment paradigm. It is also possible that some of these children's behaviours belong in a very different domain, unconnected to attachment. Some children have been found to show an absence of pro-social behaviour and to be 'callous unemotional' at the age of 7 years. These aspects appear, from a twin study (Viding *et al.* 2005), to be highly heritable and therefore point to a genetic vulnerability in these children. The findings await replication on non-twin siblings of these children. These children may well, in addition, also have experienced maltreatment by their parents from whom these difficulties will have been acquired.

Summary

The definitions of attachment disorders in international classifications and another version of attachment disorders have been described. The former is contained in ICD-10 and DSM-IV-TR and minor differences between the two classifications have been outlined. The other version is one found on many websites and in some books and publications. This version is not discernibly related to attachment theory, is based on no sound empirical evidence and has given rise to interventions whose effectiveness is not proven and which may be harmful.

Note

1   At 21.04.05 the number of items generated by Google in searching the term 'attachment disorder' was 78,400.

13 Research on Attachment Disorder

The scientific study of attachment disorder is a recent enterprise, with the important exception of the work of Tizard, Hodges and colleagues during the 1970s and 1980s. Only a handful of samples of children whose lives started in adversity have been studied, some longitudinally, specifically with the aim of furthering our understanding of the phenomenon (European Commission Daphne Programme 2005). The most important and most recent of these studies are presented and appraised in this chapter. Before commencing this appraisal, however, it is necessary to consider some issues regarding research.

Issues regarding research methods
In appraising the scientific literature concerning attachment disorder the following concerns regarding research methods have been encountered.

The timing of the assessment of attachment behaviour for children who have moved to a new placement
As previously described, the separation from or loss of an attachment figure arouses intense emotions including protest and despair. It seems inappropriate, therefore, to assess a child's attachment early into a new placement. Not only is the child adjusting to the separation or loss, but he or she is also dealing with the potential formation of a new attachment. The period during which the child is in transition is not the time to assess attachment as an entity, other than as an entity in transition. The duration of what is regarded as the period of transition will vary with a child's age and maturity.

The reliability of the source of the information on which an assessment of attachment behaviour is made

The most rigorous method of assessment of attachment behaviour is direct observation of the child. This, however, is the most time-consuming and, therefore, most expensive method. If this is not possible, information gained from the child's principal caregiver(s) will, in all likelihood, be acceptably reliable. Beyond that, the chances of reliability recede.

The assessment of attachment behaviour in the presence of the principal caregiver

As previously described, attachment behaviour can be directed towards unfamiliar figures in the absence of the attachment figure. Therefore, if the research question in any way concerns the nature of the child's attachment behaviour towards their primary caregiver, which in research on attachment disorder it certainly does, the caregiver must be involved in the assessment.

The certainty that the relationship between the child and carer is an attachment relationship

As O'Connor and Zeanah (2003) point out, the strange situation was designed to study individual differences in the attachment between the child and caregiver; it is based on the assumption that an attachment exists. This is understandable as Ainsworth's studies focused on children who had lived with their parent(s) from birth. With regard to children who have moved away from their original caregiver(s), however, no such assumption can be made. As O'Connor elsewhere (2002, p.779) points out, 'It is therefore essential to be able to define what constitutes a selective attachment relationship.' As yet it would appear that no such reliable measure exists.

Small sample sizes

A difficulty in research on attachment disorder is that, of the number of children included in the study, only a few may be assessed as having a specific disorder. This is especially true of the inhibited disorder type.

The evidence

In this review of studies, only findings related to attachment disorder – inhibited and disinhibited – are described. The studies often include assessments of other aspects of the children's functioning, which are not included.

Young children in residential nurseries in the UK and their later development

During the 1970s and 1980s, Tizard, Tizard, Joseph, Rees and Hodges[1] published a series of papers concerning the attachment status and subsequent development of a group of children who had lived uninterruptedly in residential nurseries from the age of 4 months or less until at least 2 years of age. Hodges (1996) describes the nursery environment as follows:

> Children in the nurseries received very little continuity of care, although staffing levels were high. By age two, an average of twenty-four different caregivers had looked after the children for at least a week. Even within the course of a single five-day period, an average of six different caregivers, excluding night staff, worked with each 'family group' of six children… As part of their training, staff rotated between 'family groups' of children. They went on and off duty, to college, on holiday, and eventually they left for good. All these moves were unpredictable from the point of view of the children. In this most basic of all parameters for the development of an attachment relationship, the nurseries were utterly unlike an ordinary family. (p.65)

Another important feature of this institutional environment was that the caregiving was emotionally detached. Staff very rarely reported feelings of pleasure, affection, anxiety or anger about a child. The development of a close attachment between children and the staff was explicitly discouraged, Hodges describes, 'since a child who became strongly attached to one adult tended to disrupt the smooth running of the groups' (pp.65–66). Moreover, it was 'thought unfair both to children and to staff members to allow attachments to develop since they would inevitably be broken when the staff member left' (p.66).

In other respects, the nurseries provided excellent care. The children were very well physically cared for and stimulation and play facilities were provided. As Hodges describes, 'this was maternal deprivation in a rather pure form' (p.64). She adds that this form of care is no longer current, partly as a result of Tizard's work.

Most of the children left the institutions between the ages of 2 and 7 years. Most of the children were placed in adoptive families, some returned to their biological parent(s). For most children this was the first opportunity to form selective attachments to a consistently available adult.

The children's behaviour and development was compared to a group of 2-year-olds raised in families.

In the nursery at age 2 years

Most of the children would run to be picked up when almost any nurse entered the room and would cry and try to follow when she left. Two-thirds of the family-reared children did not show such behaviour with regard to their mothers. The children's evident 'insecure' attachment behaviour was 'very unlike even usual "insecure" attachment patterns' (p.67).

Hodges describes the attachment behaviour of the nursery children as

> diffusely affectionate towards a large number of people – virtually anyone familiar, although they had a clear hierarchy of preferences. They generally showed a preference either for a particular nurse, or for the mother in those cases where she visited at least weekly. (p.67)

However, the children had very little contact with their preferred adults, on most days seeing their preferred nurse for only a few minutes and their mother not at all. The comparison family-reared children showed attachment behaviour to a small number of people, the average being four. Their principal attachment figure was usually the mother.

The nursery-reared children were shy and wary of strangers. The family-reared children were relatively at ease with strangers, 'reflecting their experience with a much wider social network' (p.67). However, in other respects, the nursery children's development differed little from the family-reared children.

COMMENT

If organisation is defined as a repeatable strategy for obtaining proximity to a figure when alarmed, it would seem from the descriptions given that the nursery children's attachment behaviours were anxiously organised. This is suggested by their display of behaviours such as following, running to a figure, indicating a wish to be picked up. As Hodges proposes, it seems that attachment behaviour was organised around a consistent style of caregiving (provided by different caregivers), that is a generalised pattern of the expectable care of many care-givers, 'the behaviour of each conforming more or less to the same pattern' (Hodges 1996, p.67), rather than the expectations of a specific figure. There is no indication of inhibited attachment disorder.

Why were the nursery children shy and wary with strangers, in contrast with the family-reared children who were relatively at ease with strangers? Hodges suggests that the family-reared children's relative ease with strangers reflects their experience with a much wider social network in comparison with the children in the nurseries, whose environment was restricted, predictable and devoid of novelty which included strangers.

At age 4½ years
ADOPTED CHILDREN

Twenty-four children had been adopted. Initial clinging and following behaviours had ceased for most of the children, although they were more demonstratively affectionate and attention-seeking than the family-reared children. Of the adoptive mothers, 83 per cent felt that their child was deeply attached to them. Some children were over-friendly towards strangers and would allow strangers to comfort them.

CHILDREN RETURNED TO BIOLOGICAL PARENT(S)

The majority of children continued to be very clinging. Hodges suggests that this behaviour seemed to reflect a continuing sense of insecurity; many mothers had been ambivalent about their child's return and threatened to send the child back to the nursery. The children were also more demonstratively affectionate and attention-seeking than the family-reared children. Some children were over-friendly towards strangers and would allow strangers to comfort them.

CHILDREN WHO REMAINED IN INSTITUTIONS

Of these 26 children, 70 per cent were said by staff 'not to care deeply about anyone' (p.69), suggesting the possibility of inhibited attachment disorder. They tended to be immature and clinging in their attachment behaviour and were more attention-seeking than the children placed in families.

FAMILY-REARED CHILDREN

Over-friendliness towards strangers was not reported for any of the family-reared children.

COMMENT

There are some indications that the attachment behaviour of the majority of the ex-institutionalised children was organised. However, 17 per cent of the adopted children were *not* felt by their adoptive mothers to be deeply (*sic*) attached, suggesting continuation of an inhibited attachment disorder. The behaviour of many of the returned children seemed to reflect a continuing sense of insecurity. In addition, some adopted and some children returned to biological parents, but none of the family-reared children, were reported to be over-friendly to strangers. The behaviour of a number of the ex-institutionalised children therefore showed continued disinhibition. The finding that none of the family-reared children were reported to be over-friendly towards strangers indicates that these children were appropriately selective.

At age 8 years
ADOPTED CHILDREN

The majority of adoptive mothers felt that their adopted child was closely attached to them. The children were less disinhibited in their attachment behaviour and would no longer accept comfort from a stranger. However, approximately a third of the children were reported to be over-friendly towards strangers. The children's teachers reported attention-seeking behaviour, restlessness, disobedience, quarrelsome behaviour and unpopularity with peers.

CHILDREN RETURNED TO BIOLOGICAL PARENT(S)

The children were less cuddly towards their parents than any other group and only half of the mothers felt their child was closely attached to them. Later placement tended to be associated with less attachment to the mother (this was not found in the adopted group). The children were more likely than any other group to accept comforting and affection from strangers. The children's teachers reported attention-seeking behaviour, restlessness, disobedience, quarrelsome behaviour and unpopularity with peers. The children in this group showed the greatest difficulty.

COMMENT

Hodges reports that there was no evidence to suggest that the difference between the adoptive and returned-home children was explained by differences in the children themselves prior to placement. 'It seemed related to the very different family settings offered by the adoptive and the biological parents' (p.69). Hodges offers an explanation for the differences between the two groups in the development of attachment bonds. The adoptive parents' desire to have a child contrasted with the ambivalence of many of the biological parents. Moreover, many of the adoptive parents had initially wanted to adopt a baby and therefore may have been more tolerant of dependent behaviour. The biological parents, however, expected more independence in their returned young child than the parents of the family-reared children.

Given that the nursery-reared children were developing their first attachments at an older age than normal, responsiveness to attachment behaviour which appears immature and age-inappropriate may be important for attachment formation. It would seem that this was particularly lacking for the returned children. Hodges suggests that this may explain the finding at age 8 in the returned children, but not the adopted children, that there was a tendency for later placement to be associated with fewer reports of attachment to the mother. Returned children may have been more likely to receive responsive caregiving if they returned when still very young, which may have decreased with the child's increasing age.

There are indications that more of the adopted children were appropriately selective than the children returned to biological families.

At age 16 years
The adopted children and children returned to biological parents were matched to children who had never been adopted or in care.

ADOPTED CHILDREN
Family relationships seemed satisfactory for most of the children and their parents and differed little from matched children. The children were not more 'cuddly' than matched comparison children. The great majority of parents viewed the child as closely attached to them. However, the children had more difficulty with siblings than comparison children. One-fifth to two-fifths of parents reported unselective friendliness towards peers.

CHILDREN RETURNED TO BIOLOGICAL PARENT(S)
Difficulties in family relationships were reported much more frequently among the children returned to their biological parent(s) than the adopted or matched children. The returned children were less often seen as attached to their parents; they showed less affection towards their parents than the other groups, they wanted less involvement in family discussions and identified themselves less with their parents. They had particularly great difficulty with sibling relationships. One-fifth to two-fifths of parents reported unselective friendliness towards peers.

BOTH GROUPS
At 16, the ex-institutionalised adolescents with adoptive or biological parents shared important characteristics which distinguished them from the comparison adolescents. Hodges describes five main features:

- orientation towards adult attention
- poor peer relationships
- less likelihood of a special friend
- less turning to peers as confidants
- unselective friendliness towards peers.

The nursery-raised adolescents were very much more likely to show four or five of these characteristics than the comparison adolescents. Hodges suggests that these characteristics may be regarded as an 'ex-institutional syndrome'. However, she points out that this syndrome occurred in only half the ex-institutional group and she gives an important warning: 'it should also be emphasised that in general the behaviour characteristics it represents are *differences* from the comparison group and do not all imply difficulties' (p.73).

COMMENT

Hodges reports that although over-friendly behaviour at age 8 was not related to friendliness towards strangers at 16, there was 'a significant association between overfriendliness to *adults* at age eight, and unselective friendliness towards *peers* at sixteen' (p.72). At 16, the children returned to biological parents continued to have greater difficulties in family relationships than the adopted children. However, difficulties in peer relationships were reported for both groups of adolescents, although the children returned to biological parents showed greater difficulties than the adopted children. It seems likely that these differences are explained by the differences in the post-nursery environment.

Indiscriminate friendliness towards peers in adolescence can be viewed as a legacy of early institutional experience. In adolescence, social orientation is increasingly towards peers, from whom future attachment figures will emerge in adulthood.

Children from Romanian orphanages adopted in Canada
At age 1½ years to 3 years and 1 month (Chisholm et al. 1995)
Children who were adopted from Romanian orphanages following the overthrow of the Ceausescu regime in late 1989 suffered severe early deprivation. The conditions in the state-run orphanages were deplorable. Chisholm *et al.* describe the child-to-caregiver ratios as ranging from 10:1 for infants to 20:1 for children over 3 years old. The children 'were exposed to a series of inatten-

tive caregivers, preventing them from establishing attachment relationships' (p.1092).

SAMPLES
Romanian orphanage group (RO)
This group consisted of 46 children who had spent at least 8 months in a Romanian orphanage prior to their adoption in Canada. The children's ages at the time of parent interview ranged from 17 to 76 months (median 30 months); they had been in their adoptive homes between 4 and 25 months (median 11 months).

Canadian-born, non-adopted, never institutionalised comparison group (CB)
The comparison group consisted of 46 children, each of whom was matched in age and gender to a child in the Romanian orphanage group.

Early-adopted Romanian children comparison group (RC)
A second comparison group consisted of 29 children who would have grown up in Romanian orphanages had they not been adopted in Canada before the age of 4 months. The ages of the children at adoption ranged from 0 to 4 months (mean age 2.3 months).

MEASURES
Attachment security
There were 23 items with the highest[2] and lowest[3] loadings on the security scale of the Attachment Q-sort.

Indiscriminately friendly behaviour

(a)   whether a child wandered without distress

(b)   how friendly a child was to strangers

(c)   whether a child was ever shy

(d)   what a child typically did upon meeting new adults

(e)   whether a child would be willing to go home with a stranger.

Each item was scored 0 or 1; total possible score 0 to 5.

Lack of investment in the role of parent
This was a 7-item sub-scale of the Parenting Stress Index (Abidin 1990). The underlying construct of this sub-scale has been described by Abidin as consistent with Bowlby's idea of internal working models of attachment.

RESULTS
Attachment security
The RO children scored significantly lower than the CB children ($p<0.006$), and lower than their RC matches ($p<0.05$). The RC children's security scores did not differ significantly from those of their matched CB children. Items that were significantly more characteristic of the RO children than the CB or RC children were 'wants to be put down, and then fusses or wants to be picked right back up' and 'when upset tends to stay where he/she is and cries'.

Indiscriminately friendly behaviour
The RO children showed significantly more indiscriminately friendly behaviours than the RC children. As examples of these differences, 61 per cent of the RO children compared with 34 per cent of the RC children 'typically approached new adults', and 52 per cent of the RO children compared with 28 per cent of the RC children were 'willing to go home with a stranger'.

There were no significant correlations between the children's scores of indiscriminate friendliness and their attachment security, for either the RO group or the RC group.

Lack of investment in the role of parent
A significant negative association was found between the RO children's attachment security and their parents' lack of investment in parenting ($p<0.01$).

Chisholm *et al.* write that the reason for the lack of association between parents' reports of indiscriminately friendly behaviour and children's attachment security is unclear. The authors suggest that indiscriminate friendliness may serve 'an adaptive function for children developing an attachment later than is usual' (p.293). It seems likely that the parents of the Romanian orphanage children found such behaviour endearing rather than alarming. However, if indiscriminate friendliness continued as the children grew older, it would be expected that parents would be concerned about the safety of a child 'who wanders unconcernedly and is willing to go home with a stranger' (p.293). In addition, parents might feel disappointment 'when the parent–child relationship fails to grow deeper over time' (p.293).

COMMENT

The item 'when upset tends to stay where he/she is and cries', which was more characteristic of the RO children, suggests some failure to enact organised behaviour, indicating continued inhibited RAD.

The absence of a correlation between attachment security and indiscriminate friendliness indicates that these are independent dimensions.

At age 4 years 5 months to 9 years 2 months (Chisholm 1998)

In this follow-up study, the assessment reported in the above 1995 paper is referred to as Time 1 and this follow-up assessment is referred to as Time 2.

SAMPLES (AS IN THE 1995 STUDY)

Romanian orphanage group (RO)

Canadian-born, non-adopted, never institutionalised comparison group (CB)

Early adopted Romanian children comparison group (EA) (aged 50 to 64 months)

MEASURES

Attachment security: behavioural assessment
A separation–reunion procedure, developed with the aid of Crittenden, was videotaped and coded using the Preschool Assessment of Attachment (PAA) (Crittenden 1992). Patterns that were both less common and more extreme were viewed as atypical insecure patterns.

Attachment security: interview assessment
The measure used in the 1995 study, based on the Attachment Q-sort (AQ-sort).

Indiscriminately friendly behaviour: five-item measure
The five-item assessment used in the 1995 study.

Indiscriminately friendly behaviour: two-item measure
The two most extreme items from the five-item assessment, 'child wanders without distress' and 'child would be willing to go home with a stranger'.

Other measures included the Child Behavior Checklist, the Parenting Stress Index, the Stanford-Binet Intelligence Scale, as well as assessments of the child's past experience in the orphanage and present general behaviour.

RESULTS

Attachment security: Time 2 (PAA)
The frequency of insecure attachment patterns in the RO group was 63 per cent, and 42 per cent and 35 per cent in the CB and EA groups respectively. Significantly more RO children than CB or EA children showed atypical insecure patterns. Of the RO children, 12 per cent were assessed as defended/coercive (A/C), whereas no children in the CB or EA groups were assessed as having this attachment pattern. In addition, 9 per cent of the RO and none of the CB or EA children were assessed as 'insecure (other)'.

Attachment security: Time 1–Time 2 comparison (AQ-sort)
Within-group analyses found that children in the RO group scored significantly higher on attachment security at Time 2 than Time 1 (p.1099).

Indiscriminately friendly behaviour: Time 2
The RO children scored significantly higher than the CB and EA children on both measures of indiscriminate friendliness.

Indiscriminately friendly behaviour: Time 1–Time 2 comparison
On the five-item measure, the RO children displayed as much indiscriminately friendly behaviour at Time 2 as at Time 1, unlike the EA children whose scores were significantly lower. Seventy-one per cent of RO parents described their child as 'overly friendly', with 90 per cent reporting little or no improvement in this behaviour over time.

In her discussion, Chisholm states that, contrary to the claims of Spitz (1945) and Goldfarb (1955) concerning institutionalised children, the Romanian orphanage children 'were able to form attachment relationships with their adoptive parents' (p.1102).

With regard to the study's provision of 'substantial evidence that indiscriminately friendly behavior is characteristic of children who have experienced early institutionalization' (p.1103), Chisholm asks the question, 'what function would this behavior have post-adoption?' (p.1103). She presents two possible answers.

First, recalling Crittenden's findings that children who suffered early neglect, upon achieving locomotion, unrestrainedly sought stimulation and novel experiences, Chisholm suggests that the indiscriminate friendliness of the RO children 'might also reflect a need for stimulation after their unstimulating early lives' (p.1103). A second possibility is that indiscriminate friendly behaviour was reinforced in the children by their parents' pleasure in their friendliness and the attention they received from strangers following their adoption.

Chisholm concludes, 'Given that even RO children classified as secure display indiscriminate friendliness, I cannot agree that their indiscriminate friendliness should be equated with attachment disorder' (p.1104). Much of this behaviour 'is not directly linked to their attachment to parents' (p.1104). Finally, Chisholm suggests that, although the children's experience in the orphanages constituted a risk factor, early institutional care alone did not foretell later attachment insecurity; other stressors were required.

COMMENT

Perhaps foremost among the findings of interest is that concerning the continuing *absence* of an association between attachment security and indiscriminate behaviour. This strongly indicates that attachment formation/organisation and disinhibition are independent dimensions of attachment behaviour. Chisholm attempts to explain the persistence of indiscriminate behaviour as being adaptive in the new environment.

An alternative view of persistent indiscriminate behaviour is that it is not adaptive and that it represents a real difficulty for these children. Her findings indicate that security-promoting parenting, for many children raised in the orphanages, did not protect against the persistence of indiscriminate behaviour.

Deprived children from Romania adopted in the UK
At age 4 years (O'Connor et al. 2003b)

This study examined the quality of attachment with an adoptive caregiver at age 4 years in children adopted in the UK before and after 6 months of age, following early severe deprivation in Romania, and a group of non-deprived UK-born adoptees, placed by 6 months.

SAMPLES
Romanian adoptees

This sample consisted of children adopted from Romanian instutitions (n=93) and very deprived homes (n=18) (not necessarily birth homes) adopted into UK families between February 1990 and September 1992:

- 58 placed before 6 months

- 59 children placed between 6 and 24 months.

Six children were excluded when it was learned that they had entered the UK after 24 months. Thus, Romanian adoptees n=111.

Comparison sample
The comparison sample consisted of 52 UK-born children placed into adoptive families between 0 and 6 months.

MEASURES
Child–parent attachment
A modified separation–reunion assessment designed by Marvin and Rutter (1994) to mildly stress the child's attachment system was carried out in the child's home.

Children were classified as secure, insecure-avoidant, insecure-dependent (ambivalent), insecure-disorganised and insecure-other. This latter classification was given when a child was clearly insecure but did not fit into one of the insecure categories. Examples were:

- display of both strong avoidant and strong dependent attachment behaviour patterns

- display of a fearful, 'compulsive-compliant' pattern.

This category included other atypical and clearly insecure patterns.

'Nonnormative behavioural patterns' in the separation–reunion procedure
These were defined as patterns that contradict expected patterns or sequences of attachment behaviour. Examples:

- immediate sociability toward the stranger followed by wariness

- immediate exploration followed by wariness

- confused sequence of behaviours with no detectable or predictable sequential pattern.

Disinhibited attachment behaviour
The behaviours displayed were:

- definite lack of differentiation between adults

- clear indication that the child would readily go off with a stranger

- definite lack of checking back with the parent in anxiety-provoking situations.

For some analyses, the researchers distinguished the children as organised or 'nonorganised'.

RESULTS

Distribution of attachment classifications in separation–reunion procedure

Of late-placed Romanian adoptees, 51 per cent received classifications of insecure-other, compared with 16 per cent for the UK early-adopted children and 34 per cent for the early-placed Romanian children.

Significant differences were also found in the distribution of attachment classifications based on an organised (secure, avoidant, dependent) versus not-organised (insecure-disorganised/controlling, insecure-other) distinction. Significant group differences were not found for the secure/not secure distinction.

Distribution of nonnormative patterns in separation–reunion procedure

Nonnormative behaviour was found to be significantly more common in both the early- and late-placed Romanian children compared with the early placed UK adoptees and 34 per cent of early-placed Romanian adoptees ($p<0.01$).

Associations between attachment classifications, nonnormative behaviour and disinhibited attachment disturbance

Nonnormative behaviour was significantly more often found among children classified as insecure-other.

Children reported as severely disinhibited with strangers were primarily classified as insecure-other.

A small group of nine children showed nonnormative behaviour despite being classified as secure or organised insecure. In addition, three children classified as secure and one child classified insecure-avoidant showed severe disinhibition.

AUTHORS' CONCLUSIONS

Among other conclusions, the authors suggest that children classified as insecure-other do not show a predictable interrelatedness in the 'organization or patterns of behaviour most closely associated with attachment theory', namely attachment, affiliation, fear/wariness and exploration (p.34). This is in contrast to children who developed a discriminating attachment relationship early in life.

COMMENT

This brief review cannot do justice to this important paper. The authors' finding that the late-placed ex-institutionalised children 'exhibited a form of insecurity that was not similar to those forms of insecurity identified in prior research on normal and at-risk samples' (p.29) is reminiscent of Zeanah *et al.*'s 2005 finding (see the author's conclusions on p.211).

The behaviour described in the 'insecure-other' classification used by the researchers, and found in a majority of late-placed children, has some resemblance to disorganised behaviour.

At age 6 years (O'Connor, Rutter and the English and Romanian Adoptees Study Team 2000)

In this paper, O'Connor *et al.* report the assessments at age 6 of Romanian children adopted in the UK and a comparison sample of UK-born adopted children. In addition, longitudinal data at ages 4 and 6 years are presented.

SAMPLES

Romanian adoptees
This group consisted of children adopted into UK families: one group was placed before 6 months of age; another group was placed between 6 and 24 months (as in the O'Connor *et al.* 2003b study).

Late-placed Romanian adoptees
This group were the children who entered the UK between 24 and 42 months (assessed at 6 years only).

Comparison sample
The comparison sample consisted of UK-born children placed into adoptive families between 0 and 6 months (as in the O'Connor *et al.* 2003b study).

MEASURES

Disinhibited attachment behaviour
The behaviours displayed were:

- definite lack of differentiation between adults

- clear indication that the child would readily go off with a stranger

- definite lack of checking back with the parent in anxiety-provoking situations.

Inhibited attachment disturbance
Characteristic behaviours include a lack of emotional responsiveness and social reciprocity with caregivers, summarised as 'indicates distress but does not come for comfort'.

Other aspects of the child's development and functioning which were assessed included behavioural and emotional problems, cognitive ability and quality of peer relations.

RESULTS
Attachment disorder behaviours at 6 years: Romanian samples
A moderate overlap among the four attachment disturbance items (three disinhibited, one inhibited) was found. The overlap was consistently greater between the disinhibited items than between the disinhibited items and the single inhibited behaviour item.

Within the Romanian samples, 14 per cent of children were rated as showing 'marked' disinhibited behaviour on the first item of the disinhibited measure (definite lack of differentiation between adults), 12 per cent on the second item (clear indication that the child would readily go off with a stranger) and 14 per cent on the third item (definite lack of checking back with the parent in anxiety-provoking situations). With regard to the single inhibited item, 12 per cent showed 'some/mild' inhibited behaviour and 3 per cent showed 'marked' inhibited behaviour. This compares with 8 per cent and 2 per cent respectively in the UK sample.

An examination of the similarity of individuals across items was carried out using cluster analysis. The authors report that 'The cluster patterns reinforce the correlational evidence for a disjunction between inhibited and disinhibited behaviors' (p.706).

As the inhibited behaviour item was infrequent, unrelated to the disinhibited behaviour items and failed to distinguish a subgroup of children, it was dropped from further analysis.

Attachment disorder symptoms and deprivation at age 6 years
A significant correlation was found in the samples of Romanian adoptees, between the total number of attachment disturbance symptoms at age 6 and duration of deprivation ($p<0.001$). However, the authors point out that there was 'substantial variability in duration of deprivation among those who exhibited severe attachment disturbance' (p.710).

Age 4 to age 6 comparison
Individual differences in disinhibited behaviour were stable from age 4 to age 6. None of the UK adoptees showed marked/severe disturbance at both ages.

In their discussion, the authors make an important point about the requirement of pathological care in ICD-10 and DSM-IV-TR criteria for attachment disorder:

> the finding that approximately 70 per cent of the children exposed to profound deprivation of more than 2 years did not exhibit marked/severe attachment disorder indicates that grossly pathogenic care is not a sufficient condition for attachment disorder behavior to result. (p.710)

The finding that attachment disturbance was evident even when deprivation was limited to the early months of life suggests that 'early deprivation may have long-term effects on the formation of subsequent selective attachment behavior' (p.710).

COMMENT

This study provides further evidence for the persistence of disinhibited behaviour in a sizeable minority of children who experienced early deprivation. Assessment of attachment organisation was not reported in this paper. However, the researchers sought to identify inhibited attachment disturbance with the single item regarding a failure to elicit comfort when distressed. Their finding that few (3%) children showed this behaviour suggests that this behaviour remits with a change to sensitive caregiving.

At age 4 years, 51 per cent of 80 Romanian adoptees were assessed as non-organised (9 per cent disorganised/controlling and 42.5 per cent 'insecure-other'). What has happened to these children at age 6 years?

It is possible that the single 'inhibited' item did not pick up, at age 6, the atypical nature of the children's attachment behaviour, which had been captured by the assessment at age 4. The description of the 'insecure-other' category in the 2003 paper, describing the adoptees at age 4 years, resembles disorganised behaviour.

Children living in residential nurseries in Bucharest

Smyke, Dumitrescu and Zeanah 2002

The objective of this study was 'To determine whether signs of disordered attachment were greater in young children being reared in more socially depriving caregiving environments' (p.972).

SAMPLES

Standard care group (ST)

This group consisted of 32 Romanian children living in a residential institution in Bucharest, receiving standard care. The children were cared for by more than 20 different staff working rotating shifts and responsible for large numbers of children (often three caregivers for 30 children on each shift). The majority of the children had been placed at the institution in the first few months of life, for 'social' reasons. The children's ages ranged from 11 to 68 months.

Pilot programme group (PI)

The pilot programme group consisted of 29 Romanian children living in the same residential institution in Bucharest, receiving more consistent caregiving in a 'pilot' unit. The children were divided into groups numbering 10 to 12. Each group was cared for by carers drawn from a pool of only four caregivers and most of the time only carers from this pool looked after the children during their waking hours. Age range: from 18 to 70 months.

Never-institutionalised group (NI)

This was a comparison group of 33 children who lived with their biological parents. Age range: 12 to 47 months.

MEASURES

The Disturbances of Attachment Interview (DAI) (Smyke and Zeanah 1999). The original schedule describes the DAI as a semi-structured interview designed to be administered by clinicians to caregivers who know the child and the child's behaviour well. If possible, it should be administered to the child's primary caregiver. Specific probes are not intended to be exhaustive and clinicians should feel free to probe further.

The interview consists of questions and probes concerning the following 12 items:

1. having a discriminated, preferred adult

2. seeking comfort when distressed

3. responding to comfort when offered

4. social and emotional reciprocity

5. emotion regulation

6. checking back after venturing away from the caregiver

7. reticence with unfamiliar adults

8. willingness to go off with relative strangers

9. self-endangering behaviour

10. excessive clinging

11. vigilance/hypercompliance

12. role reversal.

Examples of DAI questions and probes are:

Having a discriminated, preferred adult: 'Does he or she have one special adult that he or she prefers? Who is it? How does he show that he prefers that person? Could you give me a specific example? Are there any other adults that are special, like this? Who does he prefer most of all?'

Social and emotional reciprocity: 'Does he or she share things back and forth with you, let's say talk with you or show you that he or she's excited about something, or is he or she one to not really share back and forth? Does he or she take turns talking or gesturing with you?'

For this study, RAD-inhibited/emotionally withdrawn type was rated using items 1 to 5; RAD-disinhibited type was rated using items 1, 6, 7 and 8.

Other information gathered about the child included the reason for institutionalisation, language development, aggressive behaviour and stereotypies.

RESULTS

The study found that the children in the ST group had higher scores on signs of attachment disorder than children in the PI and NI groups. With regard to the indiscriminate RAD scale, children in the ST group had higher scores than those in the PI group; children in the PI group had higher scores than children who had never been institutionalised.

A four-cluster solution cluster analysis, 'to sort results by individual children rather than by variables' (p.977), distinguished the combined sample of 94 children as follows:

Cluster 1: no attachment disorder (n=70).

Cluster 2: unattached, inhibited/withdrawn (n=6). These children appeared not to be attached, were inhibited and emotionally withdrawn, but were somewhat emotionally responsive.

Cluster 3: attached/highly indiscriminate (n=9). These children had a preferred caregiver, but failed to seek comfort when distressed and scored highly on indiscriminate behaviour.

Cluster 4: unattached, inhibited/withdrawn and indiscriminate (n=9). These children had no preferred figure and were moderately inhibited/withdrawn and indiscriminate.

In their discussion, the authors write that the cluster analysis 'challenges the DSM-IV-TR and ICD-10 conceptualisations of disordered attachment' (p.980), pointing out that indiscriminate behaviour was a component of all the clusters except cluster 1.

COMMENT

In the DAI, question 2a – 'failure to seek or respond to comfort from preferred caregiver when hurt, frightened or distressed' – addresses two questions simultaneously: (1) Does the child seek comfort (i.e. is the child inhibited)? (2) Is the child discriminating in the choice of adult from whom s/he is seeking comfort (i.e. is the child disinhibited)?

The study's finding, that for some children both inhibited/withdrawn and indiscriminate behaviour was found, provides further evidence for the possible co-existence of the two types of attachment disorder.

Zeanah et al. 2005

This study examined and compared attachment in institutionalised and community children in Bucharest.

SAMPLES

Institutionalised group
The institutionalised group consisted of 95 children who had spent on average 90 per cent of their lives in institutions. Age range: 12 to 31 months (mean age=23.85).

Community group
The community group was a comparison group of 50 children living with their parents, recruited from paediatric clinics. Age range: 12 to 31 months (mean age=22.25).

MEASURES

Attachment quality and formation
Strange situation procedure. Children in the institutionalised group were assessed with their 'favourite' caregivers. 'If no favorite caregiver could be identified, the child was seen with a caregiver who worked regularly with the child and knew the child well' (p.1018).

A five-point scale for rating attachment formation, that is the stage reached in the process of forming an attachment, was developed. The scale particularly focused on child behaviour in the strange situation that did not fit the established attachment patterns (including disorganisation) and the extent to which the child showed a preference for familiar caregivers.

Attachment disorder
The Disturbances of Attachment Interview (DAI), previously described (see page 206). For this study, RAD-inhibited/emotionally withdrawn type was rated using items 1 to 5 (score 0 to 10); RAD-disinhibited type was rated using items 6, 7 and 8 (score 0 to 6).

Caregiving environment
The Observational Record of the Caregiving Environment (ORCE) (NICHD Early Child Care Research Network 1996, 1997, 2003) was adapted in two ways. First, instead of using the 'live coding' approach of the NICHD study, subjects were videotaped, in order to facilitate later coding by blind coders. Second, qualitative items were added, such as marked dysregulation, stereotypical behaviour and communicative gesture.

The ORCE was used in both institutional and home settings. Children were videotaped with their caregiver for one-and-a-half hours. The institutionalised children were videotaped with their favourite caregiver.

Cognitive abilities
The Bayley Scales of Infant Development.

Child behaviour problems and competence
The Infant–Toddler Social and Emotional Assessment (Carter and Briggs-Gowan 2000). This 195-item questionnaire was administered to caregivers. In this report the authors include only the competence score, derived from six sub-scales, namely attention, compliance, imitation/play, mastery motivation, empathy and pro-social peer relations.

RESULTS
Signs of RAD
The institutionalised children had significantly higher levels of emotionally withdrawn/inhibited RAD and indiscriminately social/disinhibited RAD than the community children ($p<0.001$ and $p<0.01$ respectively). There appeared to be no relationship between length of time in the institution and signs of either type of RAD.

Strange situation classifications
No resistant children were found in either the institutionalised or community groups. The frequency of the avoidant classification was similar in both groups (3 per cent in the institutionalised group and 4 per cent in the community group). Eighteen children or 19 per cent of the institutionalised children were classified as secure, compared to 74 per cent of the community children. This, however, included 14 children whose attachment formation was rated as not having reached a stage at which the A, B, C, D classification could be applied meaningfully. The proportions were reversed, however, for disorganisation, with 65 per cent of the institutionalised children classified as disorganised compared to 22 per cent of the community children. Finally, 13 per cent of the institutionalised children could not be classified; this did not apply to any of the community children.

Thus, only 22 per cent of the children in institutions had organised attachments, compared to 78 per cent of children living with parents. This difference was significant ($p<0.001$).

Attachment formation

On the attachment formation scale, all the children in the community group were rated as showing clear A, B, C or D attachment patterns, whereas only 3 per cent of the children in institutions were so rated.

Quality of caregiving

Only quality of caregiving significantly predicted attachment formation rating in the institutionalised children ($p<0.006$).

Attachment formation rating and quality of caregiving were the only significant factors associated with increasing the odds of an institutionalised child having an organised attachment ($p<0.009$ and $p<0.047$ respectively).

Quality of caregiving was related to emotionally withdrawn/inhibited RAD in the institutionalised group ($p<0.001$), but not related to indiscriminately social/disinhibited RAD.

AUTHORS' CONCLUSIONS

According to the authors, a most important finding of the study was that when children with weakly formed attachments had discernible attachment patterns, the patterns appeared to be anomalous or incompletely developed. They conclude from this that 'the meaning of secure and disorganised classifications of attachment in the community and institutionalised groups are different' (p.1024).

They tentatively conclude that the majority of the children in institutions were unable to form selective attachments to their caregivers. They suggest that the implication of this is that in high-risk samples such as maltreated children, the degree of attachment formation should be assessed as well as attachment classifications.

They further conclude that the results suggest that 'clinical disturbances, as reflected in signs of RAD, are related to how fully developed and expressed attachment behaviors are' (p.1024) rather than the organisation of a particular pattern.

COMMENT

The attachment classifications on points 2 and 3 of the attachment formation rating scale, which were based on minimal displays of attachment behaviour and were therefore 'forced', should perhaps be treated with caution.

The attachment formation rating scale may also be useful in understanding the development of non-institutionalised children who do not have an available preferred caregiver due to severe neglect.

US children in high-risk populations and maltreated children

Boris et al. 2004

The objective of this study was to assess the reliability and validity of attachment disorder subtypes in high-risk samples.

SAMPLES

Foster care

This was a sample group of 20 children from a clinical service treating children in foster care for state-verified ill treatment.

Homeless shelter

This was a sample of 25 children living with their young mothers in an inner-city homeless shelter.

Head start programme

There was a comparison group of 24 children of low-income mothers in a Head Start programme.

The mean ages of the children at the time of the research assessment were 33, 29 and 35 months respectively. It is not reported how long the fostered children had been living with their new families.

MEASURES

Attachment disorders were assessed using Zeanah and Boris's alternative criteria and the DSM-IV-TR and ICD-10 diagnostic criteria. In addition, the strange situation procedure and the Attachment Q-sort were used.

Inter-rater reliability in diagnosing attachment disorder using the alternative criteria and DSM-IV-TR, ICD-10 criteria were acceptable, with the exception of the diagnosis of attachment disorder with role reversal, where reliability was below acceptable levels.

RESULTS

There is little difference in the distribution of 'indiscriminate sociability', 'self-endangering', 'inhibited' and 'disinhibited (ICD)' types of 'disorder' between the maltreated and homeless shelter groups. However, ten children in the maltreated sample and one in the homeless shelter group were assessed as having disrupted attachment disorder[4]. The disorder most frequently classified was *role reversal*, interestingly found predominantly in the homeless shelter group. However, for many of the analyses, children whose sole indicator of a disorder was 'role reversal' were reclassified as having no disorder.

The authors report that 'Children from the maltreatment sample were significantly more likely to meet criteria for one or more attachment disorders than children from the other groups ($p < 0.001$)' (p.568).

Findings are also presented for the distribution of attachment disorder/no attachment disorder according to secure, insecure or disorganised attachment classification. Surprisingly, 46 per cent of children classified as having an attachment disorder were also classified as secure. Of the insecure and disorganised children, the percentage classified as having an attachment disorder was 21 per cent and 33 per cent respectively.

COMMENT

As will be discussed in the next chapter, there are reasons to suggest that '*disrupted attachment disorder*' should not be considered or defined as a disorder.

Role reversal is recognised as an aspect of behaviour in disorganised children whereby the child begins to take control of aspects of the parent–child relationship. Thus, role reversal in the parent–child relationship clearly represents a distortion of attachment behaviour, although this is usually captured in the disorganised (D) classification (see also p.29). Bowlby was clear that parental orientation towards the child as an attachment figure 'is almost always not only a sign of pathology in the parent but a cause of it in the child' (1969/1982, p.377). In fact, the authors themselves cast doubt on the appropriateness of including this type as an attachment disorder.

The findings that 46 per cent of children classified as having an attachment disorder were also classified as secure remain unexplained.

Zeanah et al. 2004

The objective of this study was to identify RAD reliably in maltreated toddlers in foster care, to determine if the two types of RAD are independent and to estimate the prevalence of RAD in ill-treated toddlers.

SAMPLE

The sample consisted of 94 children living in foster care who had experienced ill treatment.

MEASURES

Assessment of attachment disorder was made using the first eight items from the Disturbances of Attachment Interview (DAI) (Smyke and Zeanah 1999) described earlier (p.206). DSM-IV-TR criteria for RAD and ICD-10 criteria for RAD and DAD were also used.

The procedure for data collection was as follows. Fourteen clinicians from an intervention programme were responsible for the comprehensive assessment of the 94 children, their biological parents and foster parents, three months after the child came into foster care. For 67 per cent of the children, the clinician had assessed the children 2 to 20 months previously. The remainder of the children were current cases. These *clinicians* were interviewed by the research group, regarding each child's attachment behaviour at the time of the assessment, using the DAI. In addition to this procedure, for each child, three experienced child and adolescent psychiatrists applied DSM-IV and ICD-10 criteria for attachment disorders to the clinician interview data.

COMMENT

This procedure raises two questions. First, the DAI was intended to be administered to primary caregivers. Its administration to others (clinicians) who knew the child less well undermines the reliability of the information. Second, for the majority of children the clinicians retrospectively recalled the child's behaviour 2 to 20 months previously. Again, this raises a question about the reliability of the information.

RESULTS

With regard to the findings on diagnoses based on ICD-10 and DSM-IV criteria, the study found that 35 per cent of the children were diagnosed as having ICD-10 RAD, 22 per cent as having ICD-10 DAD and 17 per cent as having both. Using DSM-IV-TR criteria, 38 per cent of the children were diagnosed as having either the withdrawn/inhibited or the indiscriminate/disinhibited type. (The co-existence of both types of disorder according to DSM-IV-TR RAD criteria is not reported.)

In order to examine how the signs of attachment disorder were grouped together in the children, the authors analysed the ratings from the eight DAI items using cluster analysis. Selecting a four-cluster solution as the most appropriate, the signs of attachment disorder were clustered as follows:

Cluster 1 (mixed attachment disorder signs; n=20)
No preferred attachment figure and signs of both emotionally withdrawn and indiscriminate RAD.

Cluster 2 (no attachment disorder signs; n=37)

Cluster 3 (emotionally withdrawn/inhibited attachment disorder signs; n=22)
'Some evidence of preferred caregiver' (in text) but strong indication of preferred caregiver in Figure 1.[5]

Cluster 4 (indiscriminate/disinhibited attachment disorder signs; n=15)
'Some evidence of having a preferred caregiver' (in text) but strong indication of preferred caregiver in Figure 1.[6]

COMMENT

This appraisal raises methodological concerns regarding this study. However, even more importantly, there seems to be some discrepancy between the findings as presented in the cluster analysis figure and as presented in the text. Specifically, the text does not draw attention to the surprising finding illustrated in the figure that children who showed signs of emotionally withdrawn/inhibited attachment disorder (cluster 3) also showed quite strong evidence of *having a preferred caregiver*. This would not conform to the implicit requirement for RAD, that is not having a preferred attachment figure, as stated in the Practice Parameter for RAD (AACAP 2005).

The finding of signs of disinhibited attachment disorder alongside some evidence of a preferred caregiver (cluster 4) is more easily explained. A child who has experienced severe neglect or many changes of carers may subsequently develop an attachment to a new, responsive caregiver but an absence of wariness towards strangers may persist. However, this suggested explanation, in turn, runs contrary to the implicit requirement for RAD, that is not having a preferred attachment figure, as stated in the Practice Parameter for RAD (AACAP 2005).

There is therefore lack of clarity about the diagnosis of RAD in this sample. Specifically, the question is: can RAD be found in the presence of a preferred figure? If a diagnosis of RAD requires lack of a preferred attachment figure, then the finding of 38 per cent maltreated children with RAD is difficult to understand.

There is a further issue. Thirty-eight per cent of the children were diagnosed by the three psychiatrists as having either inhibited or disinhibited RAD, according to DSM-IV. However, using the DAI and the cluster analysis, 84 per cent of the children had either one or both signs of RAD. This discrepancy is not explained.

Given that this study is almost unique in reporting the prevalence of RAD in maltreated, as opposed to neglected, children and is quoted in the Practice Parameter (AACAP 2005), further clarification would be helpful.

Summary

The studies appraised in this chapter concern three different groups of children and include both longitudinal and cross-sectional studies. The longitudinal studies all concern groups of children reared initially in institutional settings, in England and in Romania. The English group of children were either restored to their families or placed in adoptive families. The Romanian children were adopted respectively into families in Canada and in the UK. The cross-sectional studies involve children in Romanian orphanages and children maltreated and at risk in the US.

The findings from all of these studies indicate that: (1) the inhibited and disinhibited forms of attachment disorder may coexist under conditions of extreme neglect; (2) the inhibited form mostly remits in children adopted out of institutions; (3) the disinhibited attachment disorder can endure even after children are placed with sensitive caregivers; (4) the disinhibited form can continue alongside structured attachment behaviour towards the child's permanent caregivers; (5) these attachments may be of the A, B, C or D type, or may be atypical.

Notes

1 The following summary is based on Hodges 1996, with the author's permission.

2 For example, 'child uses you as a base from which to explore'.

3 For example, 'child is demanding and impatient with you'.

4 Two types of disrupted attachment disorder distinguished in a table are included neither in the alternative criteria presented, nor described in the text.

5 This discrepancy is not explained in the paper.

6 This discrepancy is not explained in the paper.

14 The Nature of Attachment Disorder

There continues to be some lack of clarity about the nature of attachment disorders. One aspect about which there is consensus is that, whatever the precise nature of these difficulties, they only arise following very adverse early caregiving experiences in the child's life, to the extent that one might conceptualise the disorders as 'post severe caregiving adversity disorders'. This is, however, unsatisfactory, as a disorder cannot be characterised by its antecedents alone.

No discriminated attachment figure

The adverse early caregiving environment is most probably one of severe neglect characterised by lack of a consistent and available caregiver. However, the term maltreatment has also been used to describe the affected children's early experiences (e.g. Boris *et al.* 2004) and, indeed, ICD-10 (but not DSM-IV-TR) includes psychological and physical abuse and injury as well as neglect. This is problematic since maltreatment includes both neglect (omission) and abuse (commission). As will be discussed below, the postulated explanation for how attachment disorders evolve is based on an absence of an available or responsive caregiver to whom to attach. While abuse can occur alongside serious neglect or changes of caregiver, abuse on its own would be insufficient to explain attachment disorder. Abuse is associated with a developed, albeit disorganised, attachment. It is therefore safer to assume that it is absence-omission which is implicated as the pre-condition for attachment disorders. This can occur in three caregiving contexts: (1) (some) institutions, (2) repeated changes of primary caregiver and (3) extremely neglectful identifiable primary caregivers who show persistent disregard for the child's basic attachment needs. It is also important to note that severe early neglect and unavailability of a consistent caregiver are necessary but not sufficient to explain the development of an attachment disorder, since not by any means all children reared under these conditions develop an attachment disorder.

Attachment disorders are not synonymous with a post-institution syndrome. In a study of Greek infants raised in residential group care (Vorria *et al.* 2003), these young children did develop selective attachments. Moreover, not all children raised in Romanian orphanages, whose development has been thoroughly studied (see previous chapter), develop attachment disorders.

Under the circumstances of absence of an available or responsive caregiver, attachment behaviours in the child are not fully developed and expressed. Such disturbances must have begun before the age of 5 years. The fault does not lie in the child (e.g. due to developmental delay or pervasive developmental disorder). However, in these very adverse circumstances, *some* children are particularly vulnerable to developing an attachment disorder. The prevalence is unclear but is probably quite rare, other than in populations of children being reared in the most extreme, deprived settings such as some orphanages. In the Minnesota longitudinal study of a high-risk sample, 'only 2 or 3 of the 180 children...studied would have truly fitted these categories' (of attachment disorder) (Sroufe *et al.* 2005a, p.275).

Bowlby wrote (1969, p.357):

> Disturbances of attachment behaviour are of many kinds. In the Western world much the commonest, in my view, are the results of too little mothering, or of mothering coming from a succession of different people. Disturbances arising from too much mothering are less common: they arise, not because a child is insatiable for love and attention, but because his mother has a compulsion to shower them on him.

Before considering the nature of the difficulties subsumed under the term attachment disorder, it is necessary to define a *disorder* and, specifically, its distinction from attachment *disorganisation*. A clear operational definition of a clinical disorder is a condition 'requiring treatment, as opposed to risk factors for subsequent disorders', given in the Practice Parameter for the Assessment and Treatment of Children and Adolescents with Reactive Attachment Disorder of Infancy and Early Childhood (AACAP 2005, p.1208). Attachment disorganisation is a risk factor.

Both DSM-IV-TR and ICD-10 distinguish between two forms of attachment disorder: inhibited/reactive and disinhibited (see Chapter 12).

The nature of the difference between inhibited and disinhibited RAD

Given that the two forms of attachment disorder emanate from the same preconditions, what is the nature of the difference between the two forms of attachment disorder?

DSM-IV-TR stipulates that reactive attachment disorder can take the form of *either* inhibited or disinhibited behaviour. The wording used to describe the two sub-types presents them as clearly incompatible: thus, the inhibited form is described as 'failure to initiate or respond...to most social interactions, as manifest by excessively inhibited...responses'. The disinhibited form is characterised by 'indiscriminate sociability [and]...excessive familiarity with relative strangers'. Extending the behaviours to 'most social interactions' places them beyond the attachment paradigm. By contrast, some empirical evidence (reviewed in the previous chapter) has shown the *co-existence* of the two forms in a few children. These studies do not provide an explanation for this finding. However, the wording in the measures used in, for instance, the Disturbances of Attachment Interview allows for the co-existence of the two forms. It refers to behaviours more closely related to attachment – proximity and comfort seeking and accepting, and selectivity of attachment figures and relatedness to strangers. These questions follow Bowlby who stated the following:

> The kind of behaviour described [attachment behaviour] is characterised by two main features. The first is maintaining proximity to another animal, and restoring it when it has been impaired; the second is the specificity of the other animal. (Bowlby 1969, p.181)

He thus postulated *two* components of attachment behaviour, namely proximity-seeking attachment behaviour to a figure and specificity of figure. By definition, in a fully formed attachment, these two must co-exist. The absence of one or both must therefore constitute a disturbance of attachment.

Different mechanisms – and different trajectories

Disinhibited behaviour is concerned with the persons towards whom behaviour is directed, that is selectivity. Disinhibited behaviour, therefore, refers to a lack of inhibition in approaching unfamiliar figures and even directing attachment behaviour towards them.

Inhibition refers to attachment and social *behaviour* and not to the *target* of the behaviour. The child is inhibited in seeking and accepting comfort and in social interaction more generally.

The trajectories of the two types of attachment disorder are also different. While disinhibited attachment disorder appears to be enduring, the inhibited form tends to remit with the advent of an available caregiver.

Once it is clear that 'disinhibited' and 'inhibited', in the terms of attachment disorder, are not opposites of the same concept, but are in fact different concepts, it becomes clear that they can co-exist in the same child.

Disinhibited attachment disorder

Disinhibition is the lack of discrimination and specificity of the attachment figure. The basis of discrimination is familiarity. Bowlby writes that

> The immense importance in the lives of animals and men of the parameter familiar–strange has been fully recognized only during the past two decades… In very many species, it is now known, whatever situation has become familiar to an individual is treated as though it provided safety, whereas any other situation is treated with reserve. (Bowlby 1979, p.115)

Various terms are used to describe that attachment behaviour is directed towards a particular person or persons. Bowlby used the term 'specificity' (for example, *The Making and Breaking of Affectional Bonds*, p.130). Selectivity is another term frequently used. Figures towards whom differential attachment behaviours are directed are referred to as discriminated, preferred or selected figures and the attachments which are a consequence of these behaviours are referred to as discriminated or selective attachments. Once an attachment is consolidated, an attachment figure is by definition a selected figure and an attachment is by definition a selective attachment.[1]

FEAR OF STRANGERS

Referring to evidence from several studies including Ainsworth's study of Ganda infants, Bowlby (1969) describes three phases in the infant's development in the discrimination of familiar and unfamiliar figures:

(a) the infant shows no visual discrimination between strangers and familiars

(b) the infant responds to strangers positively and fairly readily, although not as readily as to familiars; the phase usually lasts six to ten weeks

(c) the infant sobers at the sight of strangers and stares; this phase usually lasts four to six weeks.

Only after these phases does the infant show *fear* of strangers, such as orientation and movement away from the stranger, whimpering, crying and a facial expression of dislike. The age when unmistakable fear on sight of strangers first appears varies from infant to infant and according to the criteria used. It is seen in a few infants as early as 26 weeks, in a majority by eight months and in a small minority not until the second year. There is some evidence that the later selective attachment develops, the later also does fear of strangers. Bowlby reports Schaffer's (1966) finding that the more people an infant habitually encounters, the later the onset of fear.

It is likely that stranger-wariness can only form once the child has begun to form a selective attachment. Until that time, the infant or young child who has no available attachment figure due to extreme neglect and/or a succession of carers cannot 'afford' not to show interest in *any* person, even if unfamiliar, as they are potential attachment figures. Furthermore, faced with a succession of carers, the infant experiences a blurring of distinction between familiar figures and strangers. If the child continues not to have the opportunity to form a selective attachment by about three years of age at the latest, the biologically determined sensitive period for developing stranger-wariness *may* have passed and the capacity to beware of strangers, or 'select out' unfamiliar figures for attachment behaviour, may never develop. These children will therefore remain socially disinhibited, even after they have been placed with new caregivers to whom the child is now showing a recognisable pattern of attachment behaviour within the A, B, C, D classification.

Inhibited attachment disorder

In inhibited attachment disorder, the children present as emotionally constricted and uncommunicative, socially withdrawn and with difficulties in emotional self-regulation. They do not seek and accept comfort at times of threat, alarm or distress and behave as if their attachment system has been deactivated even at times when it should become activated.

Attachment behaviour being innate, the *capacity* for it cannot be lost, unlike the disinhibited type. With the advent of an available caregiver, the attachment system can become activated and the previously inhibited attachment disorder can remit. The evidence from children over the age of 5 years who have been adopted from orphanages is that these children almost invariably go on to show formed attachment behaviour towards their primary caregivers. These attachment behaviours can be reliably categorised into the A, B, C, D patterns although, for some children, the patterns are distorted.

By contrast, there are some children older than 5 years who continue to show inhibited attachment disorder following placement in good, permanent alternative families. They continue to find closeness and intimacy of relationships with their new, good primary carers very difficult and appear to resist seeking proximity and accepting comfort when threatened. These children have not come from institutions but have experienced frequent changes of caregivers as well as significant neglect and would have shown inhibited RAD earlier in their life. Having experienced disruptions and changes of caregiving, it is likely that such a child would require a prolonged period of time to begin to trust in the permanency of their caregiving relationship before their attachment behavioural system will begin to operate.

Alternative criteria for disorders of attachment

Thus far, the discussion has concerned attachment disorder in which, at least implicitly if not in the formal classifications, there is no discriminated attachment figure. Zeanah and colleagues have proposed an alternative set of criteria for disorders of attachment, which they describe as drawn from developmental attachment research and modified by clinical experience (Zeanah and Boris 2000). Revising earlier versions (Zeanah, Mammen and Lieberman 1993; Lieberman and Zeanah 1995), the 2004 update (Boris *et al.* 2004) of the alternative criteria comprises three categories of attachment disorders:

1.   'No discriminated attachment figure'

2.   'Secure base distortions'

3.   'Disrupted attachment disorder'.

No discriminated attachment figure

Zeanah and colleagues have here retained their definition of a disorder as behaviour sufficiently harmful to the child to require treatment, and the requirement for early, very adverse caregiving experiences. The category of 'No discriminated attachment figure' remains as the inhibited/disinhibited attachment disorder (as above). These difficulties extend to all social interactions.

Secure base distortions

In including 'Secure base distortions' they have extended the ambit of attachment disorder to include the existence of an, albeit significantly distorted, relationship with a discriminated attachment figure. This is in contrast to the criteria for RAD in DSM-IV, which imply the absence of a clearly identifiable preferred attachment figure (Practice Parameter, AACAP 2005). As the Practice Parameter points out, Zeanah *et al.* (1993) have criticised the DSM-IV criteria as 'inadequate to describe children who had seriously disturbed attachment relationships rather than no attachment relationships at all' (AACAP 2005, p.1209).

The new category of 'Secure base distortions' includes the following four types:

(a)   attachment disorder with self endangering, presumed to attract the attention of an attentive caregiver

(b)   attachment disorder with inhibition: lack of exploration and excessive clinginess when the child is in the presence of the attachment figure and a less familiar adult

(c)   attachment disorder with compulsive compliance: excessive vigilance and anxious hypercompliance directed towards the attachment figure

(d)   attachment disorder with role reversal: inverted caregiving.

The observed disturbances are specific to interactions with the attachment figure rather than generalised to all social relationships. They are captured in the Disturbances of Attachment Interview (DAI) (Smyke and Zeanah 1999), described in the previous chapter.

Disrupted attachment disorder
In their alternative criteria, Zeanah and colleagues go further and include the reaction to an abrupt removal from a primary attachment figure as a further category. However, Zeanah and Boris (2000, p.363) themselves comment that when a young child is showing blunted affect and social withdrawal in foster care, it might be difficult to distinguish between inhibited RAD and disrupted attachment disorder.

Comment
Item (a) in Zeanah *et al.*'s alternative criteria is of particular interest. 'Lack of exploration and excessive clinginess' is presented as evidencing a disturbed or disordered relationship with a discriminated figure. However, such behaviour in the child also may be interpreted as indicating an intense expression of ambivalent/resistant (C) insecure attachment, sufficiently severe to be regarded as a disorder.

Items (b) and (c) have only rarely been found in clinical samples.

The behaviours described in item (d) (attachment disorder with role reversal) strongly resemble the transformation of earlier disorganisation. Inter-rater reliability has proved difficult to establish on this item.

In 'disrupted attachment disorder' the child, who is suddenly removed from the care of the primary attachment figure, displays symptoms along the spectrum from protest to despair to detachment. This does not refer to attachment formation or organisation, but rather to a process of change following loss. The sequential process of grief and mourning in response to the loss of an attachment figure described by Bowlby (1980) and Robertson and Robertson (1989) is a normal response to an 'abnormal' experience. It is debatable whether this should be termed a disorder. The purpose of defining this as a 'disorder' can only be understood as an alerting sign about the child's distress.

The alternative criteria thus depart from ICD-10 and DSM-IV-TR in not confining the condition to a lack of a preferred attachment figure and including very disturbed interactions specifically with an identified caregiver.

Disorganised and inhibited RAD

Several descriptors of the child's behaviour in both ICD-10 RAD (infant may approach with averted look, gaze strongly away while being held, or respond to caregivers with a mixture of approach, avoidance and resistance to comforting) and DSM-IV-TR Inhibited Type (the child may respond to caregivers with a mixture of approach, avoidance and resistance to comforting) closely resemble the behaviour of children who have formed disorganised attachment. This has been an issue for researchers and attachment theorists (e.g. van IJzendoorn and Bakermans-Kranenburg 2003) who suggest that inhibited RAD may be viewed as an extreme indication of disorganisation.

Reactive attachment disorder in children over the age of 5?

As was described in Chapter 12, not only is attachment disorder said to be widely recognised but its stated attributes are considerably wider than, and different from, the strict definitions discussed here. Many of the children to whom this label is given are older than 5 years. These are undoubtedly troubled children who may well have experienced maltreatment in their earlier life (Hanson and Spratt 2000). They may, however, not be correctly described as having a reactive attachment disorder. One criterion for attachment disorders in

ICD-10 and DSM-IV-TR is an onset before the age of 5 years, but evidence of attachment disorder behaviours, as defined here, before the age of 5 is often not available. A further, implicit, criterion for attachment disorder is severe neglect coupled with the absence of a discriminated attachment figure and/or a succession of caregivers. Many children who experience serious maltreatment have done so while living with a primary caregiver to whom they have formed an, albeit disorganised, attachment. It is also worthy of note that ICD-10 and DSM-IV-TR criteria for reactive and inhibited attachment disorder *do not* include descriptors such as lying, lack of remorse, lack of conscience, cruelty and other negative attributes commonly found in the 'alternative discourse' on attachment disorder and 'attachment disorder checklists' previously described (and see Chaffin *et al.* 2006).

It is now clear that the disinhibited form of attachment disorder can be found alongside a seemingly formed attachment relationship. However, by definition, the inhibited form cannot coexist with a formed attachment. Many of the older children who are described as having an attachment disorder do have an attachment to their caregivers. Whilst these newly formed attachments may be secure in response to the sensitive caregiving which the children are belatedly receiving, elements of previous disorganisation are slow to recede (see Chapter 17).

What is an alternative way of understanding some of the difficulties of these older children who have experienced early maltreatment and many of whom may now be living with alternative caregivers?

Correlates and transformations of disorganised attachment

Oppositional, aggressive behaviour towards adults and peers is a recognised sequel to earlier disorganised attachment. Following an early finding of disorganised attachment, a significant proportion of the same children show coercive controlling behaviour towards their caregivers in middle childhood.

Abusive experiences

Physical abuse, hostility and exposure to domestic violence are recognised precursors of both disorganised attachment and aggressive behaviour.

DEPRIVATION AND NEGLECT

One motivation towards stealing is a feeling of deprivation, which may continue to persist and lead to taking food or objects from others and seeking attention in a way which appears compulsive.

Insensitive caregiving – affect regulation

In the course of the caregiving response to an infant's attachment needs, the sensitive caregiver modulates the affect of the distressed or frightened child. Regulation of affect is thus a by-product of sensitive caregiving. When this is diminished or absent, the infant does not experience regulation of his or her aroused feelings and may not develop the capacity to do so. Frequent temper and angry outbursts and misery seen in these troubled children are thus indirectly related to their attachment experiences.

Insensitive caregiving – development of empathy

The caregiver's sensitive response to the infant's distress, expressed in the attachment bid for comfort and security, requires empathy by the caregiver towards the child. This is lacking in maltreating relationships and hampers the child's development of empathy. Lack of empathy is thus a further concomitant aspect of unfulfilled attachment needs.

The development of untruthfulness

Much of the untruthfulness to which some children resort relates to their difficulty in owning up to their misdeeds. Low self-esteem and a bad sense of self that many of these children feel are not conducive towards taking responsibility. On the basis of their past experiences, many of these troubled children continue to be fearful of the consequences of being found to have behaved inappropriately. This fearfulness may also be an aspect of post traumatic stress disorder, related to past trauma of abuse (Lieberman and Amaya-Jackson 2005).

While therefore related to their past experiences, which also affected the children's attachments, many of the difficulties which previously maltreated children show are not a part of the attachment behavioural system or paradigm.

Lastly, a minority of these children, may have difficulties which are located within the autistic spectrum or amount to hyperkinetic disorder, and which emanate from the child.

Summary

Alongside some continuing uncertainty about the precise nature of attachment disorders, three criteria are clear: the difficulties are evident before the age of 5 years, the child will have experienced severe neglect or frequent change of caregiver and will not, at a crucial time in their development, have a discriminated attachment figure. The inhibited and disinhibited forms, which arise from the same preconditions and can co-occur, are distinct both in their nature and trajectories. Both forms extend across social relationships beyond the attachment behavioural system. While the inhibited attachment disorder may well remit with a positive change in caregiving, the disinhibited form may persist. Some aspects of attachment disorders bear resemblance to disorganised attachment.

There is far less clarity about the presentation of attachment disorders over the age of 5 years. Not all the agreed criteria are verifiable and many behaviours currently included within that term are not aspects of attachment disorders (Chaffin *et al.* 2006). Some are transformations of disorganised attachment while others are sequels of the maltreatment which the child had previously experienced.

Note

1   In evolutionary terms, selectivity promotes evolutionary fitness; that is, natural selection favoured infants who, when alarmed, turned to selected, familiar figures rather than unselected, unfamiliar figures.

Part Five

Attachment Theory-based Interventions (and Some that are Not)

15 Introduction

Part Five describes and reviews the main findings about the effectiveness (where evaluated) of a number of interventions which are either based on attachment theory or which include the term 'attachment'. Part Four described the dichotomy between an academic and evidence-based approach to attachment disorders and a wide, loose approach to attachment disorders. A similar dichotomy is found when considering the current state and evidence base for interventions aimed at enhancing attachment security and ameliorating less than optimal attachment behaviour and organisation.

As described in Chapter 4, caregiving and caregiver sensitivity are the principal determinants of the child's attachment security. There have therefore been many reported studies of attachment theory-based interventions, mostly with parents of young children, the aim of these interventions being the enhancement of the quality of the caregiver's interaction with the child. The reviews here include meta-analyses, and some individual studies which illustrate the nature of the interventions.

Some of these studies are termed preventive, while others are reactive. Even the preventive ones mostly fall into the class of secondary prevention (Browne, Davies and Stratton 1988), which aims at vulnerable or high-risk groups, but before harm has occurred. In attachment terms, this would mean that the child is likely to form a disorganised attachment unless there is a change and improvement in the caregiver sensitivity. These are either parent–child dyads who are living in stressful social circumstances or where the parents possess risk factors for insensitive caregiving (e.g. drug or alcohol abuse, very troubled and abusive childhood histories or past unresolved trauma or loss).

Reactive interventions, also termed tertiary prevention (Browne *et al.* 1988), are those which aim at minimising or reversing harm which is already established. In attachment terms, the aim would be to change disorganised into organised attachment, and insecure into secure patterns. In practice, it is not always clear into which class an intervention falls – whether it constitutes secondary or tertiary prevention – as the attachment organisation of the infants or young children is not always measured at the outset.

Another means of enhancing the quality of caregiving for the child is to change the caregiver. This is achieved when a child is placed with alternative parents, either in a kinship, fostering or an adoptive placement. Evidence from a number of studies concerning the efficacy of a change of caregiver is considered later (Chapter 17).

An alternative form of intervention is direct work with the child, either individually or together with their caregivers. As has been described in Parts Three and Four, children with insecure-organised, and particularly with disorganised, attachments are troubled in many spheres of their functioning. Their difficulties reflect aspects or sequelae of their attachment dis/organisation such as controlling behaviour, are correlates of insecure and disorganised attachment and/or are directly due to earlier abusive and neglectful experiences. Much of this therapeutic work is not directly, or even indirectly, based on attachment theory. None of it has been evaluated systematically and some is harmful. This work will be reviewed in a subsequent chapter.

16 Evidence-based Interventions: Enhancing Caregiver Sensitivity

In setting out to enhance caregiver sensitivity, the target for change is the mother's or primary caregiver's sensitivity. However, since the sensitivity needs to be tailored to that particular child, the intervention needs to include observation of the mother with the child. The issue is not the mother–child interaction but the mother's interaction with the child. Some of this work therefore requires the presence of the child, while, for instance, feedback to the mother using video will be with the mother alone. Within the parameters of attachment theory, the child's behaviour or emotional state are not a focus for intervention although these aspects are central to the evaluation of the efficacy of the intervention.

The intervention studies included in the following meta-analyses by Bakermans-Kranenburg, van IJzendoorn and Juffer[1] (2003) were not restricted to a particular population. The authors point out that some samples were middle-class families with healthy infants, but studies with clinical and at-risk populations were included as well. Moreover, the meta-analyses include studies where children were living with their birth families and some studies where children had moved from their birth families to live with alternative caregivers. From the descriptions of the samples presented (Table 1, p.198), it seems that only a very small number of studies of adopted children are included in the meta-analyses, and that the majority of the samples are of at-risk or clinical populations.

Bakermans-Kranenburg, van IJzendoorn and Juffer (2003) 'Less is more: meta-analyses of sensitivity and attachment interventions in early childhood'

In introducing this important paper, the authors state their motivation for carrying out this meta-analysis.

> The time has come for a quantitative synthesis of the data that have been collected in a myriad of uncoordinated efforts and to try and come to evidence-based conclusions about what are the best intervention practices. (p.196)

Findings from van IJzendoorn, Juffer and Duyvesteyn's 1995 exploratory meta-analysis of 12 studies which measured the effect of intervention on maternal sensitivity and on infant–mother attachment are briefly described. The interventions were found to be rather effective in enhancing sensitivity (effect size: d=0.58),[2] but a smaller effect was found regarding attachment security (d=0.17). Short-term interventions with a confined focus were found to be relatively successful in affecting attachment (d=0.48), in contrast with long-term interventions, which seemed to be ineffective (d=0.00). However, the small number of studies led the authors to be cautious regarding these findings and they viewed the conclusions as hypotheses for testing in a larger-scale meta-analysis.

In the 2003 meta-analyses, the authors sought to prove or disprove four hypotheses:

1. Early intervention on parental sensitivity and on infant attachment security is effective.

2. Type and timing of the intervention programme make a difference.

3. Intervention programmes are always and universally effective.

4. Changes in parental sensitivity are causally related to attachment security.

Studies to be included in the meta-analyses were collected systematically using three search strategies. First, PsycLIT and MEDLINE were searched with relevant key words; second, references of the collected literature were searched; third, experts in the field were consulted. The selection criteria were intended to include as many intervention studies as possible, regardless of research design qualities. 'The idea was to test the influence of design features empirically and not to exclude any quantitative studies on a priori grounds' (p.197).

Instruments for assessing sensitivity included in the meta-analyses
These instruments were:

- the Ainsworth sensitivity rating scales (Ainsworth, Bell and Stayton 1974)

- the Home Observation for Measurement of the Environment (HOME; Caldwell and Bradley 1984)

- the Nursing Child Assessment Teaching Scale (NCATS; Barnard *et al.* 1988)

- the Erickson rating scales for maternal sensitivity and supportiveness (Egeland *et al.* 1990).

Studies that used other measures of maternal interactive behaviour were also included if the measures were clearly related to sensitivity.

Sample sizes
Seventy published studies were traced, presenting 88 intervention effects on sensitivity (n=7,636) and/or attachment (n=1,503).

Coding system
Intervention studies were coded according to the following:

1. *Design characteristics.* Sample size, randomisation, absence or presence of a control group and attrition rate.

2. *Features of the parents and children.* Features of both the involved parents, for example socio-economic status (SES), adolescence, clinical reference (*sic*), and at high risk due to factors such as poverty, social isolation and single parenthood. Features of the children included prematurity, irritability and international adoption.

3. *Focus of the intervention.* Whether the intervention aimed at:

   - enhancing parental sensitivity; for example, one intervention provided adolescent mothers with a videotape to help them enhance their sensitivity during mealtimes

   - affecting parents' mental representations; for example, one intervention aimed at reconstructing depressed mothers' representation of self in relation to their own parents

- providing social support; for example, in one intervention experienced mothers provided support and practical help to highly anxious mothers
- any combination of the above.

4. *Intervention characteristics.* The number of sessions, the child's age at the beginning of the intervention, the status of the person carrying out the intervention (professional or non-professional), whether intervention took place in the parents' home and whether video feedback was used as an intervention tool.

Results
SENSITIVITY

Findings regarding sensitivity were based on the analyses of 81 studies involving 7,636 families. Three studies that focused on interventions involving both mothers and fathers were not included. A core set of 51 randomised control group studies was established involving 6,282 mothers with their children. The effect of intervention on maternal sensitivity in random studies was moderate but significant (d=0.33, p<0.001). The effect size for all 81 studies was 0.44. The effect of the non-random studies was even larger (d=0.61). Thus, because non-randomised studies suggested inflated effects, almost all the findings reported concern the core set of 51 randomised studies.

Randomised studies

It was found that interventions that focused on sensitivity only were more effective (d=0.45, p<0.001) than interventions which combined sensitivity and support (d=0.27, p<0.001).

Other findings, all of which were significant at p<0.001, were:

- Interventions with video feedback (d=0.44) were more effective than without (d=0.31).

- Interventions with fewer than five sessions (d=0.42) were as effective as interventions with 5 to 16 sessions (d=0.38) and more effective than interventions with more than 16 sessions (d=0.21).

- Interventions starting after the child was 6 months old (d=0.44) were more effective than prenatal interventions (d=0.32) or interventions during the child's first 6 months (d=0.28).

- Four studies that relied not on personal contact with the client as a means of intervening, but the provision of soft baby carriers, use of the 'kangaroo' method (holding the infant close to the parent's chest), a workbook on responsiveness or a videotape, showed the largest effect size ($d=0.62$). However, the difference was not significant.

- The effect of interventions conducted at home ($d=0.29$) was not significantly different from those conducted elsewhere ($d=0.48$).

- Short interventions focusing on sensitivity only were most effective ($d=0.47$).

- Lower effect sizes were found for studies that used the HOME or NCATS as outcome measures than those which used Ainsworth's or Erickson's rating scales.

- The effect size was significantly larger for studies without attrition than for studies in which participants were lost.

Total set of 81 studies

Similar results were found as in the core set of randomised studies. The three studies involving fathers (n=81) could be analysed in this total set of studies (including non-randomised). It was found that the studies involving fathers were significantly more effective ($d=1.05$) than studies without fathers ($d=0.42$). However, given the small number of participants in the three studies involving fathers, this analysis must be considered as exploratory.

In a multiple regression analysis of study outcomes in the total set of 81 studies it was found that 'sensitivity-focused interventions and a later start of the intervention predicted higher effect sizes, even after controlling for characteristics of the sample' (p.205) such as low SES or adolescent mothers.

In a replication of the meta-analyses on a subset of randomised samples suffering multiple problems, it was found that interventions from non-professionals showed a larger effect size than those from professionals ($d=0.42$ and $d=0.26$ respectively).

ATTACHMENT

Twenty-nine intervention studies whose outcome measure was attachment security, involving 1,503 participants, were analysed. The effect size for attachment security was small but significant (for all studies $d=9.19$, $p<0.05$; for 23 randomised control group studies $d=0.20$, $p<0.05$). The authors present other findings in relation to three questions.

(1) What interventions were most effective in enhancing infant attachment security?
Based on analyses of the core set of 23 randomised intervention studies (n=1,255), the following findings are reported.

- The combined effect size for attachment security was small but significant ($d=0.20$, $p<0.05$).

- Interventions aimed at enhancing sensitivity (without focusing on support or representation) were the only interventions to show a significant effect size ($d=0.39$, $p<0.01$).

- Interventions of fewer than five sessions showed a significant effect size on infant attachment security ($d=0.27$).

- Interventions starting after the age of 6 months showed a significant effect size ($d=0.31$) and the difference compared with other interventions was significant.

- Interventions that did not use video feedback showed a significant effect size ($d=0.25$) and the difference compared with other interventions was significant.[3]

- Most sample characteristics (e.g. SES) were not significant moderators.

(2) Are shorter and behaviourally focused attachment interventions also more effective in groups with multiple risks, or do troubled families require more intensive interventions?
The meta-analyses were repeated on 15 randomised studies of families with multiple problems. The findings were:

- The combined effect size was similar to that found in the total randomised set ($d=0.19$).

- Interventions aimed at sensitivity only appeared the most effective ($d=0.34$) in enhancing infant attachment.

- Similar results were found for the number of sessions, the children's later ages at the beginning of the intervention and the use of video feedback.

- Behaviourally focused interventions appeared the most effective.

(3) Are successful interventions which aim to enhance sensitivity also more effective in enhancing infant attachment security?

> The studies with the largest effect sizes for sensitivity ($d>0.40$) were also the most effective in enhancing the children's attachment security ($d=0.45$, $p<0.001$) ... In fact, the only intervention studies that yielded a significant effect size on attachment security were the studies with a large effect size on sensitivity (when data on sensitivity were available). (p.208)

Conclusions

In their discussion of these findings the authors make a number of important points. Attachment disorganisation was not addressed because the interventions did not focus on preventing or changing disorganisation or on parents' frightened or frightening behaviour. Attrition in the control group (not experiencing the intervention) may jeopardise the comparison with the experimental group. The authors point out that intervention studies sometimes suffer from methodological flaws. On the basis of their analyses, the authors describe the design of 'the ideal intervention study' (p.211).[4] There may be a sleeper effect on attachment security; that is, changes in maternal sensitivity may not have had time to affect attachment security at the time of testing. The authors conclude, 'Interventions with an exclusively behavioral focus on maternal sensitivity appear to be most effective not only in enhancing maternal sensitivity but also in promoting children's attachment security' (p.212).

Three studies, included in the meta-analyses above, have been singled out to illustrate intervention processes which have shown good results.

Cohen et al. (1999) 'Watch, wait and wonder: testing the effectiveness of a new approach to mother–infant psychotherapy'

This intervention study involved mothers and infants attending a community mental health service as a result of child or parent difficulties. Thus, the intervention was reactive.

The authors point out early in this paper that although the infant's activity is regarded as a catalyst for the psychotherapeutic work evaluated in this study, the primary work is between the mother and the therapist. That is, the infant's presence, activity and play 'can stimulate and provide a motive for maternal change' (p.433).

The 'Watch, wait and wonder' (WWW) technique is based on the notion of the infant as an initiator in infant–parent psychotherapy and works at both the behavioural and the representational levels. The authors describe the therapy as follows:

> For half the session the mother is instructed to get down on the floor with her infant, to observe her infant's self-initiated activity, and to interact only at her infant's initiative, thus acknowledging and accepting her infant's spontaneous and undirected behavior and also being physically accessible to him. This fosters an observational reflective stance in the mother and places her in the position of being optimally, or at least more, sensitive and responsive... At the same time, the infant himself has the therapeutic experience of negotiating his relationship with his mother, and thus begins to master his environment. In the second half of the session, the mother is asked to discuss her observations and experiences of the infant-led play. The therapist does not instruct...but provides a safe, supportive environment (i.e. a sensitive and responsive environment). (p.434)

In the evaluation, the WWW approach was compared to another form of psychodynamic psychotherapy (PPT). This therapy 'involved discussion between the mother and the therapist throughout the whole session while mother and infant played, but without any instructions' (p.437).

The researchers hypothesised that infants in the WWW group would be more likely to become securely attached, show more cognitive development and regulate emotions during cognitive tasks.

The sample comprised 67 infants aged 10 to 30 months and their mothers referred to a regional centre for children's mental health. Presenting problems included feeding, sleeping, behavioural regulation, maternal depression and 'feelings of failure in bonding or attachment' (p.436). Mostly the problems were of long standing. Assignment to the two treatment groups was random. The strange situation was used to assess infant attachment. Other assessments included measures of mother–infant interaction, and maternal perception of parenting, psychological wellbeing and working alliance with the therapist.

There was no significant difference between the groups in the distribution of attachment classification prior to treatment, with 38 per cent of infants classified as insecure (A or C), 22 per cent secure (B) and 39 per cent disorganised (D). (As very few infants were classified as avoidant, the A and C categories were combined in the analyses.) Changes in attachment security at the end of treatment are presented in Table 16.1.[5]

Table 16.1 Changes in attachment security at the end of treatment		
	WWW Group n=34	**PPT Group** n=32
Shift from organised insecure to secure	20.6% (7)	3% (1)
Shift from disorganised to organised	14.7% (5)	9.3% (3)
No change in attachment classification	50% (17)*	59.4% (19)**
Shift to insecure or disorganised	14.7% (5)	28.1% (9)

Note

* Including two children who stayed secure.

** Including three children who stayed secure.

Infants in the WWW group were significantly more likely to shift to a secure or organised attachment classification than infants in the PPT group ($p<0.03$).

Despite these findings, no differential treatment effects were found in maternal sensitivity as measured by the scale used in the study, which the authors point out was unexpected. An apparently comprehensive set of measures of sensitivity were used in this study (the Chatoor Play Scale), including ratings of 'Dynamic Reciprocity and Dyadic Conflict', 'Maternal Intrusiveness' and 'Maternal Unresponsiveness'. However, it is likely that the measures used did not focus on those crucial aspects of caregiver response to attachment, which are being shown to be the actual precursors to secure attachments (Cassidy *et al.* 2005).

van den Boom (1994) 'The influence of temperament and mothering on attachment and exploration: an experimental manipulation of sensitive responsiveness among lower-class mothers with irritable infants'

The foci for intervention in this study were mothers and firstborn infants from low-SES families in the Leiden area of the Netherlands. The families were located through the birth register of the University Hospital. The infants were selected for irritability by administering a neonatal behavioural scale on the tenth and fifteenth day after birth. The assessment was administered to 588 infants in order to find the predetermined number of 100 irritable infants.

The mother–infant dyads were randomly assigned to the intervention and control groups. Further, half of the intervention and half the control subjects received a pre-treatment assessment and half did not. Three intervention sessions, in the home and lasting approximately two hours, took place at three weekly intervals when the infant was between 6 and 9 months old. The intervention was mothering/skill based. It focused on responsiveness to negative and positive infant cues and was implemented during everyday interactions. Intervention was guided by the four components of sensitive response elaborated by Ainsworth, namely perceiving an infant signal, interpreting it correctly, selecting an appropriate response and implementing the response effectively. Attention was devoted to achieving an 'optimal attunement of maternal behavior with infant signals' (p.1468).

It was found that the interaction effects were significant for all maternal components, that is for responsiveness ($p<0.001$), stimulation ($p<0.001$), visual attentiveness ($p<0.01$) and control ($p<0.001$). 'In sum, mothers who participated in the intervention did differ in meaningful ways from the control group mothers, and the differences were rooted in their responsive and stimulating orientation toward their infants' (p.1469).

It was also found that intervention infants scored significantly higher than control infants on sociability, self-soothing and exploration, and they also cried less.

The strange situation procedure carried out at 12 months showed a significant association between intervention group and attachment classification ($p<0.001$), with 78 per cent of control infants classified as insecure (A, C or D) compared with 38 per cent of intervention infants. Control infants were most likely to be classified as insecure-avoidant (52%).

van den Boom (1995) 'Do first-year intervention effects endure? Follow-up during toddlerhood of a sample of Dutch irritable infants'

In a follow-up of the intervention reported in the 1994 paper, assessments of 82 mothers and their children were carried out when the children were aged 18 and 24 months, and of 79 mothers and children at 3½ years. A host of assessments were used at the different time periods, including the Maternal Sensitivity Scales (Ainsworth *et al.* 1971) at 18 months, the Bayley Scales of Infant Development at 24 months and the Child Behavior Checklist at 42 months.

At 18 months, a significant association was found between treatment group and attachment classification ($p<0.001$), with only 26 per cent of infants in the non-treatment group, compared with 72 per cent in the treatment group classified as secure. At 3½ years, children of mothers who participated in the intervention were more secure than control children ($p<0.05$) according to the Attachment Q-sort.

At 24 months, mothers in the intervention group were significantly more accepting, accessible, cooperative and sensitive. In addition, children from the intervention group showed fewer behaviour problems and were better able to maintain a positive relationship with peers than children from the control group.

Thus, effects of the intervention were enduring. Moreover, the enduring effects on some dimensions of parent and child behaviour at follow-up were 'carried by earlier effects on attachment' (p.1813); that is, the effects were mediated by attachment.

Van den Boom suggests that behavioural specification in the intervention is necessary, as the concept of sensitivity is 'too abstract and too coarse to capture the subtle nuances of parental behavior' (p.1813). In addition, the timing of the intervention is important: 'By intervening at that point in development when mothers lose confidence in their mothering, it is possible to prevent negative cycles of interaction to develop' (p.1813).

Benoit et al. (2001) 'Atypical maternal behavior toward feeding-disordered infants before and after intervention'

The objective of this study was to determine whether inappropriate caregiver behaviours measured by the AMBIANCE (Atypical Maternal Behavior Instrument for Assessment and Classification) (described in Chapter 9) would decline as a result of intervention. The behaviours comprise the following: (a) affective communication errors, (b) role/boundary confusion (role reversal), (c) frightened/disoriented behaviour, (d) intrusiveness/negativity and (e) withdrawal.

The effects of two interventions were compared.

Play-focused intervention (modified Interaction Guidance)

A modification of Interaction Guidance (McDonough 2000) was used. Interaction Guidance is an intervention designed to reach families that have been difficult to engage, are burdened by social adversity such as poverty, have a 'limited capacity for introspection' and have 'resisted previous offers of help using more traditional psychotherapeutic methods' (p.617). The modification involved the inclusion of an individually tailored educational component such as information about regulatory difficulties in the infant.

Mothers and infants attended five consecutive weekly sessions lasting 90 minutes, each session involving approximately 15 minutes of videotaped interaction, followed by 75 minutes of discussion, education and feedback.

Feeding-focused intervention (behaviour modification)

Infants and their primary feeders attended seven consecutive weekly sessions lasting 90 minutes, each session involving 'training on behavioral techniques to eliminate specific problem behaviors in a predetermined sequence' (p.618).

Sample

The play-focused group comprised 14 mother–infant dyads (one pair was later excluded) referred to an infant psychiatry clinic for assessment of feeding difficulties. The mean age of the infants was 18.2 months. These 14 pairs were matched with a comparison group, which comprised of some participants in another, randomised-controlled trial regarding tube-fed infants (mean age 12.5 months). The comparison participants where parents randomised to receive the brief feeding-focused intervention in this trial were included.

Procedure

Atypical maternal behaviour during a five-minute play interaction was coded using the AMBIANCE pre- and post-intervention for both groups.

Results

A significant decrease in atypical maternal behaviours was found in the play-focused group from pre- to post-intervention ($p<0.01$), whereas atypical behaviours in the feeding-focused remained stable ($p<0.75$).

A significant decrease in level of disrupted communication was found from pre- to post-intervention in the play-focused group ($p<0.002$) but not the feeding-focused group ($p<0.21$). Post-intervention, mothers in the play-focused group were more likely to be classified 'nondisrupted' than mothers in the feeding-focused group ($p<0.05$).

In conclusion, the authors say that, whilst the present data is suggestive rather than conclusive, the results provide preliminary evidence for the efficacy of Interaction Guidance and indicate that sensitivity-focused interventions may also reduce disrupted behaviours which may contribute to disorganised infant attachment.

The following two studies were not included in the meta-analyses reviewed above because they concerned the parents of older, preschool children.

Toth et al. (2002) 'The relative efficacy of two interventions in altering maltreated preschool children's representational models: implications for attachment theory'

This study concerns an evaluation of two developmentally informed 'preventive' interventions for maltreated preschool children and their mothers. The interventions were designed to modify children's internal representations of self and self in relation to other and were evaluated using a Story Stem task. Treatment occurred over a period of approximately 12 months.

The interventions are described as based on 'competing' models. One model involves psychoeducational interventions, the aim of which is to teach positive parenting. In the other model, interventions focus on the processing of maternal attachment history as it affects the parent–child relationship. This study was designed to test which of these approaches is more effective in promoting good outcomes for the child.

Intervention models

PRESCHOOL PARENT PSYCHOTHERAPY (PPP)

This model 'highlights the importance of parent–child attachment in fostering positive child development, improved parent–child interaction, and decreases in child maltreatment' (pp.882–883). Mothers and their preschool-age children were seen for weekly 60-minute sessions with a clinical therapist, the majority of which were clinic-based. 'In the language of attachment theory, PPP is designed to provide the mother with a corrective emotional experience in the context of the relationship with the therapist' (p.891). The therapist provides a holding environment for the mother and child in which new experiences of self in relation to others and to the child may be internalised.

The therapist 'strives to alter the relationship between mother and child', which requires that the therapist 'attend to both the interactional and the representational level' (p.891). Through observation and empathy, the mother is assisted in recognising how her representations are enacted in her interactions with her child. The authors emphasise that PPP therapists do not 'model appropriate mother–child interactions or seek to modify parenting behavior or verbalizations through didactic instruction' (p.891). Instead, they strive to link maternal conceptualisations of relationships to mothers' childhood caregiving experiences.

PSYCHOEDUCATIONAL HOME VISITATION (PHV)

Mothers participated in 60-minute sessions (mostly home-based) with clinical therapists. An initial goal of this intervention was to conduct a comprehensive risk assessment of risk and protective factors operating in the family. To this end, therapists were trained in the provision of a model 'that strove to address how factors at different levels of proximity to the family (e.g. behavioral, psychological, sociological, and/or economic) interact to form a system of influences on functioning' (p.892). The implementation of change used a combination of social support, psychoeducational strategies and cognitive behavioural techniques. In general, the sessions focused on parent education regarding child development and developmentally appropriate parenting skills, along with the development of adequate maternal self-care skills. 'Therapeutic sessions were grounded in the present and were didactic in nature, providing mothers with specific information, facts, procedures, and practices' (p.892).

In addition to parent services, children in this intervention group were enrolled in a ten-month, full-day preschool programme where they were taught school readiness and adaptive peer relationship skills.

COMMUNITY STANDARD (CS)

The CS group was a comparison group receiving standard services and resources available through the Department of Social Services (DSS). Variability in services received during the treatment period was found; 60 per cent of the children were in full- or part-time day-care, 50 per cent were enrolled in a preschool programme and approximately 13 per cent of the children participated in individual psychotherapy. Services received by some mothers included individual psychotherapy, counselling, parenting services and practical assistance such as obtaining food or shelter.

Sample

The sample comprised 122 mothers and their preschool children. Eighty-seven of the families had a documented history of maltreatment. Maltreating families were randomly assigned to the interventions groups. The PPP group comprised 23 families, the PHV group comprised 34 families and the CS group comprised 30 families. In addition, 35 non-maltreating families (NC) served as comparisons.

Measures

Eleven Story Stems were selected from the MacArthur Story Stem Battery (Bretherton *et al.* 1990b) (described in Chapter 8) and the Attachment Story Completion Task (Bretherton *et al.* 1990a). All the children were administered the set of Story Stems before (at baseline) and after the intervention.

The codings of maternal representations from the children's narratives included positive mother, negative mother, controlling mother, incongruent mother and disciplining mother. Codes were combined to create two composite variables, namely adaptive maternal representations and maladaptive maternal representations.

The children's representational codes of self included positive self, negative self and false self.

In addition, a modified version of a global relationship expectation scale was used to capture the children's expectations of the mother–child relationship.

An abbreviated version of the WPPSI-R was used to assess the children's intelligence.

Results

Adaptive maternal representation scores increased significantly from baseline to post-intervention across the four study conditions and maladaptive maternal representations significantly decreased. Children's levels of positive self-representations increased significantly over time across the four conditions, while negative and false self-representation scores remained stable. In addition, mother–child expectation scores significantly increased across the four study conditions.

In paired-samples t test analysis, a highly significant post-intervention decrease in maladaptive maternal representations was found in the PPP intervention group ($p<0.001$). A marginally significant post-intervention decease in maladaptive maternal representations was found in the PHV group ($p<0.079$). No significant post-intervention differences in maladaptive maternal representation scores were found in paired t tests in the CS and NC conditions.

In paired t tests a considerable decline was found in children's post-intervention negative self-representations ($p<0.001$) in the PPP intervention condition, whereas children in the PHV, CS and NC groups showed no significant change. However, *t* tests found a significant post-intervention increase in the children's positive self-representations in the PPP, CS and NC groups ($p<0.001$ in all three cases), whereas only a marginal increase was found in the PHV children ($p<0.10$).

The authors conclude: 'These results suggest that an attachment-theory informed model of intervention (PPP) is more effective at improving representations of self and of caregivers than is a didactic model of intervention directed at parenting skills' (p.877).

Marvin et al. (2002) 'The Circle of Security project: attachment-based intervention with caregiver–preschool dyads'

The Circle of Security study also concerns a theory-based intervention and is included because of its importance, despite the evaluation still being in progress.

The Circle of Security is depicted as a circle around which the child moves *away from* the secure base provided by the caregiver in order to explore, and back to the safe haven provided by the caregiver when feeling threatened or needing comfort. The secure base and safe haven are drawn as a safe pair of hands. The child's needs are summarised as requiring supporting exploration, watching over, helping and experiencing enjoyment with the child, welcoming the child's return, protecting, comforting and delighting in the child and organising the child's feelings.

The authors point out that certain needs on the Circle of Security can activate painful feeling states in caregivers that lead to 'an internal warning or sense of danger' (p.109). This may cause the caregiver to move into a defensive strategy by *miscuing* the child about the child's need. Over time, the authors state, the caregiver's miscuing defensive strategy triggers a sense of danger in the child, leading the child also to miscue. This sets up a self-perpetuating feed-back loop 'in which both the child and the parent avoid the need by miscuing each other' (p.109).

During the intervention, caregivers learn that all parents experience signals perceived as especially dangerous to themselves when the child's need requires the parent to step out of their defensive strategy. The parent also learns that this defensive strategy is linked to her own childhood experiences of caregiving. In the intervention, video clips of a tranquil scene accompanied by soft music and then a modified version of the 'Jaws' soundtrack are used. This leads to an understanding of how much subjective experience can affect their feelings about their child's needs.

Specific treatment protocols are assigned to particular patterns or strategies of attachment–caregiving interactions and internal working models. Four distinct dyadic patterns (with sub-patterns) have been identified:

1. *The secure (child)-autonomous (parent) pattern*: both partners easily approach and interact when the child is distressed.

2. *The insecure, avoidant-dismissing pattern*: both partners tend to minimise intimate attachment–caregiving interactions, often through a defensive focus on exploration. They therefore feel least comfortable when the child's attachment behaviour is activated.

3. *The insecure, ambivalent-preoccupied pattern*: both partners tend to minimise the child's exploration, focusing instead on attachment–caregiving interactions and the child's over-dependence. They therefore feel least comfortable when the child's exploratory behaviour is activated.

4. *Insecure, 'disordered' (disorganised or insecure-other) patterns*: the parents' 'heightened fear of and/or anger towards the child's attachment behaviour leads to disorganization and/or abdication of the executive caregiving role' (p.113). This caregiver pattern appears to be related to lack of resolution of parental early or ongoing trauma.

Assessment

Child–caregiver dyads are assessed before intervention and within ten days of the completion of the 20-week intervention. The assessment comprises:

-   infant or preschool version of Ainsworth's strange situation (Ainsworth *et al.* 1978; Cassidy, Marvin and the MacArthur Working Group 1992)

-   observation of caregiver and child in reading and tidying task

-   the Circle of Security Interview with the caregiver: the interview lasts one hour, is videotaped and consists of questions about the child, selected questions from the Parent Development Interview (Aber *et al.* 1989) and selected questions from the Adult Attachment Interview (George *et al.* 1984)

-   caregiver-completed questionnaires regarding child behaviour problems, anxiety and depression, parenting stress and stressful life events.

Classification

The child's attachment pattern is coded according to Ainsworth's classification for infants (described in Chapter 3) or the Preschool Attachment Classification System (also described in Chapter 8).

The parent's caregiving is classified using the Caregiver Behavior Classification System (described in Chapter 9).

Intervention

Individualised intervention goals are developed on the basis of the classifications, ratings and clinical observations. The authors give the following example of usual intervention goals for dismissing caregivers: 'increased appreciation of how much their children need them; increased skill at reading and registering their children's subtle distress signals; and decreased miscuing under circumstances in which a child's attachment behavior is activated' (p.115). Caregivers usually have individualised goals within this set of shared goals.

The intervention takes place in small groups of five or six caregivers and is videotaped. The intervention protocol sets out a programme for the intervention across the 20 weeks. This consists mainly of different phases of theory-building and tape reviews of the strange situation, including selected vignettes of parent–child dyads.

The authors report that preliminary results of data analysis of 75 dyads that have completed the protocol suggest a significant shift from disordered to ordered child attachment patterns (55 per cent to 20 per cent), an increase in the number of children classified as secure (32 per cent to 40 per cent), and a decrease in the number of caregivers classified as disordered (60 per cent to 15 per cent). Further results are anticipated.

Summary

Several studies have shown the efficacy of interventions which focus on the caregiver–child interaction, in particular focusing on caregiver sensitivity and therefore behaviour towards the child, in improving the security of attachment of young children to their caregivers. This has included both preventive work with high-risk groups and a reactive therapeutic response to dyads where significant difficulties have already emerged.

Notes

1   Centre for Child and Family Studies and Data Theory at Leiden University, the Netherlands. For more than ten years the Centre for Child and Family Studies at Leiden University has been carrying out research concerning attachment theory and attachment-based interventions. This body of research includes an impressive number of meta-analyses. The Centre's research is concentrated into three main areas, attachment studies, theory and methods, and data theory. Themes in the attachment studies area include adoption, psychopathology and intervention. Much of this work is listed and summarised on the Centre's website at: www.childandfamilystudies.leidenuniv.nl/ index.php3?c=92.

2   The authors explain that Cohen defined d as the difference between the means divided by standard deviation of either group (Cohen 1988). By convention a positive effect size represents improvement and a negative effect size represents deterioration or an effect opposite to the predicted direction. Very broadly, an effect size of $d=0.2$ is viewed as a small effect, an effect size of $d=0.5$ is viewed as a medium effect and an effect size of $d=0.8$ is viewed as a large effect, although these boundaries should not be treated rigidly.

3   This finding is contradicted in a recent study (Juffer, Bakermans-Kranenburg and van IJzendoorn 2005) in which the authors report that their short-term preventive programme with video feedback and a book lowered the rate of disorganised attachment.

4   'The ideal intervention study emerges as a randomized design with a dummy-treated control group and a pretest to detect and compensate for possible randomization failures. The intervention should be carefully described in a protocol, and implementation and evaluation of the intervention should be independent' (pp.211–212).

5   Based on Cohen *et al.* (1999), p.442.

17 Evidence-based Interventions: Change of Caregiver

Change in caregiver can only be contemplated if there is near certainty that it is not possible to enhance the original caregiver's sensitivity sufficiently to meet the child's needs, within the timescale of the child. As O'Connor and Zeanah state, 'there is no intervention more radical than adoption' (2003, p.225).

The review of studies by Rushton and Mayes presents evidence from a number of studies concerning the efficacy of a change in caregiver.

Rushton and Mayes (1997) 'Forming fresh attachments in childhood: a research update'

In this paper, Rushton and Mayes review research concerning the development of the relationship between older, later-placed maltreated children and their new parents. In their introduction, the authors caution against the overuse of the diagnosis of reactive attachment disorder in explaining the difficulties of these children. 'However, we need to be careful that a wide range of adjustment difficulties are not carelessly ascribed to the attachment process when they could be the result of numerous other experiences and adversities' (p.121). The authors point out that they found no published studies of older children where attachment was assessed directly through interviews, observation or testing of the child. Thus, all the studies reviewed examined attachment through indirect assessment.

Ten studies were reviewed. From the early 1970s to the mid-1980s only four follow-up studies examined attachment relationships. All reported high rates of successful adoption as indicated by (1) a high rate of parental satisfaction (78%) in a study of 91 children in Wisconsin, (2) a high rate of having had a close emotional relationship with adoptive parents in childhood (86%), as retrospectively reported by adopted adults who had been 'hard to place' older children, (3) high rates of report by mothers that their adopted children were 'deeply attached' to them (81 per cent at age 16 years), and (4) a high rate of intact placement at four years after placement (97%) among a sample of 257 'special needs' adopted children in the United States who were all at least 8 years old at the time of placement. In the latter two studies difficulties with peer relationships were also reported.

Rushton and Mayes point to a number of methodological weaknesses in these studies, but nevertheless conclude that they provide important evidence 'to legitimate the policy of placing children in families even late in childhood' (p.123). However, whilst emphasising that these studies provide evidence that children *can* form fresh attachments, because the samples were all based on surviving placements, they do not indicate failures of attachment and whether such a factor might be associated with placement breakdown.

Moving on to 'the next decade of evidence' (p.123), Rushton and Mayes review a 1988 study in which 63 late-placed children whose placements were stable four years later were compared with 57 children whose placement had disrupted. Using a 13-item 'Attachment Rating Scale', which was completed by parents, the study assessed changes in attachment behaviour during the placement. The study found a significant association between an increase in attachment behaviours during the placement and placement stability. A number of attachment behaviours were identified which were significantly associated with disruption. 'These included: a lack of spontaneous affection; an inability to be comforted when hurt; an insatiable need for attention; and a lack of care or preference for their parents' (p.123).

In a study which compared 13 children who were placed in foster care with 19 children who returned home, it was found that two years later, although nine of the foster parents reported a good relationship with the child, half of the children were primarily attached to their birth parents and wished to return home. Only three of the children who had returned home had a good relationship with their parents.

In a four-year follow-up study of 71 families in Iowa, 'attachment difficulties' were found to be present for 10 per cent of the children. However, Rushton and Mayes point to a number of methodological limitations in this study, not least a 75 per cent rate of attrition by the end of the fourth year.

In a sample of 120 adoptive parents who were interviewed when the children had reached early adulthood, 93 per cent reported a positive parent–child relationship, although the figure during adolescence was 75 per cent. The quality of the parent–child relationship in adolescence was reported to be associated with the quality of parenting in infancy.

Finally, Rushton and Mayes report two of their own studies. In the first, in a sample of 18 boys, most had developed 'genuinely affectionate' relationships with their parents eight years after placement, although three placements disrupted in early adolescence, with attachment issues and physical aggression. In a later study of 61 late-placed children, 73 per cent had shown the ability to make a satisfactory relationship with a parent by the end of the first year in placement.

Rushton and Mayes conclude with an expression of concern that poorly presented articles may give the impression that difficulties occur in most late-placed maltreated children and that the majority do not respond to a positive change in caregiving. Accumulating evidence indicates that this is not the case.

One important aspect of the success for the child of a change in caregiver is the new caregiver's sensitivity to the child. The following two studies examine determinants of the new parents' capacity to relate sensitively and appropriately to the child.

Dozier et al. (2001) 'Attachment for infants in foster care: the role of caregiver state of mind'

This research investigated the concordance between foster mothers' attachment state of mind and foster infants' attachment quality. Three possibilities were explored:

1. After a period of consolidation, foster infants organise their attachments around the availability of the new caregivers.

2. Earlier caregiving experiences and discontinuities in care may eclipse current caregiver characteristics.

3. There is some concordance between foster mother state of mind and infant attachment when children are placed into care before approximately one year of age.

The sample comprised 50 foster-infant–mother dyads. The infants had been placed with their caregivers between birth and 20 months; the mean age at placement was 7.7 months. The foster mothers completed the Adult Attachment Interview (AAI). The foster infants and foster mothers participated in the strange situation procedure between ages 12 and 24 months. The foster children had been in placement at least three months.

Analysing the data in a variety of ways, the researchers found the following. In a two-way analysis of concordance between foster mother state of mind and foster infant attachment in which each variable was treated dichotomously (autonomous/non-autonomous state of mind and secure/insecure attachment) and unresolved mothers with a secondary autonomous classification were included in the autonomous group, a match or concordance of 72 per cent ($p<0.01$) was found. Repeating this analysis with unresolved/autonomous mothers included in the non-autonomous group, the finding was 68 per cent concordance, which remained significant ($p<0.05$).

In a four-way analysis of concordance between foster mother state of mind (autonomous; dismissing; preoccupied; unresolved/non-autonomous) and infant attachment (secure; avoidant; resistant; disorganised) the finding was 56 per cent ($p<0.05$) when unresolved/autonomous mothers were included in the autonomous group, and 52 per cent ($p<0.05$) when they were included in the non-autonomous group.

With regard to disorganised attachment, 21 per cent of foster mothers with autonomous states on mind had children with disorganised attachments, whereas 62.5 per cent of non-autonomous foster mothers had disorganised children. This difference was significant ($p<0.01$). Age at placement was not associated with infant attachment.

In their discussion, the authors describe these results as striking. The attachment security of foster infants was concordant with foster mothers' state of mind 'at levels similar to that seen among biologically intact dyads' (the authors having compared their levels of concordance with those found in van IJzendoorn's 1995 meta-analysis of children with their biological parents). The study's findings have important implications, both for practice and for theory.

> These results suggest that when placed in the first year and a half of life, foster children can organise their attachment behaviours around the availability of their new caregivers. When placed later than birth, most children in our sample had been exposed to neglect, and some to abuse, as well as up to five changes in caregivers. Nonetheless, when placed with autonomous caregivers, these children often formed secure attachments. (p.1474)

Moreover,

> This study's findings provide compelling evidence that it is maternal characteristics, rather than shared temperament or other genetically linked characteristics, that primarily determine children's attachment strategies. (p.1474)

Steele et al. (2003a) 'Attachment representations and adoption: associations between maternal states of mind and emotion narratives in previously maltreated children'

This study investigated the influence of the adoptive mother's state of mind on the attachments, as expressed in narrative story-completions, of a sample of older adopted and previously maltreated children.

The sample comprised 43 adoptive mothers of 61 children. The children's ages ranged from 4 to 8 years (mean=6 years). All the children had suffered serious adversity. The number of prior placements experienced by the children ranged from 2 to 18.

Maternal states of mind were assessed using the Adult Attachment Interview (AAI). The children's expectations and perceptions of family roles, attachments and relationships were assessed using the Story Stem Assessment Profile and coding system.

The AAI classification of the 43 mothers was as follows:

autonomous-secure   71%

insecure-dismissing   23%

insecure-preoccupied   5%

Of the 43 interviews, 21 per cent were assessed as unresolved regarding past loss or trauma.

Quantitative results are presented regarding those themes in the children's Story Stem completions which were most indicative of placement with an adoptive mother whose AAI was (1) autonomous-secure as opposed to insecure and (2) unresolved with regard to past loss or trauma. Additionally, excerpts from interviews with mothers and their children's story completions are presented.

1. The themes in the children's story completions which were associated with insecure (dismissing or preoccupied) AAI ratings were: catastrophic fantasies, child aggression, adult aggression, throwing out or throwing away, bizarre or atypical content, child injured or dead and adult injured or dead. These seven themes were highly correlated with one another and the items were thus summed to create a single composite 'aggressiveness' score.

    The composite 'aggressiveness' score correlated significantly with AAI ratings of mothers' inability to recall childhood and mothers' derogation of their own fathers. Child aggressiveness was also negatively correlated with high AAI scores indicative of an 'autonomous-secure' pattern. Thus, 'mothers who were truthful, relevant, and thoughtful when discussing their attachment histories tended to have children who tended not to use aggression as a theme to resolve the conflict inherent in the story-completion task' (p.193).

2.   The themes in the children's story completions associated with mothers' AAI ratings of lack of resolution of past loss or trauma were: higher scores for 'parent appearing child-like', adult aggression and 'throwing out or throwing away', and lower scores for realistic mastery and 'sibling or peer helps'. Further analyses suggested the following:

(a)   unresolved mourning in a parent may exacerbate the emotional worries of a recently adopted child

(b)   children of adoptive mothers with unresolved loss or trauma appear less able to use an organised strategy in dealing with conflict in the story

(c)   children placed with 'unresolved' (or insecure) mothers were not significantly different with respect to past adversity. Indeed, there was a trend that children so placed were the least damaged in the overall group.

In their discussion, the authors consider the 'somewhat surprising' finding that, given the adverse histories of the children, within three months of placement the adopter's state of mind with regard to attachment showed significant influences on the child. They point out that children who have experienced abuse and/or neglect may have different kinds of representations of caregiving. These may be the result of the experience of caregiving responses that are at times nurturing and at other times abusive, either in the same caregiver or in successive caregivers. One of the possible costs of such multiple, contradictory representations in the child is the child's 'hyper-vigilance to the state of mind of the caregiver' (p.200). The present study found that unresolved parents 'carry a state of mind which conveys a lack of organisation around the topic of loss' (p.201). Thus, both the children and the unresolved parents are vulnerable. When the vulnerability in the children is met by that in the unresolved parents, the vulnerability in both is heightened.

The authors point out that the majority of these very difficult placements survived after two years. Furthermore, 'there is no long queue of absolutely optimal adults willing to take on the challenges of adopting a "hard to place" child' (p.202). Moreover, some children might not be best placed with a secure, reflective adult who may perhaps need 'a certain measure of reciprocity of positive interactions' (p.202). Adults, who defensively keep at a distance negative aspects of their own childhood and view only the positive, might serve some children quite well.

The authors conclude that the present study may be helpful in targeting the currently promised support for adopters in a more strategic way.

The following study provides evidence of some positive changes in children's representations, behaviour and adjustment one and two years after placement for adoption.

Hodges et al. Changes in attachment representations over the first year (Hodges et al. 2003b) and second year (Hodges et al. 2005) of adoptive placement: narratives of maltreated children

(The Hodges *et al.* 2003b article and Hodges *et al.* 2005 chapter are companion papers to the Steele *et al.* 2003a study, described above.)

The 2003 paper reports on the children's development in relation to the adoptive parents' attachment organisation and the child's history of maltreatment.

Two groups of children were studied. A late-placed group comprised 33 children in 25 families. The mean age at placement was 6.08 years and the mean length of time in placement at the Year 1 assessment was 4.2 months. The mean number of placements prior to adoption was 5.3. Most children had suffered multiple forms of abuse. The second group comprised 31 children who were adopted in infancy. The mean age at placement was 3.73 months. The mean age at Year 1 assessment was 5.75 years. These children had not experienced the abuse or discontinuities of care suffered by the late-placed children.

As soon as possible after placement, the Story Stem Assessment Profile and other assessments were carried out with the child. At the same time, the parents were interviewed and other data were collected. This assessment was repeated one and two years later (findings from the second follow-up are reported below). The mean score for each theme was calculated.

The authors report findings for each narrative theme regarding differences in the children's mental representations between the infancy adopted and later-adopted groups, and differences between the Year 1 and Year 2 assessments of the late-adopted children.

With regard to 'engagement versus avoidance manoeuvres' in the story completion task, late-placed children were considerably more likely to avoid the task than the infancy-placed children. By Year 2 the late-placed children's scores had decreased and there were no significant difference between the groups.

With regard to 'disorganisation within narrative', the late-placed group showed significantly more 'catastrophic fantasy' and 'bizarre/atypical responses' than the infancy-placed group and this did not significantly change at Year 2.

The late-placed children showed significantly more extreme aggression than the infancy-placed children. Again this had not decreased in the late-placed group at Year 2.

With regard to 'representation of parents/adults', a comparison between the groups at Year 1 across the eight rating categories found that the later-adopted group showed many more negative representations of parents and parent–child relationships. Thus, the infancy-placed children had significantly higher scores on 'adult helps' and 'adult affectionate' and the late-placed children had significantly higher scores on 'adult aggressive', 'adult rejects' and 'adult unaware'.

With regard to the six rating categories of 'representation of child', the infancy-placed children scored significantly higher on 'child helps sibling/peer' and 'realistic mastery' (in coping) at Year 1 than the late-placed children. The late-placed children's scores on both these items had significantly increased at Year 2.

Finally, with regard to 'positive adaptation', the late-adopted children scored lower on 'magic/omnipotence' ('story resolution by a wishful modification of reality' (p.367)) than at Year 1.

The authors conclude that the assessments of the later-adopted children at the two time points showed some positive changes, 'though it was clear that the children's internal working models of attachment relationships were far from transformed' (p.360). They offer three possible interpretations of the findings. First, the antecedent of inconsistent maltreating parental behaviour may lead to a representation in the child's internal working model that parents are not to be trusted and may 'turn' aggressive and rejecting. Such a model, the authors state, 'would be very resistant to disconfirmation' (p.360). Second, the children may avoid 'laying themselves open' to further experiences of rejection. This 'robs the new parents of the opportunity to respond in a different way' (p.360) and robs the child of the opportunity of happier experiences of caregiving. A third possibility is that some aspects of the new parent's behaviour will be perceived 'through the lens' of the child's internal model, and therefore viewed or inter-preted by the child as abusive or rejecting, thereby confirming the model.

In Hodges *et al.* (2005) the authors include findings regarding the progress of the children after two years in their adoptive families. They report that 'it was clear that the consolidation of positive aspects was continuing but that there was considerable stability in various negative representations' (p.109). There was an increase in the overall score which combined ratings indicating security, for both the early and late-placed groups. Insecurity, however, remained almost unchanged. The authors explain this apparent contradiction by pointing out that, although the children who had experienced early adversity became increasingly secure as they settled into adoptive families, 'other possibilities and experiences remained part of their mental representations' (p.111). Moreover, although the children in the maltreated group were progressing, they had not 'made up the gap' with the non-maltreated children.

Hodges *et al.* conclude that the study suggests that children develop new, positive representations in competition with the existing negative representa-tions. 'The old expectations and perceptions remain as vulnerabilities in that they can easily be triggered by events and interactions that seem to confirm their validity' (p.115). This has important implications for adopters and those seeking to help them. 'Adopters can be helped by having, as it were, a preview of the script that the child's behaviour is using and the roles that they are being allotted within it' (p.115). This may allow them to disconfirm the child's under-lying negative expectation.

Summary

The studies reported here indicate that even relatively late placement with new, permanent caregivers is a powerful and effective intervention for children who have experienced significant maltreatment in their earlier years. The child's attachment behaviour pattern and representation show a significant association with the state of mind in respect of attachment of the new primary caregivers. While there is an increase in attachment security in the children, insecure and disorganised representations persist alongside.

These findings point towards the need for ongoing support and guidance for adoptive and other permanent alternative caregivers, both in understanding the children's continuing difficulties based on their enduring internal represen-tations of attachment and sensitively modulating their responses to the children.

18 Interventions with No Evidence Base

Direct intervention with the child

There are no reports of systematically evaluated, direct interventions with the child, which are based on attachment theory. Based on the theory and understanding of attachment disorders, children with attachment disorders and insecure/disorganised attachments show difficulties in their social interactions which have often become extended beyond the relationship with their primary caregivers. These children's internal working models will have come to skew their views and expectations of others and determine the children's consequent maladaptive social responses. On theoretical grounds there is, therefore, a place for direct therapeutic work with the child in which these internal working models can be explored. This would not, however, address attachment formation or attachment relationships.

Hughes (2004) presents 'An attachment-based treatment of maltreated children and young people' (p.263). He describes the therapist's attunement to the child, which is followed by the therapist 'co-regulating' the child's affective states, 'co-constructing' meanings for the child's experiences and, together with the child, constructing a narrative of the child's experiences. Hughes considers favourably having the child's primary caregiver actively present in the therapy, providing that if this caregiver was the maltreating parent, they have taken responsibility for the maltreatment. As Trowell (2004) comments, Hughes is clearly a very experienced and sensitive clinician. However, the therapy remains unevaluated and is not sufficiently systematised to be applied in an intervention trial. Moreover, while Hughes refers to and describes aspects of attachment theory, there is little application of the theory during the therapy, which reads like good therapeutic work with children who have been abused and neglected.

261

Brisch (2002), in his book entitled *Treating Attachment Disorders*, outlines and provides clinical examples of therapy in a number of constellations, which he includes under the term 'attachment disorder'. The case studies describe good outcomes and are of clinical interest.

Impaired selectivity

As has been described in Chapter 14, impaired selectivity (disinhibition) appears to persist in some children despite placement in well-functioning and caring families, where the parenting which the children have received over many years is sensitive and good. There have been no reports of specific or effective treatment for this difficulty.

Clinical experience would indicate that the most likely effective intervention consists of a combination of limiting the number of caregivers for the child, at least on initial placement, careful monitoring of the child's movements and a cognitive behavioural approach in which the child is reminded and 'trained' in becoming aware of who is familiar and unfamiliar and helped to 'remember' to beware of unfamiliar persons.

'Attachment therapy'

'Attachment therapy' is a very different approach which is being offered by a number of centres who identify or 'diagnose' attachment disorders in the loose way described in Chapter 12. This approach appears to be a response to the desperation of (mainly) alternative caregivers of some very troubled and troubling children who had previously been seriously maltreated. These therapies are not based on an accepted version of attachment theory and there is no objective evaluation of them. Under the overall heading of attachment therapy, a variety of different treatment approaches are offered. These include work directed at parents' interactions with the children, such as behaviour management, life-story work and work on the meanings of the child's experiences, and some approaches are directed at the child and may or may not include the child's current primary carer.

Attachment therapy often, however, also includes some other interventions including a number of variants of holding, e.g. holding time (Welch 1988) and therapeutic holding (Howe and Fearnley 2003), as well as others such as rage-reduction therapy (Cline 1991) and rebirthing. Mercer *et al.* (2003) and the Report of the APSAC Task Force on Attachment Therapy, Reactive Attachment Disorder, and Attachment Problems (Chaffin *et al.* 2006) describe both the entirely unevaluated nature of these therapies and the fact that some child deaths have occurred in the course of these treatments in the USA.

Speltz (2002), in a paper written for the American Professional Society on the Abuse of Children (APSAC),[1] traces the history of attachment therapy. A similar account is presented in Mercer, Sarner and Rosa (2003), *Attachment Therapy on Trial: The Torture and Death of Candace Newmaker*. Speltz points out that holding therapy has its roots in the controversial techniques developed by Robert Zaslow in the 1970s (Zaslow and Menta 1975)[2] for individuals with autism. Mercer *et al.* (2003) explain that Zaslow considered attachment as

> an involuntary emotional response to the face and eyes of another person, occurring when the face was presented under the proper circumstances. These circumstances involved experiences of pain, fear, and rage, following which relief was associated with the experience of eye contact. If an infant did not experience this cycle of events, Zaslow thought, he or she would not form an attachment, would not make eye contact with other people, and would show symptoms of autism rather than normal emotional and intellectual development. (p.75)

Abused children would have experienced pain and rage, without relief.

> However, Zaslow thought, a technique of creating pain and rage and combining them with eye contact could cause attachment to occur, even if the individual was long past the period of life when attachment normally happens. (p.75)

There is no empirical evidence to support Zaslow's theory. The concept of suppressed rage has, nevertheless, continued to be a central focus explaining the children's behaviour (Cline 1991).

In the *Handbook of Attachment Interventions* (Levy 2000), Levy and Orlans (p.252) describe the Holding Nurturing Process (HNP) thus:

> The primary goal of this intervention is to enhance trust, safety, and emotional connection by facilitating a positive completion of the first-year attachment cycle. For example, the child expresses anger and frustration while maintaining eye contact and safe physical containment with an empathic parent.

This volume is replete with authoritative explanation and advice but contains no accounts of objectively evaluated outcomes of attachment therapy. Interestingly, Zaslow is not referenced.

The practice of holding therapy is not confined to the USA. For example, the website of the Keys Attachment Centre in the UK describes 'therapeutic holding' in its Treatment Protocol for Children and Young People with Serious

Attachment and Trauma Difficulties (Keys Attachment Centre undated). The child lies with his head on the lap of the lead therapist, his right arm behind the therapist's back and his legs across the co-therapist's knees. The child's vulnerability is acknowledged. The child's head is held in such a way as to keep his eyes focused on the therapist. The likely physical and emotional discomfort which this may cause the child is acknowledged.

'At times', the document states, 'the child/young person will yell whilst being held in therapy, "Let me go, you're hurting me"' (p.5). This response, it is suggested, 'may be a strategy to gain release, or an experience of psychological pain that is somatised, or a function of anxiety over being held whilst unable to gain release' (p.5). The therapist will always make sure that the child is not being physically hurt or in physical pain. Assured that the child is physically safe, the therapist will empathetically respond that the child or young person is safe and that 'the sense of pain represents their anxieties, distress and/or psychological pain, deep rooted in their past' (p.5).

This approach is in theoretical contradiction to attachment theory as formulated by Bowlby, whose central message concerning therapy was that the therapist should provide a secure (i.e. not frightening) base. It is, however, consistent with Zaslow, although Zaslow is not referenced or mentioned.

It is sometimes written that holding therapy does not involve restraint. For example, Howe and Fearnley (2003) write, 'Therapeutic holding (but not restraint) seeks to reproduce a meaningful, intense, fully open relationship with the angry but hurt child' (p.381). They distinguish restraint as being 'reactive', occurring when someone seeks to control an aggressive or threatening child, whereas holding is 'consensual', that is entered into with the consent of the child. Others may not share this definition. Indeed, the description used in the account of holding therapy above, 'being held whilst unable to gain release', would seem to many an appropriate definition of restraint. Myeroff, Mertlich and Gross (1999), discussed below, in their account of holding therapy, describe the child's position across the therapist's lap as allowing for 'close proximity, eye contact, and physical restriction' (p.307). Elsewhere they describe that 'when the child becomes activated with anger or despair' the parent or therapist 'continues to contain the child physically' (p.304).

Only one published study which purports to be an evaluation of holding therapy has been found (Myeroff et al. 1999). In this study the comparison sample was inadequate (families who contacted the Attachment Center at Evergreen, Colorado, but did not attend), the children were not randomly assigned to treatment conditions, and the pre- and post-treatment assessment of the children depended on a questionnaire (the Child Behavior Checklist) completed by mothers.

This paper clearly illustrates the leap proponents of holding therapy make from Bowlby's theory to their advocated treatment. The authors write, 'Based on attachment theory holding therapy in part attempts to repair the postulated disruption that occurred in the formative years between the infant and primary caregiver' (p.304) (Bowlby 1980 and Egeland and Sroufe 1981 referenced). Four sentences later, explaining that holding therapy creates a representation of a 'healthy attachment cycle' for the child (now referencing Levy and Orlans 1995; Myeroff 1997), the authors continue, 'This occurs in the treatment by modeling the healthy attachment cycle in which the child will receive positive input from the therapist and care giver by way of eye contact, physical holding, and cognitive restructuring' (p.304). The theoretical basis for this latter statement is that of Zaslow, not Bowlby.

There are many ways in which 'holding therapy/attachment therapy' contradicts Bowlby's attachment theory, not least attachment theory's fundamental and evidence-based statement that security is promoted by sensitivity. Moreover, Bowlby (1988) explicitly rejected the notion of regression, which is key to the holding therapy approach:

> present knowledge of infant and child development requires that a theory of developmental pathways should replace theories that invoke specific phases of development in which it is held a person may become fixated and/or to which he may regress. (p.120)

In the practice parameter for the assessment and treatment of children and adolescents with reactive attachment disorder of infancy and early childhood (AACAP 2005) 'Interventions designed to enhance attachment that involve noncontingent physical restraint or coercion' (p.1216), including 'therapeutic holding' and 'rebirthing therapy', are not endorsed. The report of the APSAC Task Force on Attachment Therapy, Reactive Attachment Disorder, and Attachment Problems (Chaffin et al. 2006) similarly states:

> Treatment techniques or attachment parenting techniques involving physical coercion, psychologically or physically enforced holding, physical restraint, physical domination, provoked catharsis, ventilation of rage, age regression, humiliation, withholding or forced food or water intake, prolonged social isolation, or assuming exaggerated levels of control and domination over a child are contraindicated because of risk of harm and absence of proven benefit and should not be used. (p.86)

It is sometimes necessary and appropriate to restrain a child whose behaviour is about to damage the child, another person or objects. This is different from holding therapy.

Notes

1   Available at www.kidscomefirst.info/Speltz.pdf.

2   Attempts to obtain this publication have been unsuccessful.

19 Conclusions Regarding Interventions

Great concern needs to be expressed about the unevaluated 'attachment therapies', in particular holding therapy. These interventions are not within the attachment paradigm and are potentially abusive.

Consonant with attachment theory, the aim of intervention is to preserve or work towards secure attachment organisation and autonomous internal working models. This enables the child to move flexibly between seeking and receiving comfort and protection and free exploration, as circumstances require. There is now firm evidence indicating that a move towards security can be, and is most effectively, achieved by enhancing maternal/caregiver sensitivity, expressed by the mother's behaviour with the child. Much of this work has been directed at high-risk samples including maltreating parents. This secondary or tertiary preventive work is important in reducing later social, emotional and behavioural difficulties for the child. However, it may not be possible to reverse disorganised attachment.

The evidence indicates that greater attachment security is most effectively achieved by work which focuses on secure base and safe haven behaviours of the mother/primary caregiver, which are devoid of hostility to the child and which are not frightening.

There are now a number of attachment-based interventions with caregivers, not all of which have been evaluated as yet. The 'gold standard' method of evaluation which includes randomised, controlled trials; manualised interventions; baseline measures and assessments which are independent of and blind to the interventions; and sufficiently large sample sizes, are not easy to achieve. These interventions are, however, promising and several are described in Berlin *et al.* (2005).

Before caregivers can benefit from these interventions, some of their own risk factors, such as drug or alcohol abuse or significant mental ill-health, need to be addressed. Moreover, the troubled parents and families of maltreated children require a range of interventions which are not concerned with attachment. There is, however, little evidence that interventions not directly focused on caregiving will enhance attachment.

A move to, and work with, alternative, foster or adoptive parents which is based on attachment theory can benefit some very troubled children whose attachment pattern is already likely to be disorganised.

There is some limited theoretical basis, but no evidence, for the efficacy of individual therapy for children whose internal working models have led to a generalisation of their difficulties to other social relationships. This includes children who remain controlling even after they are no longer being cared for by maltreating caregivers. However, the evidence points to the far greater effectiveness of the actual experience of a relationship with sensitive, constant and non-abusive caregivers in bringing about changes in internal working models.

Attachment security or organisation is only one aspect of a child's functioning which is affected by neglect and abuse. As the term RAD, mis-applied to some older troubled children, indicates, they show difficulties in a number of other domains of functioning and with social relationships not within the ambit of attachment. Enhancing their attachment security through work with their caregivers cannot be expected to alleviate their other difficulties. These children require a full assessment of all aspects of their functioning including physical health and growth, behaviour or conduct, peer relationships, language and learning and emotional state, including the possibility of post traumatic stress disorder. Some of these children are likely to benefit from cognitive behavioural or psychodynamic psychotherapy (Kennedy 2004), depending on the nature of their difficulties.

There is also a need to look for and exclude attention deficit hyperactivity disorder (ADHD) and autism spectrum disorders. If found, they might explain some of the child's difficulties.

In conclusion, although secure attachment is not synonymous with child mental health, it is a very significant protective factor. Early interventions which promote secure attachments are preferable to reactive interventions, since disorganised attachment and its transformation to controlling behaviour appears to be more resistant to change. Current research is refining our understanding of the specific aspects of caregiving sensitive behaviour which is most likely to result in secure attachments.

References

AACAP (2005) 'Practice parameter for the assessment and treatment of children and adolescents with reactive attachment disorder of infancy and early childhood.' *Journal of the American Academy of Child and Adolescent Psychiatry 44*, 1206–1219.

Aber, J., Belsky, J., Slade, A. and Crnic, K. (1999) 'Stability and change in mothers' representations of their relationship with their toddlers.' *Developmental Psychology 35*, 1038–1047.

Aber, J., Slade, A., Berger, B., Bresgi, I. and Kaplan, M. (1985) *The Parent Development Interview.* Unpublished manuscript, Barnard College, Columbia University, New York.

Aber, J., Slade, A., Cohen, L. and Meyer, J. (1989) 'Parental representations of their toddlers: their relationship to parental history and sensitivity and toddler security.' Paper presented at the biennial meeting of the Society for Research in Child Development, Baltimore, MD.

Abidin, R. (1990) *Parenting Stress Index, Third Edition.* Charlottesville, VA: Pediatric Psychology Press.

Achenbach, T. (1991) *Manual for the Child Behavior Checklist/4–18 and 1991 Child Behavior Profile.* Burlington: University of Vermont, Department of Psychiatry.

Ainsworth, M. (1963) 'The development of infant–mother interaction among the Ganda.' In B. Foss (ed.) *Determinants of Infant Behavior II.* London: Methuen.

Ainsworth, N. (1964) 'Patterns of attachment behaviour shown by the infant in interaction with his mother.' *Merrill-Palmer Quarterly 10*, 51–58.

Ainsworth, M. (1967) *Infancy in Uganda: Infant Care and the Growth of Love.* Baltimore: Johns Hopkins University Press.

Ainsworth, M. (1969a) 'Object relations, dependency and attachment: a theoretical review of the infant–mother relationship.' *Child Development 40*, 969–1025.

Ainsworth, M. (1969b) *Maternal Sensitivity Scales: Revised.* Johns Hopkins University, Baltimore: Mimeograph. Available on the Stony Brook website: www.psychology.sunysb.edu/attachment/measures/content/ainsworth_scales.html

Ainsworth, M. (1989) 'Attachments beyond infancy.' *American Psychologist 44*, 4, 709–716.

Ainsworth, M. and Bell, S. (1974) 'Mother–infant interaction and the development of competence.' In K. Connolly and J. Brunner (eds) *The Growth of Competence.* London: Academic Press.

Ainsworth, M. and Marvin, R. (1995) 'On the shaping of attachment theory and research: an interview with Mary D.S. Ainsworth (Fall 1994).' In E. Waters, B. Vaughn, G. Poseda and K. Kondo-Ikemura (eds) 'Caregiving, cultural, and cognitive perspectives on secure-base behavior and working models: new growing points of attachment theory and research.' *Monographs of the Society for Research in Child Development 60* (2–3, Serial No. 244), 2–21.

Ainsworth, M. and Wittig, D. (1969) 'Attachment and exploratory behavior of one-year-olds in a strange situation.' In B. Foss (ed.) *Determinants of Infant Behavior IV.* London: Methuen.

Ainsworth, M., Bell, S. and Stayton, D. (1971) 'Individual differences in strange situation behavior of one-year-olds.' In H. Schaffer (ed.) *The Origins of Human Social Relations.* London: Academic Press.

Ainsworth, M., Bell, S. and Stayton, D. (1974) 'Infant–mother attachment and social development.' In M. Richards (ed.) *The Introduction of the Child into a Social World.* London: Cambridge University Press.

Ainsworth, M., Blehar, M., Waters, E. and Wall, S. (1978) *Patterns of Attachment: A Psychological Study of the Strange Situation.* Hillsdale, NJ: Lawrence Erlbaum.

American Psychiatric Association (2000) *Diagnostic and Statistical Manual of Mental Disorders, Fourth Edition, Text Revision (DSM-IV-TR)*. Washington, DC: American Psychiatric Association.

Ammaniti, M., Candelori, C., Dazzi, N., De Coro, A., Muscetta, S., Ortu, F., Pola, M., Speranza, A., Tambelli, R. and Zampino, F. (1990) *Intervista sull'attaccamento nella latenza (Attachment Interview for Childhood and Adolescence)*. Unpublished protocol, University of Rome.

Bakermans-Kranenburg, M. and van IJzendoorn, M. (1993) 'A psychometric study of the Adult Attachment Interview: reliability and discriminant validity.' *Developmental Psychology 29*, 5, 870–879.

Bakermans-Kranenburg, M. and van IJzendoorn, M. (2004) 'No association of the dopamine D4 receptor (DRD4) and -521 C/T promoter polymorphisms with infant attachment disorganization.' *Attachment and Human Development 6*, 211–218.

Bakermans-Kranenburg, M., van IJzendoorn, M. and Juffer, F. (2003) 'Less is more: meta-analyses of sensitivity and attachment interventions in early childhood.' *Psychological Bulletin 129*, 195–215.

Barnard, K., Magyary, D., Summer, G., Booth, C., Mitchell, S. and Spieker, S. (1988) 'Prevention of parenting alterations for women with low social support.' *Psychiatry 51*, 248–253.

Behrens, K. (2005) *Intergenerational Transmission of Attachment: Cultural Consideration on Responses to Challenging Situations*. Poster Symposium, Biennial Meeting of the Society for Research in Child Development, Atlanta, Georgia.

Belsky, J. (1999) 'Modern evolutionary theory and patterns of attachment.' In J. Cassidy and P. Shaver (eds) *Handbook of Attachment: Theory, Research and Clinical Applications*. New York: Guilford Press.

Belsky, J. and Cassidy, J. (1994) 'Attachment: theory and evidence.' In M. Rutter and D. Hay (eds) *Development Through Life*. Oxford: Blackwell Scientific Publications.

Belsky, J., Campbell, S., Cohn, J. and Moore, G. (1996) 'Instability of infant–parent attachment security.' *Developmental Psychology 32*, 921–924.

Benoit, D., Madigan, S., Lecce, S., Shea, B. and Goldberg, S. (2001) 'Atypical maternal behavior toward feeding-disordered infants before and after intervention.' *Infant Mental Health Journal 22*, 611–626.

Berlin, L., Ziv, Y., Amaya-Jackson, L. and Greenberg, M. (eds) (2005) *Enhancing Early Attachments: Theory, Research, Intervention, and Policy*. New York: The Guilford Press.

Bokhorst, C., Bakermans-Kranenburg, M., Fearon, P., van IJzendoorn, M., Fonagy, P. and Schuengel, C. (2003) 'The importance of shared environment in mother–infant attachment security: a behavioral genetic study.' *Child Development 74*, 1769–1782.

Boris, N., Hinshaw-Fuselier, S., Smyke, A., Scheeringa, M., Heller, S. and Zeanah, C. (2004) 'Comparing criteria for attachment disorders: establishing reliability and validity in high-risk samples.' *Journal of the American Academy of Child and Adolescent Psychiatry 43*, 568–577.

Bowlby, J. (1969) *Attachment and Loss, Volume 1: Attachment*. London: Hogarth Press and the Institute of Psycho-Analysis.

Bowlby, J. (1969/1982) *Attachment and Loss, Volume 1: Attachment, Second Edition*. London: Pimlico.

Bowlby, J. (1973) *Attachment and Loss, Volume 2: Separation: Anxiety and Anger*. London: Hogarth Press and the Institute of Psycho-Analysis.

Bowlby, J. (1979) *The Making and Breaking of Affectional Bonds*. Hove: Brunner-Routledge.

Bowlby, J. (1980) *Attachment and Loss, Volume 3: Loss: Sadness and Depression*. London: Hogarth Press and the Institute of Psycho-Analysis.

Bowlby, J. (1984) 'Caring for the young: influences on development.' In R. Cohen, B. Cohler and S. Weissman (eds) *Parenthood: A Psychodynamic Perspective*. New York: Guilford Press.

Bowlby, J. (1988) *A Secure Base: Clinical Applications of Attachment Theory*. London: Routledge.

Boyce, W., Barr, R. and Zeltzer, L. (1992) 'Temperament and the psychobiology of childhood stress.' *Pediatrics 90*, 483–486.

Bretherton, I. and Oppenheim, D. (2003) 'The MacArthur Story Stem Battery: development, administration, reliability, validity, and reflections about meaning.' In R. Emde, D. Wolf and D. Oppenheim (eds) *Revealing the Inner Worlds of Young Children; the MacArthur Story Stem Battery and Parent–Child Narratives*. Oxford: Oxford University Press.

Bretherton, I. and Ridgeway, D. (1990) 'Story completion task to assess children's internal working models of child and parent in the attachment relationship.' In M. Greenberg, D. Cichetti and E. Cummings (eds) *Attachment in the Preschool Years: Theory, Research, and Intervention.* Chicago: University of Chicago Press.

Bretherton, I., Oppenheim, D., Buchsbaum, H., Emde, R. and the MacArthur Narrative Group (1990b) *MacArthur Story-Stem Battery (MSSB).* Unpublished manual, Waisman Center, University of Wisconsin-Madison.

Bretherton, I., Ridgeway, D. and Cassidy, J. (1990a) 'Assessing internal working models of the attachment relationship.' In M. Greenberg, D. Cichetti and E. Cummings (eds) *Attachment in the Preschool Years: Theory, Research, and Intervention.* Chicago: University of Chicago Press.

Brisch, K. (2002) *Treating Attachment Disorders: From Theory to Therapy.* New York: Guilford Press.

Britner, P., Marvin, R. and Pianta, R. (2005) 'Development and preliminary validation of the caregiving behavior system: association with child attachment classification in the preschool Strange Situation.' *Attachment and Human Development 7,* 1, 83–102.

Bronfman, E., Parsons, E. and Lyons-Ruth, K. (1993, 1999) *Atypical Maternal Behavior Instrument for Assessment and Classification (AMBIANCE): Manual for Coding Disrupted Affective Communication.* Unpublished. Available from K. Lyons-Ruth, Department of Psychiatry, Cambridge Hospital, 1493 Cambridge St., Cambridge, MA 02139.

Browne, K., Davies, C. and Stratton, P. (1988) *Early Prediction and Prevention of Child Abuse.* Oxford: John Wiley.

Bureau, J. and Moss, E. (2001) 'The relationship between school-age children's attachment strategies and their representations of parent figures.' *Revue-Quebecoise-de-Psychologie 22,* 29–49.

Caldwell, B. and Bradley, R. (1984) *Home Observation for Measurement of the Environment.* Little Rock: University of Arkansas.

Carey, W. and McDevitt, S. (1978) 'Revision of the Infant Temperament Questionnaire.' *Pediatrics 61,* 735–739.

Carlson, E. (1998) 'A prospective longitudinal study of attachment disorganization/disorientation.' *Child Development 69,* 4, 1107–1128.

Carlson, E., Sroufe, A. and Egeland, B. (2004) 'The construction of experience: a longitudinal study of representation and behavior.' *Child Development 75,* 66–83.

Carter, A. and Briggs-Gowan, M. (2000) *The Infant–Toddler Social and Emotional Assessment (ITSEA).* Unpublished manual, University of Massachusetts, Department of Psychology, Boston, MA. New Haven, CT: Yale University.

Cassidy, J. (1988) 'Child–mother attachment and the self in six-year-olds.' *Child Development 59,* 121–134.

Cassidy, J. (1999) 'The nature of the child's ties.' In J. Cassidy and P. Shaver (eds) *Handbook of Attachment: Theory, Research and Clinical Applications.* New York: Guilford Press.

Cassidy, J. and Shaver, P. (1999) *Handbook of Attachment: Theory, Research, and Clinical Applications.* New York: Guilford Press.

Cassidy, J., Marvin, R. and the MacArthur Working Group (1987/1990/1991/1992) *Attachment Organization in Three- and Four-Year-Olds: Coding Guidelines.* Unpublished manuscript, University of Virginia, Charlottesville.

Cassidy, J., Woodhouse, S., Cooper, G., Hoffman, K., Powell, B. and Rodenberg, M. (2005) 'Examination of the precursors of infant attachment security: implications for early intervention and intervention research.' In L. Berlin, Y. Ziv, L. Amaya-Jackson and M. Greenberg (eds) *Enhancing Early Attachments: Theory, Research, Intervention, and Policy.* New York: The Guilford Press.

Chaffin, M., Hanson, R., Saunders, B., Nichols, T., Barnett, D. Zeanah, C., Berliner, L., Egeland, B., Newman, E., Lyon, T., LeTourneau, E. and Miller-Perrin, C. (2006) 'Report of the APSAC Task Force on Attachment Therapy, Reactive Attachment Disorder, and Attachment Problems.' *Child Maltreatment 11,* 76–89.

Chao, R. (2001) 'Integrating culture and attachment.' *American Psychologist 56,* Comment, 822–823.

Chisholm, K. (1998) 'A three year follow-up of attachment and indiscriminate friendliness in children adopted from Romanian orphanages.' *Child Development 69,* 1092–1106.

Chisholm, K., Carter, M., Ames, E. and Morison, S. (1995) 'Attachment security and indiscriminately friendly behavior in children adopted from Romanian orphanages.' *Development and Psychopathology 7,* 283–294.

Cline, F. (1991) *Hope for High Risk and Rage Filled Children: Attachment Theory and Therapy.* Golden, CO: Love and Logic Press.

Cohen, J. (1988) *Statistical Power Analysis for the Behavioral Sciences, Second Edition.* Hillsdale, NJ: Lawrence Earlbaum Associates.

Cohen, N., Muir, E., Lojkasek, M., Muir, R., Parker, C., Barwick, M. and Brown, M. (1999) 'Watch, wait and wonder: testing the effectiveness of a new approach to mother–infant psychotherapy.' *Infant Mental Health Journal 20*, 429–451.

Crittenden, P. (1979–2004) *CARE-Index: Coding Manual*. Unpublished manuscript, Miami, FL. Available from the author.

Crittenden, P. (1981) 'Abusing, neglecting, problematic, and adequate dyads: differentiating by patterns of interaction.' *Merrill-Palmer Quarterly 27*, 1–18.

Crittenden, P. (1992) *The Preschool Assessment of Attachment*. Unpublished manuscript, Family Relations Institute, Miami, FL.

Crittenden, P. (1995) 'Attachment and psychopathology.' In S. Goldberg, R. Muir and J. Kerr (eds) *Attachment Theory: Social, Developmental, and Clinical Perspectives*. Hillsdale, NJ: The Analytic Press.

Crittenden, P. (2005) 'Der CARE-Index als Hilfsmittel für Früherkennung, Intervention und Forschung. Frühförderung interdisziplinar (early interdisciplinary intervention).' *Special issue: Bindungsorientierte Ansätze in der Praxis der Frühförderung 24*, S. 99–106. English version 'Using the CARE-Index for screening, intervention and research.' Accessed July 2006 from www.patcrittenden.com

Crittenden, P. and Bonvillian, J. (1984) 'The effect of maternal risk status on maternal sensitivity to infant cues.' *American Journal of Orthopsychiatry 54*, 250–262.

De Wolff, M. and van IJzendoorn, M. (1997) 'Sensitivity and attachment: a meta-analysis on parental antecedents of infant attachment.' *Child Development 68*, 571–591.

Dozier, M., Stovall, K. and Albus, K. (1999) 'Attachment and psychopathology in adulthood.' In J. Cassidy and P. Shaver (eds) *Handbook of Attachment. Theory, Research, and Clinical Applications*. New York: Guilford Press.

Dozier, M., Stovall, K., Albus, K. and Bates, B. (2001) 'Attachment for infants in foster care: the role of caregiver state of mind.' *Child Development 72*, 1467–1477.

Durrett, M., Otaki, M. and Richards, P. (1984) 'Attachment and the mother's perception of support from the father.' *International Journal of Behavioral Development 7*, 167–176.

Egeland, B. and Carlson, E. (2004) 'Attachment and psychopathology.' In L. Atkinson and S. Goldberg (eds) *Attachment Issues in Psychopathology and Intervention*. Hillsdale, NJ: Lawrence Erlbaum Associates.

Egeland, B. and Sroufe, A. (1981) 'Attachment and early maltreatment.' *Child Development 52*, 44–52.

Egeland, B., Erickson, M., Clemenhagen-Moon, J., Hiester, M. and Korfmacher, J. (1990) *24 Months Tools Coding Manual: Project STEEP Revised from Mother–Child Project Scales*. Unpublished manuscript, University of Minnesota, Minneapolis.

Emde, R., Wolf, D. and Oppenheim, D. (2003) *Revealing the Inner Worlds of Young Children: The MacArthur Story Stem Battery and Parent–Child Narratives*. Oxford: Oxford University Press.

European Commission Daphne Programme (2005) *Mapping the Number and Characteristics of Children Under Three in Institutions across Europe at Risk of Harm*. Birmingham: Centre for Forensic and Family Psychology, University of Birmingham.

Evergreen Consultants in Human Behavior (2006) 'Symptom Checklist for Child Attachment Disorder.' www.attachmenttherapy.com/childsymptom.htm (accessed 13 June).

Fonagy, P., Steele, H. and Steele, M. (1991) 'Maternal representations of attachment during pregnancy predict the organization of infant–mother attachment at one year of age.' *Child Development 62*, 891–905.

Fonagy, P., Steele, M., Steele, H., Higgitt, A. and Target, M. (1994) 'The Emanuel Miller Memorial Lecture 1992: the theory and practice of resilience.' *Journal of Child Psychology and Psychiatry 35*, 231–257.

Fonagy, P., Target, M., Steele, H. and Steele, M. (1998) *Reflective Functioning Manual, Version 5.0, for Application to Adult Attachment Interviews*. University College, London.

Fox, N. (1977) 'Attachment of kibbutz infants to mother and metapelet.' *Child Development 48*, 1228–1239.

Fox, N., Kimmerly, N. and Schafer, W. (1991) 'Attachment to mother/attachment to father: a meta-analysis.' *Child Development 52*, 210–225.

Fraley, C. (2002) 'Attachment stability from infancy to adulthood: meta-analysis and dynamic modeling of developmental mechanisms.' *Personality and Social Psychology Review 6*, 123–151.

George, C. and Solomon, J. (1996) 'Representational models of relationships: links between caregiving and attachment.' *Infant Mental Health Journal 17*, 3, 198–216.

George, C. and Solomon, J. (1999) 'Attachment and caregiving: the caregiving behavioral system.' In J. Cassidy and P. Shaver (eds) *Handbook of Attachment: Theory, Research and Clinical Applications.* New York: Guilford Press.

George, C., Kaplan, N. and Main, M. (1984) *Adult Attachment Interview Protocol.* Unpublished manuscript, University of California, Berkeley.

George, C., Kaplan, N. and Main, M. (1985) *Adult Attachment Interview Protocol (Second Edition).* Unpublished manuscript, University of California, Berkeley.

George, C., Kaplan, N. and Main, M. (1996) *Adult Attachment Interview Protocol (Third Edition).* Unpublished manuscript, University of California, Berkeley.

Gervai, J. and Lakatos, K. (2004) 'Comment on "No association of dopamine D4 receptor (DRD4) and -521 C/T promoter polymorphisms with infant attachment disorganization"' by M.J. Bakermans-Kranenburg and M.H. van IJzendoorn. *Attachment and Human Development 6,* 219–222.

Gervai, J., Nemoda, Z., Lakatos, K., Ronai, Z., Toth, I., Ney, K. and Sasvari-Szekely, M. (2005) 'Transmission disequilibrium tests confirm the link between DRD4 gene polymorphism and infant attachment.' *American Journal of Medical Genetics Part B (Neuropsychiatric Genetics) 132B,* 126–130.

Gjerde, P. (2001) 'Attachment, culture, and *Amae.' American Psychologist 56,* Comment, 826–827.

Goldberg, S. (2000) *Attachment and Development.* London: Arnold.

Goldberg, S. Muir, R. and Kerr, J. (eds) (1995) *Attachment Theory: Social, Developmental, and Clinical Perspectives.* Hillsdale, NJ: Analytic Press.

Goldfarb, W. (1995) 'Emotional and intellectual consequences of psychologic deprivation in infancy: a reevaluation.' In P. Hoch and J. Zubin (eds) *Psychopathology in Childhood.* New York: Grune and Stratton.

Goldsmith, H. and Alansky, J. (1987) 'Maternal and infant temperamental predictors of attachment: a meta-analytic review.' *Journal of Consulting and Clinical Psychology 55,* 805–816.

Goldwyn, R., Stanley, C., Smith, V. and Green, J. (2000) 'The Manchester Child Attachment Story Task: relationship with parental AAI, SAT and child behaviour.' *Attachment and Human Development 2,* 71–84.

Green, J. and Goldwyn, R. (2002) 'Annotation: attachment disorganisation and psychopathology: new findings in attachment research and their potential implications for developmental psychopathology in childhood.' *Journal of Child Psychology and Psychiatry 43,* 835–846.

Green, J., Goldwyn, R., Peters, S. and Stanley, C. (2001) 'Subtypes of attachment disorganisation in young school-age children.' *Biennial Meeting of the Society for Research on Child Development* April 2001, Minneapolis.

Green, J., Stanley, C., Smith, V. and Goldwyn, R. (2000) 'A new method of evaluating attachment representations in young school-age children: the Manchester Child Attachment Story Task.' *Attachment and Human Development 2,* 1, 48–70.

Greenberg, M. (1999) 'Attachment and psychopathology in childhood.' In J. Cassidy and P. Shaver (eds) *Handbook of Attachment: Theory, Research and Clinical Applications.* New York: Guilford Press.

Grienenberger, J., Kelly, K. and Slade, A. (2005) 'Maternal reflective functioning, mother–infant affective communication, and infant attachment: exploring the link between mental states and observed caregiving behavior in the intergenerational transmission of attachment.' *Attachment and Human Development 7,* 299–311.

Grossmann, K., Grossmann, K. and Kindler, H. (2005) 'Early care and the roots of attachment and partnership representations.' In K. Grossmann, K. Grossmann and E. Waters (eds) *Attachment from Infancy to Adulthood: The Major Longitudinal Studies.* New York: The Guilford Press.

Grossmann, K., Grossmann, K. and Zimmermann, P. (1999) 'A wider view of attachment and exploration: stability and change during the years of immaturity.' In J. Cassidy and P. Shaver (eds) *Handbook of Attachment: Theory, Research and Clinical Applications.* New York: Guilford Press.

Gunnar, M. (1998) 'Quality of early care and buffering of neuroendocrine stress reactions: potential effects on the developing human brain.' *Preventative Medicine 27,* 208–211.

Hansburg, H. (1972) *Adolescent Separation Anxiety: Vol. 1. A Method for the Study of Adolescent Separation Problems.* Springfield, IL: Charles C. Thomas.

Hanson, R. and Spratt, E. (2000) 'Reactive attachment disorder: what we know about the disorder and implications for treatment.' *Children Maltreatment 5,* 137–145.

Hermelin-Kuttner, H. (1998) *Maternal Ego Flexibility and the Process of Adaptation to Motherhood: Conscious and Unconscious Aspects.* Unpublished doctoral dissertation, the City University of New York.

Hertsgaard, L., Gunnar, M., Erickson, M. and Nachmias, M. (1995) 'Adrenocortical responses to the Strange Situation in infants with disorganised/disoriented attachment relationships.' *Child Development 66*, 1100–1106.

Hesse, E. (1996) 'Discourse, memory, and the Adult Attachment Interview: a note with emphasis on the emerging cannot classify category.' *Infant Mental Health Journal 17*, 4–11.

Hodges, J. (1990) *Rating Manual for the 'Little Pig' Story Stem Assessment.* Unpublished manuscript, The Anna Freud Centre, London.

Hodges, J. (1996) 'The natural history of early non-attachment.' In J. Brannen and B. Bernstein (eds) *Children, Research and Policy: Essays for Barbara Tizard.* Philadelphia: Taylor and Francis.

Hodges, J., Hillman, S., Steele, M. and Henderson, K. (2004) *Story Stem Assessment Profile Rating Manual.* Unpublished manuscript, The Anna Freud Centre, London.

Hodges, J., Steele, M., Hillman, S. and Henderson, K. (2003a) 'Mental representations and defences in severely maltreated children: a story stem battery and rating system for clinical assessment and research applications.' In R. Emde, D. Wolf and D. Oppenheim (eds) *Revealing the Inner Worlds of Young Children; the MacArthur Story Stem Battery and Parent–Child Narratives.* Oxford: Oxford University Press.

Hodges, J., Steele, M., Hillman, S., Henderson, K. and Kaniuk, J. (2003b) 'Changes in attachment representations over the first year of adoptive placement: narratives of maltreated children.' *Clinical Child Psychology and Psychiatry 8*, 351–367.

Hodges, J., Steele, M., Kaniuk, J., Hillman, S. and Henderson, K. (2003c) 'Changes in children's internal representations of parental figures over the first two years of placement.' Paper presented at conference: *Attachment Issues in Adoption: Risk and Resiliency Factors.* UCL, London.

Hodges, J., Steele, M., Hillman, S., Henderson, K. and Kaniuk, J. (2005) 'Change and continuity in mental representations of attachment after adoption.' In D. Brodzinsky and J. Palacios (eds) *Psychological Issues in Adoption: Research and Practice.* Westport, CT: Praeger.

Howe, D. and Fearnley, S. (2003) 'Disorders of attachment in adopted and fostered children: recognition and treatment.' *Clinical Child Psychology and Psychiatry 8*, 369–387.

Howes, C. (1999) 'Attachment relationships in the context of multiple caregivers.' In J. Cassidy and P. Shaver (eds) *Handbook of Attachment: Theory, Research and Clinical Applications.* New York: Guilford Press.

Howes, C. and Oldham, E. (2001) 'Processes in the formation of attachment relationships with alternative caregivers.' In A. Goncu and E. Klein (eds) *Children in Play, Story, and School.* New York: Guilford Press.

Hughes, D. (2004) 'An attachment-based treatment of maltreated children and young people.' *Attachment and Human Development 6*, 263–278.

Jacobsen, T., Edelstein, W. and Hofmann, V. (1994) 'A longitudinal study of the relation between representations of attachment in childhood and cognitive functioning in childhood and adolescence.' *Developmental Psychology 30*, 112–124.

Juffer, F., Bakermans-Kranenburg, M. and van IJzendoorn, M. (2005) 'The importance of parenting in the development of disorganized attachment: evidence from a preventive intervention study in adoptive families.' *Journal of Child Psychology and Psychiatry 46*, 3, 263–274.

Kaplan, N. (1987) *Individual Differences in Six-year-olds' Thoughts about Separation: Predicted to Actual Experiences of Separation.* Unpublished doctoral dissertation, University of California, Berkeley.

Kennedy, E. (2004) *Child and Adolescent Psychotherapy: A Systematic Review of Psychoanalytic Approaches.* London: North Central London Strategic Health Authority.

Kermoian, R. and Leiderman, P. (1986) 'Infant attachment to mother and child caretaker in an East African community.' *International Journal of Behavioral Development 9*, 455–469.

Keys Attachment Centre (undated) *Keys Treatment Protocol for Children and Young People with Serious Attachment and Trauma Difficulties.* Accessed July 2006 from www.keys-attachment-centre.co.uk

Klagsbrun, M. and Bowlby, J. (1976) 'Responses to separation from parents: a clinical test for young children.' *British Journal of Projective Psychology and Personality Study 21*, 2, 7–27.

Kondo-Ikemura, K. (2001) 'Insufficient evidence.' *American Psychologist 56*, Comment, 825–826.

Konner, M. (1977) 'Infancy among the Kalahari Desert San.' In P. Leiderman, S. Tulkin and A. Rosenfeld (eds) *Culture and Infancy: Variations in the Human Experience.* New York: Academic Press.

Lakatos, K., Nemoda, Z., Toth, I., Ronai, Z., Ney, K., Sasvari-Szekely, M. and Gervai, J. (2002) 'Further evidence for the role of the dopamine D4 receptor (DRD4) gene in attachment disorganization: interaction of the exon III 48-bp repeat and the -521 C/T promoter polymorphisms.' *Molecular Psychiatry 7*, 27–31.

Lakatos, K., Toth, I., Nemoda, Z., Ney, K., Sasvari-Szekely, M. and Gervai, J. (2000) 'Dopamine D4 receptor (DRD4) gene polymorphism is associated with attachment disorganization in infants.' *Molecular Psychiatry 5*, 633–637.

Levy, T. (ed.) (2000) *Handbook of Attachment Interventions.* San Diago: Academic Press.

Levy, T. and Orlans, M. (1995) *Intensive Short-Term Therapy with Attachment Disordered Children.* Unpublished manuscript (no source given).

Levy, T. and Orlans, M. (2000) 'Attachment disorder and the adoptive family.' In T. Levy (ed.) *Handbook of Attachment Interventions.* San Diego: Academic Press.

Lieberman, A. and Amaya-Jackson, L. (2005) 'Reciprocal influences of attachment and trauma.' In L. Berlin, Y. Ziv, L. Amaya-Jackson and M. Greenberg (eds) *Enhancing Early Attachments: Theory, Research, Intervention, and Policy.* New York: The Guilford Press.

Lieberman, A. and Zeanah, C. (1995) 'Disorders of attachment in infancy.' In K. Minde (ed.) *Child Psychiatric Clinics of North America: Infant Psychiatry.* Philadelphia: Saunders.

Lyons-Ruth, K. and Jacobvitz, D. (1999) 'Attachment disorganization: unresolved loss, relational violence, and lapses in behavioral and attentional strategies.' In J. Cassidy and P. Shaver (eds) *Handbook of Attachment: Theory, Research and Clinical Applications.* New York: Guilford Press.

Lyons-Ruth, K., Alpern, L. and Repacholi, B. (1993) 'Disorganized infant attachment classification and maternal psychosocial problems as predictors of hostile-aggressive behavior in the preschool classroom.' *Child Development 64*, 572–585.

Lyons-Ruth, K., Bronfman, E. and Parsons, E. (1999) 'Maternal frightened, frightening, or atypical behavior and disorganized infant attachment patterns.' In J. Vondra and D. Barnett (eds) 'Atypical attachment in infancy and early childhood among children at developmental risk.' *Monographs of the Society for Research in Child Development 64* (3, Serial No. 259), 67–96.

Lyons-Ruth, K., Melnick, S., Bronfman, E., Sherry, S. and Llanas, L. (2004) 'Hostile-helpless relational models and disorganized attachment patterns between parents and their young children: review of research and implications for clinical work.' In L. Atkinson and S. Goldberg (eds) *Attachment Issues in Psychopathology and Intervention.* Hillsdale, NJ: Lawrence Erlbaum.

McDonough, S. (2000) 'Interaction guidance: an approach for difficult-to-engage families.' In C. Zeanah (ed.) *Handbook of Infant Mental Health, Second Edition.* New York: Guilford Press.

Main, M. (1999) 'Epilogue. Attachment theory: eighteen points with suggestions for future studies.' In J. Cassidy and P. Shaver (eds) *Handbook of Attachment: Theory, Research and Clinical Applications.* New York: Guilford Press.

Main, M. and Cassidy, J. (1988) 'Categories of response to reunion with the parent at age six: predictable from infant attachment classifications and stable over a 1-month period.' *Developmental Psychology 24*, 415–426.

Main, M. and Goldwyn, R. (1984) *Adult Attachment Scoring and Classification System.* Unpublished manuscript, University of California, Berkeley.

Main, M. and Goldwyn, R. (1994) *Adult Attachment Rating and Classification Systems.* Version 6. Unpublished manuscript, University of California, Berkeley.

Main, M. and Goldwyn, R. (1998) *Adult Attachment Scoring and Classification System.* Unpublished manuscript, University of California, Berkeley.

Main, M. and Hesse, E. (1990) 'Parents' unresolved traumatic experiences are related to infant disorganized status: is frightened and/or frightening parental behavior the linking mechanism?' In M. Greenberg, D. Cichetti and E. Cummings (eds) *Attachment in the Preschool Years: Theory, Research, and Intervention.* Chicago: University of Chicago Press.

Main, M. and Solomon, J. (1986) 'Discovery of an insecure disorganized/disoriented attachment pattern: procedures, findings and implications for the classification of behavior.' In T. Braxelton and M. Yogman (eds) *Affective Development in Infancy.* Norwood, NJ: Ablex.

Main, M. and Solomon, J. (1990) 'Procedures for identifying infants as disorganized/disoriented during the Ainsworth Strange Situation.' In M. Greenberg, D. Cicchetti and E. Cummings (eds) *Attachment in the Preschool Years: Theory, Research, and Intervention.* Chicago: University of Chicago Press.

Main, M., Hesse, E. and Kaplan, N. (2005) 'Predictability of attachment behavior and representational processes at 1, 6, and 19 years of age.' In K. Grossmann, K. Grossmann and E. Waters (eds) *Attachment from Infancy to Adulthood: The Major Longitudinal Studies.* New York: The Guilford Press.

Main, M., Kaplan, N. and Cassidy, J. (1985) 'Security in infancy, childhood, and adulthood: a move to the level of representation.' In I. Bretherton and E. Waters (eds) 'Growing points of attachment theory and research.' *Monographs of the Society for Research in Child Development 50* (1–2, Serial No. 209), 66–104.

Marvin, R. and Britner, P. (1996) *Classification System for Parental Caregiving Patterns in the Preschool Strange Situation.* Unpublished classification manual, University of Virginia.

Marvin, R. and Rutter, M. (1994) *Instructions for a Home-Based Separation–Reunion Procedure for Assessing Preschool Children's Attachments.* Unpublished manuscript, University of Virginia.

Marvin, R., Cooper, G., Hoffman, K. and Powell, B. (2002) 'The Circle of Security project: attachment-based intervention with caregiver–preschool child dyads.' *Attachment and Human Development 4,* 1, 107–124.

Marvin, R., Van Devender, T., Iwanaga, M., Le Vine, S. and Le Vine, R. (1977) 'Infant–caregiver attachment among the Hausa of Nigeria.' In H. McGurk (ed.) *Ecological Factors in Human Development.* Amsterdam: North-Holland.

Matas, L., Arend, R. and Sroufe, A. (1978) 'Continuity of adaptation in the second year: the relationship between quality of attachment and later competence.' *Child Development 49,* 547–556.

Meins, E. (1997) *Security of Attachment and the Social Development of Cognition.* Hove: Psychology Press.

Meins, E., Fernyhough, C., Fradley, E. and Tuckey, M. (2001) 'Rethinking maternal sensitivity: mothers' comments on infants' mental processes predict security of attachment at 12 months.' *Journal of Child Psychology and Psychiatry 42,* 637–648.

Mercer, J., Sarner, L. and Rosa, L. (2003) *Attachment Therapy on Trial: The Torture and Death of Candace Newmaker.* Westport, CT: Praeger Publishers.

Morelli, G. and Tronick, E. (1991) 'Efe multiple-caretaking and attachment.' In J. Gewirtz and W. Kurtines (eds) *Intersections with Attachment.* Hillsdale, NJ: Erlbaum.

Myeroff, R. (1997) *Comparative Effectiveness with Special Needs Adoptive Population.* Unpublished dissertation, Union Institute, Cincinnati.

Myeroff, R., Mertlich, G. and Gross, J. (1999) 'Comparative effectiveness of holding therapy with aggressive children.' *Child Psychiatry and Human Development 29,* 4, 303–313.

Nachmias, M., Gunnar, M., Mangelsdorf, S., Parritz, R. and Buss, K. (1996) 'Behavioral inhibition and stress reactivity: the moderating role of attachment security.' *Child Development 67,* 508–522.

NICHD Early Child Care Research Network (1996) 'Characteristics of infant child care: factors contributing to positive caregiving.' *Early Childhood Research Quarterly 11,* 269–306.

NICHD Early Child Care Research Network (1997) 'The effects of infant child care on infant–mother attachment security: results of the NICHD study of early child-care.' *Child Development 68,* 860–879.

NICHD Early Child Care Research Network (2003) 'Does quality of child care affect child outcomes at age 4½?' *Developmental Psychology 39,* 451–469.

O'Connor, T. (2002) 'Attachment disorders of infancy and childhood.' In M. Rutter and E. Taylor (eds) *Child and Adolescent Psychiatry: Modern Approaches, Fourth Edition.* London: Blackwell Scientific Publications.

O'Connor, T. and Zeanah, C. (2003) 'Attachment disorders: assessment strategies and treatment approaches.' *Attachment and Human Development 5,* 223–244.

O'Connor, T., Heron, J., Glover, V. and the ALSPAC Study Team (2002) 'Antenatal anxiety predicts child behavioral/emotional problems independently of postnatal depression.' *Journal of the American Academy of Child and Adolescent Psychiatry 41,* 1470–1477.

O'Connor, T., Heron, J., Golding, J., Glover, V. and the ALSPAC Study Team (2003a) 'Maternal antenatal anxiety and behavioural/emotional problems in children: a test of a programming hypothesis.' *Journal of Child Psychology and Psychiatry 44,* 1025–1036.

O'Connor, T., Marvin, R., Rutter, M., Olrick, J., Britner, P. and the English and Romanian Adoptees Study Team (2003b) 'Child–parent attachment following early institutional deprivation.' *Development and Psychopathology 15,* 19–38.

O'Connor, T., Rutter, M. and the English and Romanian Adoptees Study Team (2000) 'Attachment disorder behavior following early severe deprivation: extension and longitudinal follow-up.' *Journal of the American Academy of Child and Adolescent Psychiatry 39*, 703–712.

Oppenheim, D. (1997) 'The attachment doll-play interview for preschoolers.' *International Journal of Behavioral Development 20*, 4, 681–697.

Oppenheim, D., Emde, R. and Warren, S. (1997) 'Children's narrative representations of mothers: their development and associations with child and mother adaptation.' *Child Development 68*, 1, 127–138.

Patterson, G., Chamberlain, P. and Reid, J. (1982) 'A comparative evaluation of parent training procedures.' *Behavior Therapy 3*, 638–650.

Posada, G. and Jacobs, A. (2001) 'Child–mother attachment relationships and culture.' *American Psychologist 56*, Comment, 821–822.

Posada, G., Gao, Y., Fang, W., Posada, R., Tascon, M., Schoelmerich, A., Sagi, A., Kondo-Ikemura, K., Ylaland, W. and Synnevaag, B. (1995) 'The secure-base phenomenon across cultures: children's behavior, mothers' preferences, and experts' concepts.' *Monographs of the Society for Research in Child Development 60* (2–3, Serial No. 244), 27–48.

Raval, V., Goldberg, S., Atkinson, L., Benoit, D., Myhal, N., Poulton, L. and Zwiers, M. (2001) 'Maternal attachment, maternal responsiveness and infant attachment.' *Infant Behavior and Development 24*, 281–304.

Robertson, J. and Robertson, J. (1989) *Separations and the Very Young.* London: Free Association Books.

Robinson, J. and Mantz-Simmons, L. (2003) 'The MacArthur Narrative Coding System: one approach to highlighting affective meaning making in the MacArthur Story Stem Battery.' In R. Emde, D. Wolf and D. Oppenheim (eds) *Revealing the Inner Worlds of Young Children; the MacArthur Story Stem Battery and Parent–Child Narratives.* Oxford: Oxford University Press.

Robinson, J., Mantz-Simmons, L., Macfie, J. and the MacArthur Narrative Working Group (1992) *The Narrative Coding Manual.* Unpublished manuscript, University of Colorado, Boulder.

Rothbaum, F., Weisz, J., Pott, M., Miyake, K. and Morelli, G. (2000) 'Attachment and culture: security in the United States and Japan.' *American Psychologist 55*, 1093–1104.

Rothbaum, F., Weisz, J., Pott, M., Miyake, K. and Morelli, G. (2001) 'Deeper into attachment and culture.' *American Psychologist 56*, Comment, 827–829.

Rushton, A. and Mayes, D. (1997) 'Forming fresh attachments in childhood: a research update.' *Child and Family Social Work 2*, 121–127.

Rutgers, A., Bakermans-Kranenburg, M., van IJzendoorn, M. and van Berckelaer-Onnes (2004) 'Autism and attachment: a meta-analytic review.' *Journal of Child Psychology and Psychiatry 45*, 1123–1134.

Rutter, M. (1995) 'Clinical implications of attachment concepts: retrospect and prospect.' *Journal of Child Psychology and Psychiatry 36*, 4, 549–571.

Rutter, M. and O'Connor, T. (1999) 'Implications of attachment theory for child care policies.' In J. Cassidy and P. Shaver (eds) *Handbook of Attachment: Theory, Research and Clinical Applications.* New York: Guilford Press.

Sagi, A., Lamb, M., Lewkowicz, K., Shoham, R., Dvir, R. and Estes, D. (1985) 'Security of infant–mother, –father, and –metapelet attachments among kibbutz-reared Israeli children.' In I. Bretherton and E. Waters (eds) 'Growing points of attachment theory and research.' *Monographs of the Society for Research in Child Development 50* (1–2, Serial No. 209), 257–275.

Sapolsky, R. (1996) 'Why stress is bad for your brain.' *Science 273*, 749–750.

Schaffer, H. (1966) 'The onset of fear of strangers and the incongruity hypothesis.' *Journal of Child Psychology and Child Psychiatry 7*, 95–106.

Schaffer, H. (1990) *Making Decisions about Children.* Oxford: Blackwell.

Simpson, J. (1999) 'Attachment theory in modern evolutionary perspective.' In J. Cassidy and P. Shaver (eds) *Handbook of Attachment: Theory, Research and Clinical Applications.* New York: Guilford Press.

Slade, A. (1987) 'Quality of attachment and early symbolic play.' *Developmental Psychology 23*, 78–85.

Slade, A. (2005) 'Parental reflective functioning: an introduction.' *Attachment and Human Development 7*, 269–281.

Slade, A., Aber, L., Bresgi, I., Berger, B. and Kaplan, M. (2004) *The Parent Development Interview – Revised.* Unpublished protocol, the City University of New York.

Slade, A., Aber, L., Cohen, L., Fiorello, J., Meyer, J., DeSear, P. and Waller, S. (1993) *Parent Development Interview Coding System.* Unpublished manuscript, the City College of New York.

Slade, A., Belsky, J., Aber, L. and Phelps, J. (1999) 'Maternal representations of their relationship with their toddlers: links to adult attachment and observed mothering.' *Developmental Psychology 35*, 611–619.

Slade, A., Bernbach, E., Grienenberger, J., Levy, D. and Locker, A. (2002) *Addendum to Reflective Functioning Scoring Manual: For Use with the Parent Development Interview.* Unpublished manuscript, the City College and Graduate Center of the City University of New York.

Slade, A., Grienenberger, J., Bernbach, E., Levy, D. and Locker, A. (2005) 'Maternal reflective functioning, attachment, and the transmission gap: a preliminary study.' *Attachment and Human Development 7*, 283–298.

Slough, N. and Greenberg, M. (1990) 'Five-year-olds' representations of separation from parents: responses from the perspective of self and other.' In I. Bretherton and M. Watson (eds) *New Directions for Child Development: No. 48. Children's Perspectives on the Family.* San Francisco: Jossey-Bass.

Smyke, A. and Zeanah, C. (1999) 'Disturbances of Attachment Interview.' Available on the *Journal of the American Academy of Child and Adolescent Psychiatry* website at www.jaacap.com via Article Plus.

Smyke, A., Dumitrescu, A. and Zeanah, C. (2002) 'Attachment disturbances in young children. I: The continuum of caretaking casualty.' *Journal of the American Academy of Child and Adolescent Psychiatry 41*, 972–982.

Solomon, J. and George, C. (1999) 'The measurement of attachment security in infancy and childhood.' In J. Cassidy and P. Shaver (eds) *Handbook of Attachment: Theory, Research and Clinical Applications.* New York: Guilford Press.

Solomon, J., George, C. and De Jong, A. (1995) 'Children classified as controlling at age six: evidence of disorganized representational strategies and aggression at home and at school.' *Development and Psychopathology 7*, 447–463.

Speltz, M. (2002) 'Description, history, and critique of corrective attachment therapy.' *The APSAC Advisor 14*, 4–8. Accessed July 2006 from www.kidscomefirst.info/speltz.pdf

Spitz, R. (1945) 'An inquiry into the genesis of psychiatric conditions in early childhood. I: Hospitalism.' *Psychoanalytic Study of the Child 1*, 53–74.

Squire, L. (1992) 'Memory and the hippocampus: a synthesis of findings with rats, monkeys and humans.' *Psychological Review 99*, 195–231.

Sroufe, A., Carlson, E. and Shulman, S. (1993) 'Individuals in relationships: development from infancy through adolescence.' In D. Funder, R. Parke, C. Tomlinson-Keesey and K. Widaman (eds) *Studying Lives through Time: Approaches to Personality and Development.* Washington, DC: American Psychological Association.

Sroufe, A. and Fleeson, J. (1986) 'Attachment and the construction of relationships.' In W. Hartup and Z. Rubin (eds) *Relationships and Development.* Hillsdale, NJ: Erlbaum.

Sroufe, A., Egeland, B., Carlson, E. and Collins, A. (2005a) *The Development of the Person: The Minnesota Study of Risk and Adaptation from Birth to Adulthood.* New York: Guilford Press.

Sroufe, A., Egeland, B., Carlson, E. and Collins, A. (2005b) 'Placing early attachment experiences in developmental context: The Minnesota Longitudinal Study.' In K. Grossmann, K. Grossmann and E. Waters (eds) *Attachment from Infancy to Adulthood: The Major Longitudinal Studies.* New York: Guilford Press.

Sroufe, A., Fox, N. and Pancake, V. (1983) 'Attachment and dependency in developmental perspective.' *Child Development 54*, 1615–1627.

Steele, H. and Steele, M. (2003) *Friends and Family Interview Coding.* Unpublished manuscript, University College London.

Steele, H. and Steele, M. (2005) 'The construct of coherence as an indicator of attachment security in middle childhood: The Friends and Family Interview.' In K. Kerns and R. Richardson (eds) *Attachment in Middle Childhood.* New York: Guilford Press.

Steele, H., Steele, M. and Fonagy, P. (1996) 'Associations among attachment classifications of mothers, fathers, and their infants.' *Child Development 57*, 541–555.

Steele, M., Hodges, J., Kaniuk, J., Hillman, S. and Henderson, K. (2003a) 'Attachment representations and adoption: associations between maternal states of mind and emotion narratives in previously maltreated children.' *Journal of Child Psychotherapy 29*, 187–205.

Steele, M., Steele, H., Woolgar, M., Yabsley, S., Fonagy, P., Johnson, D. and Croft, C. (2003b) 'An attachment perspective on children's emotion narratives: links across generations.' In R. Emde, D. Wolf and D. Oppenheim (eds) *Revealing the Inner Worlds of Young Children; the MacArthur Story Stem Battery and Parent–Child Narratives.* Oxford: Oxford University Press.

Suess, G., Grossmann, K. and Sroufe, A. (1992) 'Effects of infant attachment to mother and father on quality of adaptation in preschool: from dyadic to individual organisation of self.' *International Journal of Behavioral Development 15*, 43–65.

Target, M., Fonagy, P. and Shmueli-Goetz, Y. (2003) 'Attachment representations in school-age children: the development of the Child Attachment Interview (CAI).' *Journal of Child Psychotherapy 29*, 2, 171–186.

Teti, D. (1999) 'Conceptualizations of disorganization in the preschool years.' In J. Solomon and C. George (eds) *Attachment Disorganization*. New York: Guilford Press.

Teti, D. and Ablard, K. (1989) 'Security of attachment and infant–sibling relationships: a laboratory study.' *Child Development 60*, 1519–1528.

Thomas, N. (2000) 'Parenting children with attachment disorders.' In T. Levy (ed.) *Handbook of Attachment Interventions*. San Diego: Academic Press.

Thompson, R. (1999) 'Early attachment and later development.' In J. Cassidy and P. Shaver (eds) *Handbook of Attachment: Theory, Research and Clinical Applications*. New York: Guilford Press.

Toth, S., Maughan, A., Manly, J., Spagnola, M. and Cicchetti, D. (2002) 'The relative efficacy of two interventions in altering maltreated preschool children's representational models: implications for attachment theory.' *Development and Psychopathology 14*, 877–908.

Trowell, J. (2004) 'Reflection on "an attachment-based treatment of maltreated children and young people".' *Attachment and Human Development 6*, 279–283.

True, M., Pisani, L. and Oumar, F. (2001) 'Infant–mother attachment among the Dogon of Mali.' *Child Development 72*, 1451–1466.

van Dam, M. and van IJzendoorn, M. (1988) 'Measuring attachment security: concurrent and predictive validity of the Parental Attachment Q-set.' *Journal of Genetic Psychology 149*, 4, 447–457.

van den Boom, D. (1994) 'The influence of temperament and mothering on attachment and exploration: an experimental manipulation of sensitive responsiveness among lower-class mothers with irritable infants.' *Child Development 65*, 1457–1477.

van den Boom, D. (1995) 'Do first-year intervention effects endure? Follow-up during toddlerhood of a sample of Dutch irritable infants.' *Child Development 66*, 1798–1816.

van IJzendoorn, M. (1995) 'Adult attachment representations, parental responsiveness, and infant attachment: a meta-analysis on the predictive validity of the Adult Attachment Interview.' *Psychological Bulletin 117*, 387–403.

van IJzendoorn, M. and Bakermans-Kranenburg, M. (2003) 'Attachment disorders and disorganized attachment: similar and different.' *Attachment and Human Development 5*, 313–320.

van IJzendoorn, M. and Kroonenberg, P. (1988) 'Cross cultural patterns of attachment: a meta-analysis of the strange situation.' *Child Development 59*, 147–156.

van IJzendoorn, M. and Sagi, A. (1999) 'Cross-cultural patterns of attachment: universal and contextual dimensions.' In J. Cassidy and P. Shaver (eds) *Handbook of Attachment: Theory, Research and Clinical Applications*. New York: Guilford Press.

van IJzendoorn, M. and Sagi, A. (2001) 'Cultural blindness or selective inattention?' *American Psychologist 56*, Comment, 824–825.

van IJzendoorn, M., Juffer, F. and Duyvesteyn, M. (1995) 'Breaking the intergenerational cycle of insecure attachment: a review of the effects of attachment-based interventions on maternal sensitivity and infant security.' *Journal of Child Psychology and Psychiatry 36*, 225–248.

van IJzendoorn, M., Sagi, A. and Lambermon, M. (1992) 'The multiple caretaker paradox: data from Holland and Israel.' In R. Pianta (ed.) *New Directions for Child Development: No. 57. Beyond the Parent: The Role of Other Adults in Children's Lives*. San Francisco: Jossey-Bass.

van IJzendoorn, M., Schuengel, C. and Bakermans-Kranenburg, M. (1999) 'Disorganized attachment in early childhood: meta-analysis of precursors, concomitants, and sequelae.' *Development and Psychopathology 11*, 225–249.

Viding, E., Blair, J., Moffitt, T. and Plomin, R. (2005) 'Evidence for substantial genetic risk for psychopathy in 7-year-olds.' *Journal of Child Psychology and Psychiatry 46*, 592–597.

Vorria, P., Papaligoura, Z., Dunn, J., van IJzendoorn, M., Steele, H., Kontopoulou, A. and Sarafidou, Y. (2003) 'Early experiences and attachment relationships of Greek infants raised in residential group care.' *Journal of Child Psychology and Psychiatry 44*, 1208–1220.

Warren, S., Huston, L., Egeland, B. and Sroufe, A. (1997) 'Child and adolescent anxiety disorders and early attachment.' *Journal of the American Academy of Child and Adolescent Psychiatry 36*, 637–644.

Waters, E. (undated) 'Assessing secure base behavior and attachment security using the Q-Sort method.' www.psychology.sunysb.edu/attachment/measures/content/aqs_method.html Accessed July 2006.

Waters, E. (1978) 'The reliability and stability of individual differences in infant–mother attachment.' *Child Development 39*, 483–494.

Waters, E. and Deane, K. (1985) 'Defining and assessing individual differences in attachment relationships: Q-methodology and the organization of behavior in infancy and early childhood.' In I. Bretherton and E. Waters (eds) *Growing Points of Attachment Theory and Research: Monographs of the Society for Research in Child Development 50*, Serial No. 209 (1–2), 41–65.

Waters, E., Crowell, J., Treboux, D., O'Connor, E., Posada, G. and Golby, B. (1993) *Discriminant Validity of the Adult Attachment Interview.* Paper presented at the Biennial Meeting of the Society for Research in Child Development, New Orleans, LA.

Waters, E., Merrick, S., Treboux, D., Crowell, J. and Albersheim, L. (2000) 'Attachment security in infancy and early adulthood: a twenty-year longitudinal study.' *Child Development 71*, 684–689.

Waters, H., Rodrigues, L. and Ridgeway, D. (1998) 'Cognitive underpinnings of narrative attachment assessment.' *Journal of Experimental Child Psychology 71*, 211–234.

Webster-Stratton, C. (1996) 'Early intervention with videotape modelling: programs for families of children with oppositional defiant disorder or conduct disorder.' In E. Hibbs and P. Jensen (eds) *Psychological Treatments for Child and Adolescent Disorders: Empirically Based Strategies for Clinical Practice.* Washington, DC: American Psychological Association.

Webster-Stratton, C., Hollinsworth, T. and Kolpacoff, M. (1989) 'The long-term effectiveness and clinical significance of three cost-effective training programs for families with conduct-problem children.' *Journal of Consulting and Clinical Psychology 57*, 550–553.

Weinfield, N., Sroufe, A., Egeland, B. and Carlson, E. (1999) 'The nature of individual differences in infant–caregiver attachment.' In J. Cassidy and P. Shaver (eds) *Handbook of Attachment: Theory, Research and Clinical Applications.* New York: Guilford Press.

Weinfield, N., Whaley, G. and Egeland, B. (2004) 'Continuity, discontinuity, and coherence in attachment from infancy to late adolescence: sequelae of organization and disorganization.' *Attachment and Human Development 6*, 73–97.

Welch, H. (1988) *Holding Time.* New York: Fireside.

Wittenborn, J. (1961) 'Contributions and current status of Q methodology.' *Psychological Bulletin 58*, 132–142.

World Health Organization (1992) *International Statistical Classification of Diseases and Related Health Problems, Tenth Revision (ICD-10).* Geneva: World Health Organization.

Zaslow, R. and Menta, M. (1975) *The Psychology of the Z-process: Attachment and Activity.* San Jose, CA: San Jose State University Press.

Zeanah, C. and Boris, N. (2000) 'Disturbances and disorders of attachment in early childhood.' In C. Zeanah (ed.) *Handbook of Infant Mental Health, Second Edition.* New York: Guilford Press.

Zeanah, C., Mammen, O. and Lieberman, A. (1993) 'Disorders of attachment.' In C. Zeanah (ed.) *Handbook of Infant Mental Health.* New York: Guilford Press.

Zeanah, C., Scheeringa, M., Boris, N., Heller, S., Smyke, A. and Trapani, J. (2004) 'Reactive attachment disorder in maltreated toddlers.' *Child Abuse and Neglect 28*, 877–888.

Zeanah, C., Smyke, A., Koga, S. and Carlson, E. (2005) 'Attachment in institutionalized and community children in Romania.' *Child Development 76*, 1015–1028.

Subject Index

Page numbers followed by 'n' and a numeral represent note numbers

Adult Attachment Interview (AAI) 33, 34, 35–36, 79, 123, 124, 129, 132–34, 170, 249, 254, 256–57
affectional bonds
    bonding 57
    caregiving, and love 57–59
    commitment 56
    versus relationships 57
    types of 58
Ainsworth sensitivity rating scales 235
APSAC Attachment Therapy, Reactive Attachment Disorder and Attachment Problems 262–63, 265
assessment
    attachment 85–86
    caregiving 86–87, 140
    versus measurement 95n1
    presentation structure 87–88
attachment
    and autism 47–48, 268
    and dependency 20
    development of 18–20
    intergenerational transmission of 49–55
    meaning of 15
    and other behavioural systems 21–22, 85
    and stress response 173
    summary 97–98
    see also insecure attachment; secure attachment
Attachment and Loss (Bowlby) 29, 39
attachment behaviour, activation and termination of 17–18
attachment behavioural system 17, 37n2
attachment classifications
    disorganised attachment
        Group D: disorganised/disoriented insecure attachment 27–30, 33
    distribution of 30–31

normative *versus* non-normative samples 168
organised attachment
    Group A: insecure-avoidant attachment 25–26
    Group B: secure attachment 25
    Group C: insecure-resistant/ambivalent attachment 26
    groups and subgroups, continuum 27
    secure base/secure haven, attachment figure as 27
    qualitative characteristics 24
    see also attachment organisation; attachment patterns
attachment disorder classifications 12
    alternative criteria 223–25
    international classifications 205, 208, 214–15
    DSM-IV-TR classification 184, 185, 212
    ICD-10 classification 183–84, 185, 212
    misunderstandings of 184, 186–87
    see also Disinhibited Attachment Disorder of Childhood (DAD); Reactive Attachment Disorder (RAD)
attachment disorder research
    children from Romanian orphanages, adopted in Canada (Chisholm *et al.*)
        age 4 to 6 comparison 203–4, 205
        attachment security 196, 197, 198, 199, 200
        indiscriminate friendly behaviour 196, 197, 199–200
        role of parent, lack of investment in 197
        sample groups 196, 198
        severe early deprivation 195–96
    children in high-risk populations, and maltreated children (Boris *et al.*)
        diagnostic criteria 212
        disrupted attachment disorder 213
        findings summary 213
        role reversal 213
        sample groups 212
        secure/attachment disorder link 213
    children in high-risk populations, and maltreated children (Zeanah *et al.*)

attachment disorder, signs of 214–15
    data collection 214
    Disturbances of Attachment Interview (DAI) 214–15
    methodological concerns 215
    sample 214
children in residential nurseries, and later development (Hodges *et al.*)
    adoptive *versus* returned-home children 193–94
    age 16 years 194–95
    anxiously organised attachment behaviour 191–92
    attention-seeking behaviour 193
    clinging behaviour 192
    indiscriminate friendly behaviour 192, 193, 194, 195
    inhibited attachment disorder 192–93
    insecure attachment behaviour 191
    institutional environment 190
    nursery-raised *versus* comparison adolescents 194–95
    returned children 194, 195
children in residential nurseries in Bucharest (Smyke *et al.*)
    attachment disorder 209
    attachment formation 209, 211–12
    attachment quality 209
    caregiving environment 209
    child behaviour problems/competence 210
    cognitive abilities 210
    disordered attachment 208
    Disturbances of Attachment Interview (DAI) 208, 209
    institutionalised *versus* community group comparisons 208–12
    quality of caregiving 211
    sample groups 206, 209
    strange situation classifications 210
deprived children from Romania, adopted in UK (O'Connor *et al.*)
    age 4 to 6 comparison 205
    at age 6 203–4
    attachment security 201, 202
    deprivation 204, 205
    disinhibited attachment behaviour 201–2, 203, 204, 205

deprived children from Romania
 cont.
  inhibited attachment
   disturbance 204
  non-normative behaviour
   201, 202
  sample groups 200–1, 203
  separation–reunion procedure
   201, 202
 research issues
  attachment relationship,
   assumption of 189
  information sources, reliability
   of 189
  principal caregiver, assessment
   in presence of 189
  sample sizes 189
  transitions, and assessment
   timing 189
attachment figures
 and attachment disorder 218–19
 as 'caregivers' 59–60
 meaning of 15
 multiple
  attachment classifications
   64–67
  monotropy concept 63, 64,
   67
  multiple caretaker paradox 63
  principle 63
  emergency situations 68
  monotropy concept 67–68
  selection of 68–69
 as professional child-carers
  60–62
 proximity-seeking behaviour 16,
  17, 22–23
 subsidiary 63
'attachment-in-the-making' phase
 (Ainsworth) 19
Attachment Interview for Childhood
 and Adolescence (AICA)
 130–31
attachment organisation
 Bielefeld Project 170, 171
 disorganised attachments, specific
  antecedents (D group)
  fear, and parental behaviour
   44–45
  maltreating parents 45
  'normal' populations 45
 early attachment, and later
  functioning 178–79
 functioning, domains of 160–61
 insecure attachment, and later
  emotional/behavioural
  difficulties 174–79
 organised attachments, specific
  antecedents (ABC groups)
  affect regulation 44

general maternal characteristics
 42–43
 intergroup differences 42
 maternal behaviour, measures
  of 41–42
 mind-mindedness 43–44
 reflective functioning 43
 sensitive responsiveness
  43–44
 pathways of influence, of
  attachment 161–65
 Regensburg Project 170,
  172–73, 174–75
 research issues 166–68
 secure attachment, and good
  functioning 170–73
 see also Minnesota Longitudinal
  Study of Parents and
  Children
attachment patterns
 secure and insecure/anxious 24,
  25, 32
 stability/predictability of
  Belsky *et al.* study 32–33
  Berkeley longitudinal study
   35–36
  continutity/discontinuity 32,
   34
  Fraley meta-analysis 34–35
  Grossman and Grossman
   samples 35
  Minnesota Longitudinal Study
   32, 33–34
  van IJzendoorn meta-analysis
   33
  Waters *et al.* sample 34
Attachment Q-sort (AQ-sort) 61, 79,
 106–9, 196, 198, 212, 243
Attachment Rating Scale 253
attachment theory (Bowlby)
 evidence base for 10
 evolutionary perspective 16–17,
  22–23
 and holding therapy 264, 265
 practitioners, relevance for
  10–11
 separation and loss 10
 see also cultures, and attachment
  theory
attachment therapy 12, 262–66
Attachment Therapy on Trial (Mercer
 et al.) 263
attention deficit hyperactivity disorder
 (ADHD) 268
Atypical Maternal Behavior
 Instrument for Assessment and
 Classification (AMBIANCE)
 45, 53, 54, 87, 145–47, 243
autism, and attachment 47–48, 268

Baltimore study (Ainsworth *et al.*)
 41–44
Bayley Scales of Infant Development
 210, 242
behaviour *see* attachment behaviour
Berkeley longitudinal study 35–36
Bielefeld Project 170, 171
bipolar disorder (maternal) 37n6

CARE-Index 87, 143–45
Caregiver Behavior Classification
 System 87, 147–50
caregiver change research
 attachment representations,
  adoptive placements
  (Hodges *et al.*) 258–60
 caregiver states of mind
  emotion narratives (Steele
   et al.) 256–57
  role of (Dozier *et al.*) 254–55
 fresh attachments in childhood,
  formation of (Rushton and
  Mayes)
  indirect assessment 252
  methodological weaknesses
   253
  placement stability 253–54
  RAD diagnosis, overuse of
   252
  successful adoption, high rates
   of 252–53
caregiving
 assessment of 86–87, 140
 bond, meaning of 15
 caregiver risk factors 268
 caregiving behavioural system
  38–39, 86–87
 child security 41
 definition of 38–39
 and other parenting domains
  39–41
caregiving behavioural system
 38–39, 86–87
child affective experience codes
 151–52
Child Attachment Interview (CAI)
 86, 124–27
Child Behavior Checklist (CBCL)
 116, 199, 242
Circle of Security project 248–50
classifications *see* attachment
 classifications (ABCD)
'clear-cut attachment' phase
 (Ainsworth) 19
cluster analysis 89
coding systems
 Adult Attachment Interview (AAI)
  130–31, 133–34

Attachment Interview for
Childhood and Adolescence
(AICA) 131
Atypical Maternal Behavior
Instrument for Assessment
and Classification
(AMBIANCE) 146–47
CARE-Index 144
Caregiver Behavior Classification
System 148–49
Friends and Family Interview
(FFI) 128
MacArthur Story Stem Battery
(MSSB) 115–16
Manchester Child Attachment
Story Task (MCAST) 122
Parent Development Interview
(PDI) 151–52
community standard (CS) 246
concurrent validity 93–94
Attachment Interview for
Childhood and Adolescence
(AICA) 131–34
Attachment Q-set (AQS) 108
Atypical Maternal Behavior
Instrument for Assessment
and Classification
(AMBIANCE) 147
CARE-Index 145
Experience of Caregiving
Interview 154
Main and Cassidy attachment
classification system 104
Manchester Child Attachment
Story Task (MCAST) 123
Separation Anxiety Test (SAT)
111, 112, 123
Story Stem Assessment Profile
(SSAP) 120
construct validity 93
Manchester Child Attachment
Story Task (MCAST) 123
Parent Development Interview
(PDI) 152
strange situation 101
convergent validity see concurrent
validity
correlation coefficient 89–90, 91
cultures, and attachment theory
academic debate 75–81
Dogon of Mali 72–73
Efe (or Pygmies) of Zambia 75
Gusii of Kenya 72
Hausa of Nigeria 74
Israeli Kibbutzim 73–74
!Kung San of Botswana 75
normativity hypothesis 71, 72
Rothbaum et al.'s paper

Chao, and definition of culture
78
culture, role of 75–76, 77
Gjerde, and evidence 79–80
Kondo-Ikemura, and cultural
bias 79
Pasada and Jacobs 77–78
Rothbaum et al.'s reply 80
US versus Japanese culture 76
van IJzendoorn and Sagi, and
evidence 78–79
Uganda study 71–72

data, categorical and continuous 90
Development of the Person (Stroufe et al.)
170
direct interventions 261–62
discriminant validity 94
Adult Attachment Interview (AAI)
134
Attachment Q-set (AQS) 108
Child Attachment Interview (CAI)
126–27
Friends and Family Interview
(FFI) 129
Manchester Child Attachment
Story Task (MCAST) 123
Story Stem Assessment Profile
(SSAP) 120
Disinhibited Attachment Disorder of
Childhood (DAD) 184, 185
disorder see attachment disorder
dissociation, and trauma 177–78
Disturbances of Attachment Interview
(DAI) 206–7, 208, 209,
214–15, 224
Dogon of Mali 72–73
doll play techniques 113
DSM-IV-TR (Diagnostic and Statistical
Manual of Mental Disorders,
Fourth Edition, Text Revision)
(American Psychiatric
Association) 47, 184, 185,
205, 208, 212, 214–15
see also Reactive Attachment
Disorder (RAD)
Dynamic Maturational Model of
attachment 30

Efe (Pygmies) of Zambia 75
effect size 90
emotional reciprocity 207
enhancing sensitivity, research
Atypical Maternal Behavior
toward feeding-disordered
infants (Benoit et al.)
behaviours 243
feeding-focused intervention
244

play-focused intervention
243–44
procedure 244
results 244–45
sample 244
Circle of Security project (Marvin
et al.)
assessment 249
caregiver, defensive strategy of
248
Circle of Security concept
248
classification 249–50
dyadic patterns 249
interventions 250
early childhood interventions
(Bakermans-Kranenburg
et al.)
attachment 237–39
coding system 235–36
hypotheses 234
instruments 234
methodological flaws 239
motivation 234
samples 233, 235
search strategies 234
sensitivity 236–37
maltreated preschool children's
representational models,
altering (Toth et al.)
intervention models 245–48
measures 247
results 247–48
sample 246–47
mother–infant psychotherapy,
effectiveness of new
approach to (Cohen et al.)
attachment security, changes in
240–41
infant as initiator 239–40
sample 240
'Watch, wait and wonder'
(WWW) technique
240–41
temperament, and mothering (van
den Boom) 241–42
follow-up study 242–43
environment of evolutionary
adaptedness (EEA) 16, 75
Erickson rating scale for maternal
sensitivity and supportiveness
235
ex-institutional syndrome 195
Experience of Caregiving Interview
87

factor analysis 90–91, 106
fear 16, 44–45
figures see attachment figures

friendly behaviour, indiscriminate 192, 193, 194, 195, 196, 197, 198, 199–200
Friends and Family Interview (FFI) 127–30

Gusii of Kenya 72

Handbook of Attachment (Cassidy and Shaver) 10, 12, 68
Handbook of Attachment Interventions (Levy) 263
Hausa of Nigeria 74
high-risk samples *see* Minnesota Longitudinal Study of Parents and Children
Holding Nurturing Process (HNP) 263
holding therapy 262–66, 267
Home Observation for Measurement of the Environment (HOME) 235, 237
hunter-gatherer societies 75
hypothalamic-pituitary-adrenal (HPA) axis stress response 173

ICD-10 (*International Statistical Classification of Diseases and Related Health Problems, Tenth Revision*) (WHO) 183–84, 185, 205, 208, 212, 214–15, 218
see also Reactive Attachment Disorder (RAD)
impaired selectivity (disinhibition) 262
Infant Temperament Questionnaire 46
Infant–Toddler Social and Emotional Assessment 210
'initial pre-attachment' phase (Ainsworth) 19
insecure attachment, and later difficulties 174–79
discussion 177–78
insecure-ambivalent/resistant attachment
anxiety disorders 175
controlling behaviour 176–77
dissociation 176
hesitance/withdrawal 175
oppositional defiant disorder (ODD) 176
insecure-avoidant attachment 174–75
aggression 174
anti-social behaviour 174
hostile behaviour 174
negative affect 174

victimisation 174
insecure-disorganised attachment 175–77
aggression 176
hostility 175
inter-rater reliability 92
Attachment Interview for Childhood and Adolescence (AICA) 131
Attachment Q-set (AQS) 107
Atypical Maternal Behavior Instrument for Assessment and Classification (AMBIANCE) 147
Caregiver Behavior Classification System 149
Child Attachment Interview (CAI) 126
Experience of Caregiving Interview 153
MacArthur Story Stem Battery (MSSB) 116
Main and Cassidy attachment classification system 104
Manchester Child Attachment Story Task (MCAST) 122
Maternal Sensitivity Scales 142
Parent Development Interview (PDI) 152
preschool strange situation 102
Separation Anxiety Test (SAT) 111, 112
Story Stem Assessment Profile (SSAP) 119
strange situation 99, 101
Interaction Guidance 243–44
intergenerational transmission, of attachment
AAI, and state of mind 49
parental sensitive responsiveness 50–52
parental state of mind 50–51
transmission gap 52, 53–55
interview techniques 124–34, 198
intra-rater reliability 92
Israeli Kibbutzim 73–74

Kaplan and Main Drawing system 69
kappa statistic 89, 91
Keys Attachment Centre 263–64
Kiddie Schedule for Affective Disorders and Schizophrenia (K-SADS) 169
!Kung San of Botswana 75

'lessening of egocentricity' 20
'Little Pig' Story Stem protocol 116, 117
London Parent–Child Project 151

MacArthur Story-Stem Battery (MSSB) 105, 114–16, 117, 118, 247
Manchester Child Attachment Story Task (MCAST) 121–23
maternal depression (chronic) 37n6
Maternal Sensitivity Scales 87, 139, 141–42, 242
Minnesota Longitudinal Study of Parents and Children 32, 33–34, 45, 166–67, 168–70, 172, 174, 175, 176, 178
monotropy 63, 64, 67–68
versus hierarchy 70n4

Narrative Story Stem techniques (NSSTs) 86, 113–23
natural selection 16
non-verbal communication 125
Nursing Child Assessment Teaching Scale (NCATS) 235, 237

Observational Record of the Caregiving Environment (ORCE) 209–10
oppositional defiant disorder (ODD) 176
organisation *see* attachment organisation

p value (probability) 92–93
Parent Development Interview (PDI) 53, 87, 150–52
Parent Development Interview-Revised (PDI-R) 150
parent training programmes 40–42
parental affective experience codes 151
Parenting Stress Index 197, 199
partial correlation analysis 90
partnership, mother–child 19–20
pathways of influence, of attachment 161–65
patterns *see* attachment patterns
Pervasive Developmental Disorder Not Otherwise Specified (PDD-NOS) 47
picture response tasks 109–13
placement stability 253–54
post-institution syndrome 219
predictive validity 94
Adult Attachment Interview (AAI) 134
Attachment Q-set (AQS) 108
Atypical Maternal Behavior Instrument for Assessment and Classification (AMBIANCE) 147

CARE-Index 145
Child Attachment Interview (CAI)
127
Friends and Family Interview
(FFI) 129–30
MacArthur Story Stem Battery
(MSSB) 116
Main and Cassidy attachment
classification system 105
Parent Development Interview
(PDI) 152
preferred adults/carers 207
Preschool Assessment of Attachment
(PAA) 198
preschool parent psychotherapy (PPP)
245–46
preventative versus reactive
interventions 231–32
psychodynamic psychotherapy (PPT)
240, 241
psychoeducational home visitation
(PHV) 246

Q-sort methodology 86, 105–9
Attachment Q-set (AQS) 106–9
description of 106

rage, suppressed 263
Reactive Attachment Disorder (RAD)
184, 185, 207, 209–11, 268
abusive experiences 226
deprivation and neglect 226
disorganised attachment 225,
226
high-risk populations 214–16
holding therapy 265–66
inhibited versus disinhibited
220–23
insensitive caregiving 227
preferred attachment figure,
absence of 224
untruthfulness, development of
227
Regensburg Project 170, 172–73,
174–75
reliability 90, 91–92
CARE-Index 145
Friends and Family Interview
(FFI) 128–29
preschool strange situation 102
research
cross-sectional versus longitudinal
studies 166–67
glossary of terms 89–95
normative versus non-normative
samples 167–68
restraint procedures 264–66

secure attachment
complex symbolic play 171
dependency, self-reliance, efficacy
172
disagreements/connectedness
171
emotional independence/ positive
attention seeking 171
empathy 172
enthusiasm/positive affect/
compliance/affective
sharing 170–71
interpersonal confidence 172
positive affect 170
positive defences 172–73
sibling harmony 172
see also insecure attachment
secure base 22, 23, 27, 76
distortions 223–24
secure haven 22–23, 27
security theory 37n1
selectivity 221
semi-structured interviews 124,
132–33, 151, 153, 206–7
sensitivity see enhancing sensitivity,
research
separation anxiety 16–17
Separation Anxiety Test (SAT) 35,
36, 69, 86, 110–13, 170
separation–reunion procedure
attachment classification system
for 103–5
strange situation 96, 99–103
significance, statistical 92–93
social reciprocity 207
specificity 221
stability see test–retest reliability
Stanford-Binet Intelligence Scale 199
Story Stem Assessment Profile (SSAP)
116–20, 258–59
strange situation 249
classifications 210
insecure attachment 25–28
procedure 86
reliability 99, 101
secure haven 22–23
separation–reunion procedure
96, 99–103
validity 101, 103
strangers, fear of 221–22

temporary relationships 60
test–retest reliability 92
Adult Attachment Interview (AAI)
134
Attachment Q-set (AQS) 108
Child Attachment Interview (CAI)
126

MacArthur Story Stem Battery
(MSSB) 116
Main and Cassidy attachment
classification system 104–5
Manchester Child Attachment
Story Task (MCAST) 122
theory see attachment theory
therapy see attachment therapy
Treating Attachment Disorders (Brisch)
262

validity 93–94
Caregiver Behavior Classification
System 150
Manchester Child Attachment
Story Task (MCAST)
122–23
Maternal Sensitivity Scales 143
preschool strange situation 103
Story Stem Assessment Profile
(SSAP) 119–20
variance, ANOVA 94–95

'Watch, wait and wonder' (WWW)
technique 240–41
WISC-III^{UK} 129

Author Index

AACAP 215, 216, 265
Aber, J. 150, 152, 249
Abidin, R. 197
Ablard, K. 172
Achenbach, T. 116
Ainsworth, M. 17, 19–20, 22–23, 24, 25, 26, 31, 39, 41–43, 44, 50, 52, 57, 59, 60, 61, 62, 68–69, 71–72, 76, 78, 87, 95n1, 96, 99, 139, 143, 160, 163, 235, 242, 249
Alansky, J. 52
Albus, K. 177
Alpern, L. 174
Ammaniti, M. 130
Arend, R. 170

Bakermans-Kranenberg, M. 30, 31, 33, 45, 48, 49, 225, 233–39
Barnard, K. 235
Barr, R. 173
Behrens, K. 80
Bell, S. 41, 139, 163, 235
Belsky, J. 32–33, 160, 164
Benoit, D. 146, 147, 243–45
Berlin, L. 268
Bokhorst, C. 47
Boris, N. 40, 212–13, 223, 224
Bowlby, J. 9–10, 16–23, 24, 29, 32, 38–40, 56, 57, 63, 64, 67–68, 72, 110, 112, 160, 163, 197, 213, 219, 220, 221–22, 264, 265
Boyce, W. 173
Bradley, R. 235
Bretherton, I. 17, 105, 114, 115
Briggs-Gowan, M. 210
Brisch, K. 262
Britner, P. 87, 102, 147, 149, 150
Bronfman, E. 45, 87, 145, 146, 147
Browne, K. 231
Bureau, J. 105

Caldwell, B. 235
Carey, W. 46
Carlson, E. 45, 169, 170, 171, 174, 177, 178–79
Carter, A. 210

Cassidy, J. 10, 29, 30, 35–36, 43, 49, 54, 59, 80, 101, 103–5, 160, 164, 241, 249
Chaffin, M. 186, 226, 228, 262, 265
Chao, R. 78
Chisholm, K. 195–200
Cline, F. 186, 262, 263
Cohen, J. 239–41
Crittenden, P. 30, 87, 143, 144, 145, 198, 199–200

Davies, C. 231
De Jong, A. 30
De Wolff, M. 52
Deane, K. 106
Dozier, M. 177, 254
Dumitrescu, A. 206–8
Durrett, M. 78
Duyvesteyn, M. 234

Edelstein, W. 110
Egeland, B. 174, 177, 178, 235, 265
Emde, R. 114
England, B. 33

Fearnley, S. 262, 264
Fonagy, P. 43, 46, 50, 124, 151
Fox, N. 64, 73–74
Fraley, C. 34–35

George, C. 30, 39, 40, 49, 102, 105, 111, 132, 152, 249
Gervai, J. 49
Gjerde, P. 79–80
Goldberg, S. 10, 21
Goldfarb, W. 199
Goldsmith, H. 52
Goldwyn, R. 37n6, 123, 133
Green, J. 37n6, 121, 123
Greenberg, M. 110, 112, 163, 168, 175, 176
Grienberger, J. 53
Gross, J. 264
Grossman, K. 173, 175
Grossman, K. and K. 35, 170, 171
Gunnar, M. 173

Hansburg, H. 110
Hanson, R. 225
Hermelin-Kuttner, H. 152
Hertsgaard, L. 173
Hesse, E. 27, 44, 49
Hodges, J. 116, 119, 120, 188, 190–95, 258–60
Hofmann, V. 110
Hollinsworth, T. 40
Howe, D. 262, 264
Howes, C. 61–62, 64, 65, 66, 67
Hughes, D. 261

Jacobs, A. 77–78
Jacobsen, T. 110, 111
Jacobvitz, D. 28, 44
Juffer, F. 233–39

Kaplan, N. 27, 49, 110, 132
Kelly, K. 53
Kennedy, E. 268
Kermoian, R. 72
Kerr, J. 10
Kimmerly, N. 64
Kindler, H. 35
Klagsbrun, M. 110, 112
Kolpacoff, M. 40
Kondo-Ikemura, K. 79
Konner, M. 75

Lakatos, K. 48, 49
Lambermon, M. 60–61, 62
Leiderman, P. 72
Levy, T. 186, 263, 265
Lieberman, A. 223
Lyons-Ruth, K. 28, 44, 45, 87, 145, 146, 147, 174

McDevitt, S. 46
McDonough, S. 243
Main, M. 17, 27–29, 30, 31, 32, 35–36, 37n2, 40, 44, 45, 49, 50, 51, 53, 65, 68, 69, 80, 96, 99, 101, 103–5, 110, 132, 133
Mammen, O. 223
Mantz-Simmons, L. 115
Marvin, R. 62, 68, 74, 87, 101, 102, 147, 201, 248–50
Matas, L. 170
Mayes, D. 252–54
Meins, E. 43, 44
Menter, M. 186, 263
Mercer, J. 262–63
Mertlich, G. 264
Morelli, G. 75
Moss, E. 105
Muir, R. 10
Myeroff, R. 264–65

Nachmias, M. 46, 173

O'Connor, T. 40–41, 46, 189, 200–5
Oldham, E. 62
Oppenheim, D. 114, 115
Orlans, M. 263, 265
Otaki, M. 78
Oumar, F. 72–73

Parsons, E. 45, 87, 145, 146, 147
Pianta, R. 102

Pisani, L. 72–73
Posada, G. 77–78

Raval, V. 52
Repacholi, B. 174
Richards, P. 78
Ridgeway, D. 114
Robinson, J. 115
Rosa, L. 263
Rothbaum, F. 75–77
Rushton, A. 252–54
Rutgers, A. 47
Rutter, M. 40–41, 67, 201, 203–5

Sagi, A. 60–61, 62, 71, 74, 78–79
Sapolsky, R. 173
Sarner, L. 263
Schafer, W. 64
Schaffer, H. 57, 222
Schuengel, C. 30, 31, 33, 45
Shaver, P. 10
Shmueli-Goetz, Y. 124
Shulman, S. 171
Slade, A. 43, 53, 54, 150, 151, 152,
    171
Slough, N. 110, 112
Smyke, A. 206–8, 214, 224
Solomon, J. 27–29, 30, 31, 39, 40,
    45, 53, 96, 99, 101, 102,
    104, 111, 152, 176
Speltz, M. 263
Spitz, R. 199
Spratt, E. 225
Squire, L. 173
Sroufe, A. 170, 171, 175, 178, 179,
    265
Stayton, D. 41, 139, 235
Steele, H. 43, 46, 50, 65, 116, 120,
    127, 128, 129, 130, 171,
    256–58
Steele, M. 43, 50, 127, 128, 129
Stovall, K. 177
Stratton, P. 231
Stroufe, A. 170
Suess, G. 175

Target, M. 124
Teti, D. 172
Thomas, N. 186
Thompson, R. 160, 170, 177
Tizard, B. 190
Tizard, J. 188, 190
Toth, S. 245–48
Tronick, E. 75
Trowell, J. 261
True, M. 72–73

van de Boom, D. 46, 241–43
van IJzendoorn, M. 30, 31, 33, 45,
    48, 49, 50, 51, 52, 60–61,
    62, 63, 64, 66, 67, 71, 75,
    78–79, 167, 225, 233–39,
    255
Viding, E. 187
Vorria, P. 219

Warren, S. 175
Waters, E. 106, 107
Waters, H. 34
Watson, J. 68
Webster-Stratton, C. 40
Weinfield, N. 33, 169, 170, 171–72,
    174, 175, 176
Welch, H. 262
Whaley, G. 33
Wittenborn, J. 105
Wittig, D. 25, 96

Zaslow, R. 186, 263, 264, 265
Zeanah, C. 40, 189, 203, 206,
    214–16, 223, 224
Zeltzer, L. 173
Zimmerman, P. 171

About FOCUS

FOCUS was launched in 1997 to promote clinical and organisational effectiveness in child and adolescent mental health services, with an emphasis on incorporating evidence-based research into everyday practice.

Please visit our website to find out more about our work (including our discussion forum and conferences): www.rcpsych.ac.uk/crtu/focus.aspx

Lightning Source UK Ltd.
Milton Keynes UK
UKOW06f0122140515

251498UK00001B/30/P